Studies in the Dead Sea Scrolls and Related Literature

Peter W. Flint, Martin G. Abegg Jr., and Florentino García Martínez,
General Editors

The Dead Sea Scrolls have been the object of intense interest in recent years, not least because of the release of previously unpublished texts from Qumran Cave 4 since the fall of 1991. With the wealth of new documents that have come to light, the field of Qumran studies has undergone a renaissance. Scholars have begun to question the established conclusions of the last generation; some widely held beliefs have withstood scrutiny, but others have required revision or even dismissal. New proposals and competing hypotheses, many of them of an uncritical and sensational nature, vie for attention. Idiosyncratic and misleading views of the Scrolls still abound, especially in the popular press, while the results of solid scholarship have yet to make their full impact. At the same time, the scholarly task of establishing reliable critical editions of the texts is nearing completion. The opportunity is ripe, therefore, for directing renewed attention to the task of analysis and interpretation.

Studies in the Dead Sea Scrolls and Related Literature is a new series designed to address this need. In particular, the series aims to make the latest and best Dead Sea Scrolls scholarship accessible to scholars, students, and the thinking public. The volumes that are projected — both monographs and collected essays — will seek to clarify how the Scrolls revise and help shape our understanding of the formation of the Bible and the historical development of Judaism and Christianity. Various offerings in the series will explore the reciprocally illuminating relationships of several disciplines related to the Scrolls, including the canon and text of the Hebrew Bible, the richly varied forms of Second Temple Judaism, and the New Testament. While the Dead Sea Scrolls constitute the main focus, several of these studies will also include perspectives on the Old and New Testaments and other ancient writings — hence the title of the series. It is hoped that these volumes will contribute to a deeper appreciation of the world of early Judaism and Christianity and of their continuing legacy today.

Peter W. Flint
Martin G. Abegg Jr.
Florentino García Martínez

BIBLICAL INTERPRETATION
AT QUMRAN

Edited by

MATTHIAS HENZE

WILLIAM B. EERDMANS PUBLISHING COMPANY
GRAND RAPIDS, MICHIGAN / CAMBRIDGE, U.K.

Wm. B. Eerdmans Publishing Co.
255 Jefferson Ave. S.E., Grand Rapids, Michigan 49503 /
P.O. Box 163, Cambridge CB3 9PU U.K.

Printed in the United States of America

10 09 08 07 06 05   7 6 5 4 3 2 1

ISBN 0-8028-3937-1

www.eerdmans.com

Contents

CONTENTS

Preface

The present volume grew out of a public conference titled "The Dead Sea Scrolls: The Bible and Biblical Interpretation at Qumran," held at Rice University on February 10, 2001. The articles by John J. Collins, Peter W. Flint, and Matthias Henze were first presented at the conference and appear here in reworked form. I am indebted to the sponsors of the conference, the Rockwell Foundation, the Center for the Study of Cultures at Rice University, and the Department of Religious Studies, for their generous support. All other contributions in this volume were added by invitation.

The general editors of the STUDIES IN THE DEAD SEA SCROLLS AND RELATED LITERATURE series, Peter W. Flint, Martin G. Abegg Jr., and Florentino García Martínez kindly accepted this volume into the series. Florentino García Martínez made valuable suggestions for its improvement. I am grateful to my student assistant, Ambreen T. Tour, for her help in preparing the manuscript for publication. I also wish to thank the Senior Editor of Wm. B. Eerdmans Publishing Company, Allen Myers, and the Associate Managing Editor, Jennifer Hoffman.

Above all, *Deo gratias.*

MATTHIAS HENZE
Rice University
August 2004

Contributors

MOSHE J. BERNSTEIN
Professor of Bible
Yeshiva University, New York, New York

SHANI BERRIN
University of Sydney

MONICA BRADY
Dead Sea Scrolls Publication Project
University of Notre Dame, Notre Dame, Indiana

GEORGE J. BROOKE
Rylands Professor of Biblical Criticism and Exegesis
School of Arts, Histories, and Cultures
University of Manchester, United Kingdom

JOHN J. COLLINS
Holmes Professor of Old Testament Criticism and Interpretation
Yale University, The Divinity School, New Haven, Connecticut

PETER W. FLINT
Canada Chair in Dead Sea Scrolls and Related Literature, and
Professor of Biblical Studies
Trinity Western University, British Columbia

Contributors

MATTHIAS HENZE
Watt J. and Lilly G. Jackson Associate Professor in Biblical Studies
Department of Religious Studies
Rice University, Houston, Texas

SHLOMO A. KOYFMAN
Yale University Medical School, New Haven, Connecticut

MICHAEL SEGAL
Department of Bible
Hebrew University of Jerusalem, Israel

JAMES C. VANDERKAM
John A. O'Brien Professor of Hebrew Scriptures
Department of Theology
University of Notre Dame, Notre Dame, Indiana

Diacritical Marks, Sigla, and Abbreviations

Abbreviations of journals, reference works, and other secondary sources generally conform to the "Instructions for Contributors" in the *Membership Directory and Handbook* of the Society of Biblical Literature (1994): 223-40. For abbreviations of Qumran sigla, see J. A. Fitzmyer, *The Dead Sea Scrolls: Major Publications and Tools for Study,* rev. ed., SBLRBS 20 (Atlanta: Scholars Press, 1990), 1-8.

Diacritical Marks and Sigla

[Daniel]	The bracketed word is no longer extant but has been restored
4QSam^a	The first of a series of 1 and 2 Samuel manuscripts found in Cave 4
2:4-5	The second extant column of the manuscript, lines 4-5
8 ii 3-4	fragment 8, column 2, lines 3-4
AMS	Accelerated Mass Spectrometry
Ant.	Josephus, *The Jewish Antiquities*
Apol.	Philo, *Apologia pro Judaeos*
b.	The Babylonian Talmud (Bavli)
B. Bat.	*Baba Batra*
B. Qam.	*Baba Qamma*
Ber.	*Berakot*
CD	The *Damascus Document*

col(s).	column(s)
Ecc. Rab.	*Ecclesiates Rabbah*
ʿ*Erub.*	ʿ*Erubin*
ET	English translation
Exod. Rab.	*Exodus Rabbah*
frg(s).	fragment(s)
Gen. Rab.	*Genesis Rabbah*
Ḥag.	*Ḥagigah*
Jub.	*Jubilees*
LAB	Pseudo-Philo, *Liber Antiquitatum Biblicarum (Biblical Antiquities)*
Lev. Rab.	*Leviticus Rabbah*
LXX	The Septuagint
m. Mak.	The Mishnah *Makkot*
Meg.	*Megillah*
Menaḥ.	*Menaḥot*
MMT or 4QMMT	Miqṣat Maʿaśeh Ha-Torah from Cave 4 at Qumran
MT	The Masoretic Text
Ned.	*Nedarim*
NJPSV	New Jewish Publication Society Version
NRSV	New Revised Standard Version
Num. Rab.	*Numbers Rabbah*
Pes.	*Pesaḥim*
Qidd.	*Qiddušin*
Roš Haš.	*Roš Haššanah*
Šabb.	*Šabbat*
Sanh.	*Sanhedrin*
Šebu.	*Šebuʿot*
SP	The Samaritan Pentateuch
TS	*Temple Scroll*
T. Sol.	*Testament of Solomon*
War	Josephus, *The Jewish War*

Journal and Series Abbreviations

AB	Anchor Bible
ABD	*Anchor Bible Dictionary*. Edited by D. N. Freedman. 6 vols. New York, 1992
ABRL	Anchor Bible Reference Library

ACW	Ancient Christian Writers. 1946-
ASOR	American Schools of Oriental Research
BASOR	*Bulletin of the American Schools of Oriental Research*
BEATAJ	Beiträge zur Erforschung des Alten Testaments und des antiken Judentums
BETL	Bibliotheca ephemeridum theologicarum lovaniensium
BHT	Beiträge zur historischen Theologie
BJS	Brown Judaic Studies
BZAW	Beihefte zur Zeitschrift für die alttestamentliche Wissenschaft
CAD	*The Assyrian Dictionary of the Oriental Institute of the University of Chicago.* Chicago, 1956-
CBQ	*Catholic Biblical Quarterly*
CBQMS	Catholic Biblical Quarterly Monograph Series
CRINT	Compendia rerum iudaicarum ad Novum Testamentum
DBSup	*Dictionnaire de la Bible: Supplément.* Edited by L. Pirot and A. Robert. Paris, 1928-
DJD	Discoveries in the Judaean Desert
DSD	*Dead Sea Discoveries*
EB	Echter Bibel
ErIsr	*Eretz Israel*
FOTL	Forms of the Old Testament Literature
HSS	Harvard Semitic Studies
HTR	*Harvard Theological Review*
HUCA	*Hebrew Union College Annual*
ICC	International Critical Commentary
IEJ	*Israel Exploration Journal*
JBL	*Journal of Biblical Literature*
JJS	*Journal of Jewish Studies*
JNSL	*Journal of Northwest Semitic Languages*
JQR	*Jewish Quarterly Review*
JSOT	*Journal for the Study of the Old Testament*
JSOTSup	Journal for the Study of the Old Testament: Supplement Series
JSPSup	Journal for the Study of the Pseudepigrapha: Supplement Series
MGWJ	*Monatsschrift für Geschichte und Wissenschaft des Judentums*

MSU	Mitteilungen des Septuaginta-Unternehmens der Akademie der Wissenschaften in Göttingen
NTL	New Testament Library
NTS	*New Testament Studies*
NTOA	Novum Testamentum et Orbis Antiquus
OED	*Oxford English Dictionary*
OTL	Old Testament Library
PEQ	*Palestine Exploration Quarterly*
RB	*Revue biblique*
RevQ	*Revue de Qumran*
SBLDS	Society of Biblical Literature Dissertation Series
SBLMS	Society of Biblical Literature Monograph Series
SBLRBS	Society of Biblical Literature Resource for Biblical Study
SCS	Septuagint and Cognate Studies
SDSRL	Studies in the Dead Sea Scrolls and Related Literature
SJLA	Studies in Judaism in Late Antiquity
SPB	Studia postbiblica
SPCK	Society for Promoting Christian Knowledge
STDJ	Studies on the Texts of the Desert of Judah
TDOT	*Theological Dictionary of the Old Testament.* Edited by G. J. Botterweck and H. Ringgren; translated by J. T. Willis, G. W. Bromiley, and D. E. Green. 13 vols. Grand Rapids, 1974-
VT	*Vetus Testamentum*
VTSup	Supplements to Vetus Testamentum
WCJS	World Congress of Jewish Studies
WUNT	Wissenschaftliche Untersuchungen zum Neuen Testament
ZAW	*Zeitschrift für die alttestamentliche Wissenschaft*

Introduction

MATTHIAS HENZE

There is hardly any scholarly discipline that has benefited from the discovery of the Dead Sea Scrolls as much as the field of Biblical Studies. Long before the discovery of the first cave in 1947, reports were known of Hebrew manuscript discoveries in the area of the Dead Sea. Eusebius, bishop and church historian of the late third and early fourth century, noted in his *Ecclesiastical History* that in compiling the Hexapla of the Psalter, the Church Father Origen (185-254) had been able to secure textual evidence beyond the versions that were known at the time. The hitherto unknown biblical manuscripts, Eusebius informs us, were "found at Jericho in a jar in the time of Antonius son of Severus" (6.16). About half a millennium later the Nestorian patriarch Timotheus I wrote in a now famous letter about the accidental discovery of "books containing the Old Testament and other works in Hebrew script," again not far from Jericho. Among the Hebrew texts, Timotheus writes, were "more than 200 psalms of David." What exactly these manuscripts mentioned by Eusebius and Timotheus contained we do not know, though both reports single out biblical scrolls, specifically psalms. It appears that we are not the first to have discovered the Dead Sea Scrolls. The excitement over the discoveries was fueled, then and now, largely by the presence of ancient biblical manuscripts.

With all of the Dead Sea Scrolls now available to the scholarly community, the full extent of their significance can be assessed in a much more differentiated way. Of the many areas within the field of Biblical Studies in which the scrolls have made invaluable contributions, three in particular stand out: (1) the history of the text of the Hebrew Bible/Old Testament; (2) the development of the biblical canon as it involves both the final stages in the formation of individual books and the emergence of the biblical canon as a whole; and (3) Jewish biblical interpretation in antiquity.

The history of the text of the Hebrew Bible/Old Testament has been richly illuminated by the biblical scrolls in particular.[1] Of the close to 900 Dead Sea Scrolls discovered in eleven caves between 1947 and 1956, about a quarter, or 222, are biblical scrolls, while approximately 670 are nonbiblical.[2] The distinction commonly made between biblical and nonbiblical scrolls presumes, of course, the existence of a closed biblical corpus as it was finalized only in post-Qumran times. Labels such as *Bible, scriptural, canonical, apocryphal,* or *pseudepigraphical* are anachronistic, and strictly speaking should not be applied to the literature of the Second Temple period, including the Dead Sea Scrolls. It is nonetheless helpful to categorize the texts from a modern perspective.

As is well known, the biblical manuscripts from the Judean Desert include fragments of all books of the Hebrew Bible/Old Testament, with the exception of Nehemiah and Esther. The vast majority of the biblical fragments were found in Cave 4, which may have served as the community's main depository for what was to become the canonical books. Leading the list of biblical books ranked according to the number of manuscript discoveries is the book of Psalms with 39 manuscripts, followed by Deuteronomy (33 manuscripts), Genesis (24 manuscripts), and Isaiah (22 manuscripts). One obvious reason why the discovery of the biblical manuscripts is so significant is their age. The Leningrad Codex, the oldest complete manuscript of the Hebrew Bible and basis of the *Biblia Hebraica Stuttgartensia* as well as of most modern English Bibles, dates from the year 1008 C.E. The Dead Sea Scrolls thus predate the Leningrad Codex by a full millennium. In some instances this brings us breathtakingly close to the original date of composition of at least some of the biblical books. A good example is a manuscript of the book of Daniel, 4QDan^c, which dates from about 125 B.C.E. As Professor Frank Moore Cross explains, "it is no more than about a half century younger that the autograph of Daniel. It is thus closer to the original edition of a biblical work than any other biblical manuscript in existence."[3]

1. See the overview by E. Tov, "Scriptures: Texts," in *Encyclopedia of the Dead Sea Scrolls,* ed. L. H. Schiffman and J. C. VanderKam, 2 vols. (New York: Oxford University Press, 2000), 832-36.

2. These numbers as well as the numbers of book manuscripts below are taken from the most recent introduction to the Dead Sea Scrolls by J. C. VanderKam and P. W. Flint, *The Meaning of the Dead Sea Scrolls: Their Significance for Understanding the Bible, Judaism, Jesus, and Christianity* (San Francisco: HarperSanFrancisco, 2002), 103.

3. Frank M. Cross, *The Ancient Library at Qumran* (Sheffield: Sheffield Academic

The biblical scrolls, now believed to come not only from Qumran but from a number of different places in ancient Israel, are commonly classified according to their textual character, i.e., based on the degree of proximity to the versions, the Proto-Masoretic Text, the Septuagint, and the Samaritan Pentateuch in particular. Especially remarkable is the coexistence in the library of Qumran of manuscripts representing different textual traditions, possibly an indication that no one fixed text or textual family was universally regarded to be *the* central text for all of ancient Israel.[4] In recent years, numerous theories have been proposed regarding the development of the biblical text. Their common goal is to move beyond the initial theory of local texts developed by Frank Moore Cross[5] by taking advantage of all the textual evidence now available.[6]

Closely related to the history of the biblical text is the second area of Biblical Studies that has changed significantly in light of the discoveries, the question of canon. The term "canon" has been used by Christians since the fourth century C.E. to designate a closed, exclusive list of inspired and therefore authoritative books that make up the Christian Bible. No equivalent term is known from the Jewish literature of the Second Temple period, including the scrolls, though the absence of a term hardly implies that the concept as such was unknown. In a series of publications Eugene Ulrich has argued that there are three aspects of canon as a *terminus technicus* that are important: (a) "canon" represents a reflexive judgment, (b) it denotes a closed list, and (c) it concerns biblical books, not the specific text form of a book.[7]

Press, 1995 [1st ed. 1958]), 43; see also J. T. Milik, *Ten Years of Discovery in the Wilderness of Judea,* trans. J. Strugnell (London: SCM Press, 1959 [1st French ed. 1957]), 28.

4. Tov, "Scriptures," 834.

5. F. M. Cross, "The Contribution of the Qumrân Discoveries to the Study of the Biblical Text," *IEJ* 16 (1966): 81-95, reprinted in F. M. Cross and S. Talmon, eds., *Qumran and the History of the Biblical Text* (Cambridge: Harvard University Press, 1975), 278-92; see also his *The Ancient Library of Qumran,* esp. chap. 4, "The Old Testament at Qumrân," 121-42.

6. The main contributors include S. Talmon, "The Textual Study of the Bible — A New Outlook," in *Qumran and the History of the Biblical Text,* 321-400; E. Tov, "The Biblical Text from the Judean Desert — An Overview and Analysis of All the Published Texts," in *The Bible as Book: The Hebrew Bible and the Judean Desert Discoveries,* ed. E. D. Herbert and E. Tov (London: British Library, 2002), 139-65; Tov, *Textual Criticism of the Hebrew Bible,* 2nd ed. (Assen and Maastricht: Van Gorcum; Minneapolis: Fortress, 2001); and the collection of essays by Eugene Ulrich that appeared in this series, *The Dead Sea Scrolls and the Origins of the Bible,* SDSRL (Grand Rapids: Eerdmans, 1999), esp. chaps. 2–6.

7. E. Ulrich, "The Canonical Process, Textual Criticism, and Latter Stages in the Composition of the Bible," in *Sha'arei Talmon: Studies in the Bible, Qumran, and the Ancient Near East Presented to Shemaryahu Talmon,* ed. M. Fishbane, E. Tov, and W. W. Fields

By "reflexive judgment" Ulrich means the deliberate process by which a communal and hence official agreement is reached that certain books are binding for their own community. These books are endowed — through a *historical* process, that is, rather than due to inherent characteristics that invariably set these books apart — with authority over the faith and practices of each member of the community. Ulrich's second aspect, that canon denotes a closed list of books, is a direct result of this. Building on the assumption that there was a corpus of works in place at Qumran whose authority was accepted by the community, scholars have set out to identify specific ways in which the Qumran authors marked their source texts as authoritative.[8] James VanderKam, for example, lists several different examples, most prominent among them perhaps those passages that, like the *Temple Scroll,* are said to come from the mouth of God. Other examples include quotations introduced by formulas that are otherwise known to introduce citations from texts of supremely high status.[9] While there can be little doubt then that the community knew of a set of uniquely authoritative writings, Ulrich does well in reminding us that a long process ("the canonical process") lies between the community's first acknowledgment that certain texts are binding for faith and practice and the actual formation of a canon. "The period from the early existence of some books with 'canonical' (in the active sense) status to the decisions about a definitive list constitutes the process toward canon, but the canon itself is a post-biblical phenomenon."[10]

Ulrich's third aspect of canon, the notion that the canonical status applies to the book as such, not to a particular wording or text form, brings us back to our earlier comments about the history of the biblical text. A good example would be the book of Jeremiah, which was considered "canonical" both in an earlier, short edition as attested in the Septuagint and in its secondary, longer and rearranged edition known from the MT, with both these textual forms attested at Qumran (see the discussion by Michael Segal below). This raises a number of intriguing issues, such as the involvement of the

---

(Winona Lake, Ind.: Eisenbrauns, 1992), 267-91, and more recently, "Canon," in *Encyclopedia of the Dead Sea Scrolls,* 117-20, with further bibliography.

8. "Authoritative Literature in the Dead Sea Scrolls," *DSD* 5 (1998): 382-402. Also, J. Barton, "The Significance of a Fixed Canon of the Hebrew Bible," in *Hebrew Bible/Old Testament: The History of Its Interpretation. I/1: Antiquity,* ed. M. Saebø (Göttingen: Vandenhoeck & Ruprecht, 1996), 67-83.

9. See M. J. Bernstein, "Introductory Formulas for Citation and Re-citation of Biblical Verses in the Qumran Pesharim: Observations on a Pesher Technique," *DSD* 1 (1994): 30-70.

10. Ulrich, "Canon," 117-18.

scribe in the composition of the biblical text, an involvement that led Shemaryahu Talmon to call him "a minor partner in the creative literary process."[11] Another issue concerns the existence of double literary editions of the same text, also an aspect on which Ulrich has written repeatedly.[12]

The third area within the discipline of Biblical Studies in which the Dead Sea Scrolls have had an enormous impact, the study of biblical interpretation during the Second Temple period, is the most amorphous of the three. The variety of the Qumran material combined with the fact that what was discovered at Qumran has to be seen in the wider context of Jewish biblical interpretation in antiquity in general lets one begin to appreciate the far-reaching significance of the discovery. Moshe Bernstein is certainly correct when he writes, "[t]he significance of the Dead Sea Scrolls in this area is based not merely upon the number of manuscripts discovered, but also on the diversity in its corpus and the way in which the collection seems to mirror Second Temple Jewish literature as a whole."[13]

Various helpful attempts have been made to categorize the material. In his recent introduction to the scrolls, James VanderKam has proposed three different types of interpretation: legal interpretation, based almost exclusively on the Torah; narrative interpretations as found particularly in *1 Enoch, Jubilees,* and in a commentary on Genesis (4Q252); and finally prophetic interpretation as found in the *pesharim,* the sectarian interpretations of biblical prophetic texts.[14] In his article on the thematic *pesharim* in this volume, George Brooke opens the discussion by proposing that there are five categories of early Jewish exegetical works in the scrolls. The first category includes legal texts; the second is interpretations in poetic, liturgical, and wisdom texts, a category of biblical interpretation all too often overlooked; the third is exhortations in which biblical passages serve as an example, either positively or

---

11. Talmon, "Textual Study," 381.

12. For example, Ulrich, "Double Literary Editions of Biblical Narratives and Reflections on Determining the Form to Be Translated," in *Perspectives on the Hebrew Bible: Essays in Honor of Walter J. Harrelson,* ed. J. L. Crenshaw (Macon, Ga.: Mercer University Press, 1988), 101-16, reprinted in *The Dead Sea Scrolls and the Origins of the Bible,* 34-50.

13. M. J. Bernstein, "Interpretation of Scripture," in *Encyclopedia of the Dead Sea Scrolls,* 376-83 (p. 376); see also his "Scriptures: Quotation and Use," in the same work, 839-42. To Bernstein's bibliography should be added the recent volume edited by J. H. Charlesworth, *The Bible and the Dead Sea Scrolls,* vol. 1, *The Hebrew Bible and Qumran* (North Richland Hills, Tex.: BIBAL Press, 2000), and the collection of essays edited by P. W. Flint that also appeared in this series, *The Bible at Qumran: Text, Shape, and Interpretation,* SDSRL (Grand Rapids: Eerdmans, 2001).

14. VanderKam and Flint, *The Meaning,* chap. 13, "Biblical Interpretation in the Dead Sea Scrolls," 293-308.

negatively, to provoke a particular kind of behavior; the fourth is interpretations of scriptural narratives; and the fifth category concerns the *pesharim*, the topic of Brooke's article.

Of the three areas in Biblical Studies to which the scrolls have made the most significant contributions — the biblical text, the biblical canon, and biblical interpretation — the present volume is concerned exclusively with the third, and even here the essays can only scratch the surface, even though it is hoped that the specific observations here offered are representative of a much broader phenomenon. The articles are arranged roughly in the canonical order of their respective topics, reaching from the creation of humankind to the reception history of the psalms at Qumran. The volume opens with a programmatic essay by Michael Segal titled "Between Bible and Rewritten Bible." Segal observes that during the late Second Temple period a number of "biblical" books still underwent textual revision, and the process of literary development continued. If scribal intervention in the biblical corpus was still accepted, Segal asks, how can we then distinguish between the transmission of the biblical texts and the literary activity that produced what modern scholars refer to as "the rewritten Bible," i.e., the creative and deliberate composition of *new* texts? The aim of Segal's article is to identify a number of characteristics, both external and internal, that are unique to rewritten compositions such as the *Temple Scroll, Jubilees,* and the *Genesis Apocryphon,* and that differ from the scribal practices attested in the textual witnesses of the Bible.

John Collins opens his article, "Interpretations of the Creation of Humanity in the Dead Sea Scrolls," by noticing that the Adam and Eve story in Genesis 1–3, a story which has profoundly influenced the understanding of human nature in the Western world, is hardly reflected at all in the remainder of the Hebrew Bible. Evidently the question of the *conditio humana* was not a particularly pressing issue for the biblical authors. However, the situation changed in the second century B.C.E., when numerous texts attest to a lively debate about the creation of humanity, specifically about the origin of sin, a debate that included the community at Qumran but reached far beyond. Collins begins with a close reading of several passages in Ben Sira, and then moves on to the scrolls, most importantly to 4QInstruction and the so-called "Instruction on the Two Spirits" in the *Community Rule.* All three texts fail to mention the fall and, in fact, deny that God has ever forbidden humanity to know good and evil — the thought that God could have forbidden humans to acquire the knowledge of good and evil would simply have been inconceivable to them. To the contrary, recognition of this distinction can be said to be one of the goals of creation, and it is because of the "spirit of flesh," as Ben Sira puts it, that humans cannot grasp this distinction.

In his article "Sinai Revisited" James VanderKam observes that the self-image of the Qumran community as found in one of the group's foundation documents, the *Community Rule,* shares a number of traits with descriptions of other Hellenistic associations. It was the biblical description of Israel at Mount Sinai, however, that provided the key elements for the sect's self-understanding. The biblical interpreters at Qumran, like other Jewish commentators of slightly later date, found in the description of Israel at Sinai in the book of Exodus, chapters 19–20 and 24 the description of an ideal society worthy of imitation. VanderKam thus argues that the Qumran community modeled itself after the likeness of Israel as it encamped at the foot of Mount Sinai, as expressed most clearly in the idealized self-image of the group in the *Community Rule.*

With the next article by Moshe Bernstein and Shlomo Koyfman, "The Interpretation of Biblical Law in the Dead Sea Scrolls: Forms and Methods," we encounter a different kind of biblical interpretation: legal exegesis. In a rather systematic way, the authors explore various ways in which the interpretation of Scripture at Qumran served as a source of, or justification for, the legal decisions made by the community. The analysis falls into two sections, with each section furnishing a significant number of examples from the scrolls: the first part of the article is devoted to various *forms* of interpretation, i.e., to the ways in which legal interpretation is presented in the scrolls, and the latter part investigates the *methods* or *types* of halakic exegesis.

In "Biblical Interpretation in the 'Pseudo-Ezekiel' Fragments (4Q383-391) from Cave Four," Monica Brady takes a fresh look at a set of particularly difficult fragments of a hitherto unknown work (or works). Previously scholars have suggested an array of different labels for these texts, ranging from "pseudo" Jeremiah to "pseudo" Ezekiel, "second" Ezekiel, "pseudo" Moses, and so forth, a confusion that is the result of both uncertainties regarding the relationship of these fragments with the biblical text and methodological problems in these studies. Brady offers a new, detailed description of the nine manuscripts in question and discusses their form and content. She concludes that the author has paraphrased and reworked the biblical material in order to compose an abbreviated summary version of the biblical text. The newly composed text is either framed by a dialogue between God and a pseudepigraphic figure, or it is cast in the form of a divine speech to said figure. Topics of major concern include sin, exile, and the hope of return from exile.

When one thinks of biblical interpretation at Qumran, one thinks immediately of the *pesharim*. While it is evident that exegesis at Qumran encompasses much more, the *pesharim* nonetheless occupy a central place, and so it seemed justified to include two articles on the topic in the present volume. In "Qumran Pesharim" Shani Berrin tackles anew the old question, "What is *pesher?*" and offers the following definition: *pesher* is "a form of biblical interpretation peculiar to Qumran, in which biblical poetic/prophetic texts are applied to postbiblical historical/eschatological settings through various literary techniques in order to substantiate a theological conviction pertaining to divine reward and punishment." She then proceeds to discuss the various characteristics of *pesher* by looking at four aspects in particular: form, content, method, and motive.

In an influential article thirty years ago, J. Carmignac divided the Qumran *pesharim* into two groups, "continuous" and "thematic."[15] The division of these works that interpret what Brooke calls "unfulfilled prophecies" has since found wide acceptance. In his article "Thematic Commentaries on Prophetic Scriptures," George Brooke challenges this long-standing distinction and proposes two reasons why it no longer serves the useful function it once did. First, the so-called "thematic" *pesharim* display a great variety in their formal presentation of both prophetic scripture and exegesis. And secondly, some of these "thematic" *pesharim* are not exclusively based on unfulfilled prophecies. After discussing a number of the thematic commentaries on prophetic scriptures, Brooke concludes his article by drawing up a list of characteristics shared by all of these compositions.

In "The Prophet David at Qumran," Peter Flint observes that even though David is said to have been endowed with prophetic qualities in the New Testament, the Psalms Targum, and some rabbinic writings, this aspect is rare at Qumran. The reason for this, Flint explains, is a prevalent suspicion at Qumran of the term "prophet" in general. Nevertheless, the large Psalms scroll states explicitly that David composed his psalms and other songs through prophecy. Also, there are three *pesharim* on the psalms, an interpretive genre otherwise reserved for the prophetic books only, which Flint takes to be additional evidence that David was indeed regarded a prophet at Qumran.

Finally, in my own article, "Psalm 91 in Premodern Interpretation and at Qumran," I argue that the Qumran community, like indeed any other Jewish group of the late Second Temple period, did not only inherit the Hebrew Bible but with it a number of fixed interpretive traditions that were closely associated with a given biblical text. More often than not, these interpretations are far from obvious, at least to a modern reader, but were shared by several interpretive communities of the time. Psalm 91 was widely understood as an apotropaic

---

15. J. Carmignac, "Le document de Qumrân sur Melkisédeq," *RevQ* 7 (1969-71): 297-333.

song that possessed the power to safeguard the faithful from malevolent spirits, whose origin can be traced back to the versions of the Hebrew Bible. The same reading is attested both in the New Testament and in early rabbinic literature. The community at Qumran knew of this tradition and used the psalm to this effect in their rituals, but the tradition did not originate at Qumran. Moreover, other apotropaic compositions that are clearly sectarian do not mention Psalm 91. These texts display a different strand of demonology, which has its origin in the fall of the watchers, a tradition known from numerous apocalyptic writings.

The volume ends with a select bibliography on biblical interpretation at Qumran and two indices.

Between Bible and Rewritten Bible

MICHAEL SEGAL

The great number of Qumran scrolls that relate to the Bible have enriched our picture of both the biblical text and biblical interpretation in the late Second Temple period. Numerous biblical manuscripts found in the Dead Sea area (but primarily at Qumran) attest to a textual fluidity in this formative period prior to the destruction of the temple. At the same time, many compositions unknown before the Qumran discoveries offer a window into the various modes and forms of biblical exegesis during this era. Of unique importance is an entire group of works that used the Bible as their basis, in which the authors added, deleted, changed, and reordered material from their source text. This literary genre was labeled "Rewritten Bible" by Vermes,[1] a title that has gained wide acceptance in scholarly discussion of these compositions. The variety of compositions found among the many lists of such works compiled by scholars attests to both the wealth of the compositions as well as the complexity involved in any attempt to classify the various texts.

The recent completion of the publication of the Dead Sea Scrolls allows for a reevaluation of and reflection upon many fields within Jewish literature.

---

1. G. Vermes, *Scripture and Tradition in Judaism: Haggadic Studies* (2nd rev. ed.; Leiden: E. J. Brill, 1973), 67-126; E. Schürer, *The History of the Jewish People in the Age of Jesus Christ (175 B.C.–A.D. 135),* ed. G. Vermes, F. Millar, and M. Goodman, 3 vols. (Edinburgh: Clark, 1973-87), III.1:308-41 (Vermes has revised this section); G. Vermes, "Biblical Interpretation at Qumran," *ErIsr* 20 (1989): 184-91.

This article was first presented as a lecture in the Greenfield Scholars Seminar of the Orion Center for the Study of the Dead Sea Scrolls and Associated Literature at the Hebrew University, January 2001. I would like to thank Prof. E. Tov for his important comments.

New texts from Qumran must be integrated with those already known, so that a new, synthesized picture of Judaism in the Second Temple period will emerge. Primacy must be given to the Bible and its interpretation, an area that occupied much of the literary energies of Jews during this time. The multiplicity of Second Temple works related to the Bible necessitates an extremely nuanced approach to this group of texts. This study will concentrate on one group of compositions from among those works defined as "Rewritten Bible" that closely follow the biblical text but introduce changes into their source. These include Chronicles,[2] the *Temple Scroll, Jubilees,* the *Genesis Apocryphon,* Josephus's *Jewish Antiquities,* and Pseudo-Philo's *Liber Antiquitatum Biblicarum (LAB).*

Motivation for Composition

By definition, each of the compositions under discussion in some way revised an earlier work. The phenomenon of rewriting assumes that readers can identify the source text underlying the revision; otherwise, the author/rewriter could have just as easily composed a completely new work. The dependence upon biblical compositions in the process of creating new works is a product of the author's desire to impute authority to his work; by associating his composition with the holiest of texts, the new work is also granted the same stamp of authority. The author's worldview and his interpretation of biblical passages are not presented as revolutionary ideas, created ex nihilo by the writer. The inclusion of this material within the framework of the biblical passages under interpretation transforms the ideas of the later writer into authoritative and accepted beliefs. They are no longer new ideas, but are found in ancient texts alongside accepted notions. Even though these rewritten compositions sometimes contain material contradictory to their biblical sources, their inclusion within the existing framework of the biblical text bestows upon them legitimacy in the eyes of the intended audience. Indeed, the rewritten composition was not composed with the purpose of *replacing* the biblical texts, for without the Bible itself the rewritten composition loses its legitimacy.

Thus the nature of the relationship between rewritten biblical compositions and their sources constitutes a paradox. On the one hand, the rewritten composition relies upon biblical texts for authority and legitimacy. The au-

---

2. Throughout this article I use the term "Rewritten Bible" in a literary sense — a work which revises an earlier biblical work — and not with canonical connotations. Thus a work such as Chronicles, which rewrote Samuel and Kings, is an example of "Rewritten Bible," and at the same time a canonical biblical book.

thor claims that any new information included in the later work already appears in earlier sources. But simultaneously, the insertion of new ideas into the biblical text, ideas that may even contradict the beliefs and concepts of the original biblical authors, undermines the very authority that the rewriter hopes to utilize. The rewritten texts ask the reader to accept the authority of their sources, but to understand those sources according to the rewritten text's interpretation.

"Rewritten Bible" versus Bible

The designation "Rewritten Bible" itself demands attention. This descriptive phrase is composed of two elements: an object, "Bible," qualified by the process of "rewriting." It is impossible to understand the phenomenon described by the combination of the two terms without an appreciation of each in its own right. Before one can begin an investigation of rewriting the "Bible," it is necessary first to address how ancient readers understood this fundamental concept. Advances in the past generation of scholarship have led to an increased appreciation of the role of scribes in the development of biblical texts, the primary catalyst being the discovery of the Dead Sea Scrolls. Scribes left their marks on two levels, the text of the biblical composition and its literary development. Regarding the former, one observes with respect to the various textual witnesses, including the Masoretic Text, the biblical scrolls from the Dead Sea, the Samaritan Pentateuch, and the ancient translations (primarily the Septuagint), that in the late Second Temple period the text of the Bible was still fluid. In almost every verse of the Bible one finds textual variants in the sundry witnesses. These variants certainly include scribal errors, but they also include intentional changes, sometimes for aesthetic reasons, at other times for exegetical purposes, and in some cases tendentious readings. These "intentional" variants are the most important for a comparison with "rewritten" biblical texts, because they exemplify the intervention of scribes in the text of the Bible, even if only on a small scale.

More significantly, when one turns to the literary forms of the books of the Bible, an even greater level of scribal intervention can be observed. In a number of biblical books, the textual witnesses provide evidence not only of textual variation but also of further literary development of the compositions.[3]

3. E. Tov, *Textual Criticism of the Hebrew Bible,* 2nd ed. (Minneapolis: Fortress, 2001), 313-50, provides an important introduction to the theoretical principles underlying the interrelationship of textual and literary criticisms, as well as specific examples of bibli-

The following two examples, illustrating this phenomenon, suggest that at times the MT was the earlier of the two editions, and at other times an expanded version. The choice of a specific edition in each witness appears to be arbitrary, the result of a process whose details remain enigmatic.

Jeremiah[4]

The book of Jeremiah has been preserved from antiquity in two separate editions, a short edition attested in the LXX and 4QJer[b,d], and a longer version found in the MT and 4QJer[a,c,e]. Some of the differences between the two relate to variants that repeat themselves throughout the book, such as the expansion of personal names, repetition of details from the immediate context, and the repetition of set formulations. In addition to these one finds much longer additions in the later edition, including a thirteen-verse prophecy describing the "offshoot of righteousness" (Jer. 33:14-26). Furthermore, the order of the verses in the two editions differs, in particular regarding the location of the prophecies against the nations (in the MT in chaps. 46–51; in the LXX after 25:13).[5] Although one should not assume that every small difference

---

cal compositions in which this phenomenon is attested. See also E. Ulrich, "The Canonical Process, Textual Criticism, and Latter Stages in the Composition of the Bible," in *Sha'arei Talmon: Studies in the Bible, Qumran, and the Ancient Near East Presented to Shemaryahu Talmon,* ed. M. Fishbane and E. Tov with W. W. Fields (Winona Lake, Ind.: Eisenbrauns, 1992), 267-91; Ulrich, "Multiple Literary Editions: Reflections toward a Theory of the History of the Biblical Text," in *Current Research and Technological Developments on the Dead Sea Scrolls: Conference on the Texts from the Judean Desert, Jerusalem, 30 April 1995,* ed. D. W. Parry and S. D. Ricks, STDJ 20 (Leiden: Brill, 1996), 78-105.

4. The secondary literature on the two editions of Jeremiah is vast. The studies of Bogaert and Tov present the most convincing arguments for the longer MT edition as an expansion of the shorter LXX version: P.-M. Bogaert, "De Baruch à Jérémie: Les deux rédactions conservées du livre de Jérémie," in *Le Livre de Jérémie: Le prophète et son milieu, les oracles et leur transmission,* ed. Bogaert, BETL 54 (Leuven: Uitgeverij Peeters, 1981), 168-73; Bogaert, "La libération de Jérémie et le meurtre de Godolias: le texte court (LXX) et la rédaction longue (TM)," in *Studien zur Septuaginta: Robert Hanhart zu Ehren,* ed. D. Fraenkel et al., MSU 20 (Göttingen: Vandenhoeck & Ruprecht, 1990), 312-22; Bogaert, "Le livre de Jérémie en perspective: les deux rédactions antiques selon les travaux en cours," *RB* 101 (1994): 363-406; E. Tov, "The Literary History of the Book of Jeremiah in the Light of Its Textual History," in *Empirical Models for Biblical Criticism,* ed. J. H. Tigay (Philadelphia: University of Pennsylvania Press, 1985), 211-37; Tov, *Textual Criticism,* 319-27.

5. A. Rofé, "The Arrangement of the Book of Jeremiah," *ZAW* 101 (1989): 390-98, has provided convincing arguments for the secondary nature of the placement of the prophecies in the LXX.

between the two editions necessarily leads to the conclusion that the shorter edition preserves the earlier reading,[6] all the evidence combined leads to such a conclusion regarding the editions in general. These two editions were included in two different collections of biblical books, the MT and the LXX, and in each the book is labeled "Jeremiah." In the eyes of ancient readers, both versions preserved the same composition, containing the prophecies of and stories surrounding Jeremiah. Thus the definition of the biblical book Jeremiah allowed for a great deal of flexibility regarding the literary form of the composition in question. Both editions were authoritative copies of the same biblical works, despite the major differences between the two.

The Pentateuch

One can identify the nature of the additional material found in the Samaritan Pentateuch when comparing the Samaritan Pentateuch with the MT version of the Torah. Besides the clearly ideological additions present in certain passages,[7] scholars have identified a number of characteristics of this version, most prominently its "harmonistic" nature.[8] Scrolls which attest to this harmonistic tendency were among those discovered at Qumran and were thus assigned the title "pre-Samaritan" texts.[9] These harmonistic additions were always based upon, or copied from, other passages in the Pentateuch, thus limiting the extent of this intervention on the part of those scribes responsible for these changes.[10] In this case, the MT repre-

---

6. As argued by A. Rofé, "The Name YHWH SEBA'ÔT and the Shorter Recension of Jeremiah," in *Prophetie und geschichtliche Wirklichkeit im alten Israel: Festschrift für Siegfried Herrman zum 65. Geburtstag*, ed. R. Liwak and S. Wagner (Stuttgart: Kohlhammer, 1991), 307-15; A. van der Kooij, "Jeremiah 27:5-15: How Do MT and LXX Relate to Each Other?" *JNSL* 20 (1994): 59-78.

7. F. Dexinger, "Das Garizimgebot im Dekalog der Samaritaner," in *Studien zum Pentateuch für Walter Kornfeld zum 60. Geburtstag*, ed. G. Braulik (Vienna: Herder, 1977), 111-33; J. Margain, "Samaritain (Pentateuque)," in *DBSup*, 9:762-73; Tov, *Textual Criticism*, 94-95.

8. R. Weiss, "Synonymous Variants in Divergences between the Samaritan and Massoretic Texts of the Pentateuch," in Weiss, *Studies in the Text and Language of the Bible* (Jerusalem, 1981), 63-189 (in Hebrew); E. Tov, "The Nature and Background of Harmonizations in Biblical Manuscripts," *JSOT* 31 (1985): 3-29; J. Tigay, "Conflation as a Redactional Technique," in *Empirical Models*, 53-96.

9. J. Sanderson, *An Exodus Scroll from Qumran: 4QpaleoExod and the Samaritan Tradition*, HSS 30 (Atlanta: Scholars Press, 1986); Tov, *Textual Criticism*, 97-100.

10. Sanderson, *Exodus Scroll*, 299.

sents a shorter edition of the Torah, expanded to a longer one in the Samaritan Pentateuch.

Another group of texts found in Cave 4 at Qumran, 4Q364-367, were labeled 4QReworked Pentateuch[b-e] by Tov and White in their official publication in DJD 13.[11] Most of the fragments of these scrolls preserve a work similar to the text of the Pentateuch, as is known to us from various textual witnesses. New elements of varying length were added into this textual framework, some half a line long, others a line or two, and even one extensive seven-line passage, quoting an expanded version of the Song of Miriam (Exod. 15:21; 4Q365, frgs. 6a col. ii and 6c). Besides these additions there is also evidence of omission of details known from the sundry textual witnesses, as well as differences in the order of verses.[12] Despite the numerous differences between these scrolls and other textual witnesses of the Torah, the vast majority of the material preserved therein offers a text strikingly similar to the Pentateuch, which used a pre-Samaritan text as its source.[13] How should one classify texts that exhibit such similarity to the known versions of the Torah, yet simultaneously attest to hitherto unknown readings and passages? As noted above, the editors of these scrolls assigned them the title "Reworked Pentateuch," and included them in a volume of para-biblical texts, clearly assuming that the changes introduced into these works warranted a new categorization. Tov and Crawford have each suggested that these scrolls should be viewed in contrast to the SP, in which additional material vis-à-vis the MT is present throughout, yet none of it is "new" material created by the scribe. The SP, accepted as an authoritative edition of the Torah, thus represents their boundary of acceptable scribal intervention, past which compositions should be described as "Reworked Pentateuch" and not the Pentateuch itself.[14] As I have previously suggested, the nature of these scrolls, a textual framework similar to known textual witnesses, expanded by new material, in addition to occasional omissions and changes in sequence, finds a close parallel in the textual history of Jeremiah discussed above. In

---

11. E. Tov and S. White, "Reworked Pentateuch," in *Qumran Cave IV.VIII: Parabiblical Texts, Part 1*, ed. H. W. Attridge et al., DJD 13 (Oxford: Clarendon, 1994), 187-352.

12. Tov and White, "Reworked Pentateuch," 191.

13. A quick glance at the table provided in E. Tov, "4QReworked Pentateuch: A Synopsis of Its Contents," *RevQ* 64 (1995): 647-53, reveals that the number of additions to these scrolls pales in comparison to the preserved Pentateuchal passages.

14. As emphasized separately by E. Tov, "Rewritten Biblical Compositions and Biblical Manuscripts, with Special Attention to the Samaritan Pentateuch," *DSD* 5 (1998): 334-54, on p. 339; S. W. Crawford, "The 'Rewritten' Bible at Qumran: A Look at Three Texts," *ErIsr* 26 (1999): 1*-8*, p. 3*.

that case the MT edition preserves the textual framework of the LXX, expanded by new material (some very extensive) and altered regarding the sequence. This comparison leads to a conclusion similar to that presented in the case of Jeremiah; the differences between these scrolls and the known textual witnesses are the work of scribes who regularly intervened in their *Vorlagen*. As Jeremiah was viewed as the same composition regardless of the edition in question, these scrolls should also be viewed as later editions of the text of the Torah.[15]

The term "Bible" itself in the late Second Temple period does not relate to a specific text of the biblical book, but rather to a literary composition. These compositions underwent revision, and as seen above continued the process of literary development. The active intervention of scribes in these texts was accepted in this period and was not viewed as an affront to the sanctity of the text. The text was of secondary importance to the composition itself, and thus scribes allowed themselves the freedom to "improve" these works.[16]

What is the meaning of "Rewritten Bible" if the category "Bible" also includes the editions produced as a result of a process of continual scribal intervention into the biblical text, and further literary development of the compositions? The rewritten texts under discussion, such as *Jubilees*, also preserve the textual framework of their source, while at the same time introducing changes, either through addition, omission, or rearrangement. But as noted above, the textual evidence available today testifies to the very same phenomena within the final strata of the literary growth of the biblical books, which leads to the question whether a true boundary can be drawn between these two categories, "Bible" and "Rewritten Bible." Was the division between these two genres, as used by modern scholars, recognized in antiquity?

Two examples from biblical collections indicate that ancient readers, or groups, did distinguish between a biblical book and its later rewriting: (1) Chronicles, a rewriting of Samuel and Kings, was included in the same

15. M. Segal, "4QReworked Pentateuch or 4QPentateuch," in *The Dead Sea Scrolls Fifty Years after Their Discovery*, ed. L. H. Schiffman, E. Tov, and J. C. VanderKam (Jerusalem: Israel Museum, 2000), 391-99; E. Ulrich, "The Qumran Scrolls and the Biblical Text," in *The Dead Sea Scrolls Fifty Years after Their Discovery: Proceedings of the Jerusalem Congress, July 20-25, 1997*, ed. Lawrence W. Schiffman, Emanuel Tov, and James C. VanderKam (Jerusalem: Israel Exploration Society, 2000), 51-59.

16. E. Ulrich, "Pluriformity in the Biblical Text, Text Groups, and Questions of Canon," in *The Madrid Qumran Congress: Proceedings of the International Congress on the Dead Sea Scrolls, Madrid, 18-21 March 1991*, ed. J. Trebolle Barrera and L. Vegas Montaner, 2 vols. (Leiden: Brill, 1992), 1:23-41, notes that "it was the sacred work or book that was important, not the specific edition or specific wording of the work" (p. 36).

canon as those books. The later work was sufficiently different from its sources to be defined as a new composition. (2) Similarly, the composition preserved in the LXX known as 1 Esdras rewrote parts of Ezra-Nehemiah and Chronicles, and yet all these compositions exist side by side in the Greek Scriptures. The question of the "biblical" status of these rewritten compositions, or employing somewhat anachronistic terminology, the canonical status of these works, is essentially a sociohistorical issue. In the case of each such work, one can ask whether a certain religious group accepted it as an authoritative work. Alternatively, one can ask whether ancient readers distinguished between the rewritten compositions and their sources on a literary level. The examples of Chronicles and 1 Esdras indicate that such a literary distinction did exist. It is therefore legitimate to investigate the nature of the differences between the two.

I suggest that it is possible to identify a number of criteria unique to rewritten biblical compositions that differ from the scribal phenomena attested in textual witnesses of the Bible. A certain tension exists in the following list. On the one hand, the most significant examples regarding the nature of the relationship between "Bible" and "Rewritten Bible" are those cases in which there is a considerable common basis between the rewritten composition and its source. At the same time, the purpose of this study is to identify those characteristics that distinguish "rewritten" biblical compositions from biblical manuscripts themselves. As a result, the compositions under investigation here are those which make up the boundary between these two groups of texts.

The criteria to be discussed can be divided into two general categories: external characteristics and those concerning the content of the rewritten compositions.

External Characteristics

Language

On the simplest level, one can posit that any composition which presumes to present a copy of its source will be composed in the same language as its *Vorlage*. Thus, for most of the Bible, this limits the discussion to rewritten texts written in Hebrew. This removes certain compositions from discussion, such as the *Genesis Apocryphon* composed in Aramaic, and Josephus's *Antiquities of the Jews* in Greek.[17] Although each of these works resembles other re-

17. In Josephus's introduction to the *Antiquities*, he writes explicitly that his in-

written compositions from a literary perspective, the difference in language demarcates a clear line between them and their source.

The Textual Relationship between the Source and Its Revision

Can one identify the source composition upon which the rewriter based his revision within the rewritten composition itself? This question does not refer to biblical allusions and references within the new composition but rather to instances in which the rewriter adopted or copied entire passages from the Bible and incorporated them into his new composition. A classical example of this technique can be identified in Chronicles. One can synoptically compare Chronicles to its sources, primarily Samuel and Kings, and easily recognize the texts which the later reviser adopted from his earlier sources.[18]

Textual kinship can be measured within two areas: textual variance and the order of verses. The working assumption of this criterion is that extensive textual dependence of the rewritten composition upon its sources attests to the intentions of the author regarding the status of the work, as well as the resulting perception of the text by its readers. However, certain methodological difficulties can be raised regarding both of these categories. In those sections in which the rewriter adopted passages from his sources, one can investigate whether he was careful to preserve even the smallest details in his new composition, or alternatively, whether he took the liberty to introduce changes into those cited passages. A conservative approach by the reviser suggests that he intended to preserve the correspondence with his source and thus possibly reveal his intentions in regard to his new composition. However, as noted above, textual variation, specifically at the level of details, was common in biblical textual witnesses, and thus cannot be used as a criterion for the description of a composition as "biblical" or "rewritten" Bible in the eyes of both ancient authors and readers. In addition, it is difficult to determine which version served as the source of the rewritten composition. This problem is apparent in the study of Chronicles — one can point to textual affiliations with different textual witnesses regarding differing details. Some of its sources are connected to the MT versions of Samuel and Kings, others to the LXX, still others to additional witnesses, such as 4QSam[a], and at other times

---

tended audience is Hellenistic readers (1.5). For the *Antiquities* one could raise the question of the relationship between that work and the Greek text on which Josephus based his rewriting. However, the external linguistic difference between the Greek rewriting and the Hebrew original still draws a clear boundary between the two.

18. A. Bendavid, *Parallels in the Bible* (Jerusalem: Karta, 1972) (Hebrew).

possibly to other witnesses unknown to us today.[19] It is therefore difficult to determine where the rewriter copied from a known textual witness, and further to determine where he introduced changes into those sources. This problem is even more acute in the case of a number of compositions which are preserved in their entirety only in translation, such as *Jubilees* (Ge'ez) and Pseudo-Philo's *LAB* (Latin), where it is difficult to assess accurately the textual relationship of the passages preserved in translation with their sources.[20]

One can also compare the order of the verses as presented in the rewritten composition to the sequence found in the sources. Thus, for example, one can compare *Jubilees* with Genesis and Exodus and highlight those instances in which the author's chronological worldview led him to reorder various passages. This is the reason why the sale of Joseph (*Jub.* 34:11-12) is described before the death of Isaac (*Jub.* 36:18), while in Genesis, the latter (Gen. 35:29) is related prior to the former (Gen. 37). Similar to the reservations raised above, one must exercise caution in using reordering as a criterion for the determination of "biblical" versus "rewritten" compositions. The same phenomenon of reordering is attested in textual witnesses of the Bible itself: LXX Exodus 35–40 presents a different order of the execution of the instructions regarding the erecting of the tabernacle;[21] the different location of the prophecies against the nations in the MT and the LXX of Jeremiah;[22] the alternate orders of the verses in Jeremiah 10 as preserved in the MT on the one hand and in the LXX and 4QJer[b] on the other;[23] and the variant sequence of the

19. F. M. Cross, "The History of the Biblical Text in the Light of Discoveries in the Judean Desert," *HTR* 57 (1964): 281-99, reprinted in F. M. Cross and S. Talmon, eds., *Qumran and the History of the Biblical Text* (Cambridge: Harvard University Press, 1975), 177-95; W. E. Lemke, "The Synoptic Problem in the Chronicler's History," *HTR* 58 (1965): 349-63.

20. D. J. Harrington, "The Biblical Text of Pseudo-Philo's *Liber Antiquitatum Biblicarum*," *CBQ* 33 (1971): 1-17; J. C. VanderKam, *Textual and Historical Studies in the Book of Jubilees* (Missoula: Scholars Press, 1977); VanderKam, "Jubilees and the Hebrew Texts of Genesis-Exodus," *Textus* 14 (1988): 71-86.

21. A. Kuenen, *A Historico-Critical Inquiry into the Origin and Composition of the Hexateuch,* trans. P. H. Wicksteed (London: Macmillan, 1886), 76-77, provides a useful chart of the differences between the two. D. W. Gooding, *The Account of the Tabernacle* (Cambridge: Cambridge University Press, 1959), ascribed the differences in the LXX to the Greek translator. Compare the convincing analysis of A. Aejmelaeus, "Septuagintal Translation Techniques — a Solution to the Problem of the Tabernacle Account," in *Septuagint, Scrolls and Cognate Writings: Papers Presented to the International Symposium on the Septuagint and Its Relations to the Dead Sea Scrolls and Other Writings* (Manchester, 1990), ed. G. J. Brooke, SCS 33 (Atlanta: Scholars Press, 1992), 381-401.

22. Rofé, "The Arrangement of the Book of Jeremiah."

23. Tov, *Textual Criticism,* 325-26.

collections of wisdom sayings found in the MT and the LXX of Proverbs.[24] This list represents only a sampling of differences between textual witnesses regarding the order of verses in biblical texts. It is thus methodologically difficult to employ verse order as a criterion to determine the status of a rewritten composition vis-à-vis the Bible.

Literary Criteria for "Rewritten Bible"

The analysis until this point could lead to the conclusion that rewritten biblical compositions have enough in common with textual witnesses of the Bible to warrant their description as further editions of the biblical books themselves. However, beyond the differences regarding the external form of the compositions (which, although significant, are all attested in biblical manuscripts), one can also identify internal differences of content in these compositions that are not preserved in textual witnesses. It is precisely these characteristics, I submit, that define a rewritten composition as a new work and not merely as a further literary edition of the source. None of the characteristics to be listed below applies equally to all the compositions under question, and none of the compositions exhibits all of the above traits. However, the presence of each criterion in a number of works, and the attestation of a number of criteria in each work, suggest that they are all relevant to the definition of rewritten biblical compositions.

Scope of the Composition

If the revised version of the biblical book is intended to be another edition of the same work, then the later text should cover the same material as contained in the source. If one takes the two editions of Jeremiah as an example, the longer MT version includes the entire LXX edition. Although one finds additions in the later edition, they do not change the general scope of the book. The longer, later edition relates to the entire composition, presenting a new edition of the complete book of Jeremiah. In contrast, rewritten compositions do not generally correspond to the scope of their sources. Chronicles

---

24. E. Tov, "Recensional Differences between the Masoretic Text and the Septuagint of Proverbs," in *Of Scribes and Scrolls: Studies on the Hebrew Bible, Intertestamental Judaism, and Christian Origins Presented to J. Strugnell,* ed. H. W. Attridge, College Theology Society Resources in Religion 5 (Lanham, Md.: University Press of America, 1990), 43-56.

presents parts of Samuel and Kings; *Jubilees* rewrites Genesis–Exodus 12; Pseudo-Philo's *Biblical Antiquities* begins with Adam and continues through David but seems to be most interested in the period of Judges. None of these works corresponds to any one biblical book, nor to any collection of works. Chronicles cannot be mistaken for Samuel and Kings, because almost all of 1 Samuel is absent. *Jubilees* could not be taken for the Pentateuch, because the final three and a half books, containing almost all of the Pentateuchal legal material, are missing. *LAB* contains material from both the Torah and the Former Prophets, and therefore can be a further edition of neither of the two. In all these examples the change in the scope of the composition created a new literary unit.

New Narrative Frame

In a number of rewritten compositions, the author has added a new narrative frame. This change places the composition as a whole into a new setting and thus offers a new ideological framework by which to understand the text. Two paradigmatic examples of this phenomenon are found in *Jubilees* and the *Temple Scroll*. Both works are rewritings of the Pentateuch, and perhaps it is for this reason that each of the authors felt a need to justify the creation of new compositions that seem to posit the existence of further Sinaitic revelation. *Jubilees* opens on the sixteenth of the third month, and describes a Sinaitic revelation to Moses through the agency of the Angel of the Presence. The first verses of this composition are taken from Exodus 24:12-18, with minor differences from the extant textual witnesses, primarily the removal of characters other than Moses. In Exodus 19–24 one encounters descriptions of a number of ascents to Sinai, and traditional commentators have debated the chronology of the events surrounding these encounters.[25] According to *Jubilees*, the revelation of the Torah and the accompanying covenantal ceremony are described in Exodus 19:1–24:11. From elsewhere in this work it can be shown that this event is dated to the fifteenth of the third month, the date of all covenants in the book.[26] Thus, by dating the new narrative frame of the book to the sixteenth of the third month, the author of *Jubilees* wished to identify this book as a separate revelation from that of the Pentateuch itself. At the same time, the author relied upon the Pentateuch, specifically the de-

25. See the comments of Rashi and Nahmanides on Exod. 24:1, 12.
26. *Jub.* 14:10 (covenant between the pieces); 15:1 (covenant of circumcision); 16:14 (birth of Isaac); 28:15 (birth of Judah); 29:7 (covenant between Laban and Jacob).

scription of Moses' ascent in Exodus 24:12-18, for a biblical source for this revelation. According to the sequence of events in Exodus 24ff., the content of the revelation during the forty-day period was the instructions regarding the construction of the tabernacle in chapters 25ff. However, according to *Jubilees* the content was none other than *Jubilees* itself.

A similar narrative framework was apparently added to the *Temple Scroll.* This scroll was preserved only from column 2 onward; the first column has not survived.[27] However, the content of the second column can perhaps be used to reconstruct the first one in the most general terms. Column 2 includes Exodus 34:10-16, with the addition of one verse from Deuteronomy 7 in the middle of that passage. Apparently, column 1 contained the first part of Exodus 34. This chapter describes the renewal of the covenant between God and Israel through the intercession of Moses, following the sin of the golden calf. This renewal included another revelation after which Moses received a second set of tablets. Thus this chapter includes both Sinaitic revelation and divine legislation of laws. If this reconstruction of the first column of the scroll is correct, then the author of the *Temple Scroll,* similarly to *Jubilees,* distinguished between his composition and the Pentateuch itself. The Torah was given in Exodus 19–24 while the *Temple Scroll* was received in Exodus 34. At the same time, the author appeals to the authority of the Torah as it provides the evidence for this revelation. According to the authors of these compositions, the Pentateuch itself allows for the possibility of divine manifestation including revelation of new laws following the initial Sinaitic theophany. By casting their compositions within a new narrative frame, the authors distinguished their works from the biblical text, while simultaneously lending authority to their writings by connecting them to the Bible itself.

Voice

Biblical narrative is generally written in third person, describing the events from a somewhat detached perspective. Both *Jubilees* and the *Temple Scroll,* besides the addition of a narrative frame at the beginning of the compositions, change the voice of the narrator throughout. *Jubilees* introduces the character of the Angel of the Presence, absent from the Pentateuch, who dictates the book to Moses in a Sinaitic revelation. The addition of angelic figures is well documented in Jewish literature of the Second Temple period.

27. E. Qimron, ed., *The Temple Scroll: A Critical Edition with Extensive Reconstructions,* Judean Desert Studies (Jerusalem: Israel Exploration Society, 1996), 11.

The insertion of an angel as an intermediary specifically into the most significant theophany in the Bible has the effect of distancing YHWH from direct
contact with worldly matters. In fact, in a number of passages *Jubilees* elimi-
nates such contact between man and God when it is present in the Bible.[28]
Regarding the question of voice, the role of the angel as narrator led to a different viewpoint in the retelling of the story. This distinction can be observed
both stylistically and in content. Regarding the style, descriptions of angels in
the Torah in the third person are transformed in *Jubilees* to first person. In
terms of content, the angels function sometimes in place of God, thus changing the nature of the relationship between human characters and the divine
realm.[29]

The *Temple Scroll* refrains from introducing any new characters into its
revision but rather rewrites passages from the Torah with God as the narrator.
This change is presumably intended to ascribe authority to the laws of the
Pentateuch, as they derive directly from the Lord. The use of the first person
in this scroll emphasizes the divine status of the statutes, and at the same time
emphasizes the difference between this work and the Torah itself.[30]

Expansion versus Abridgment

In all the cases in which one can identify two editions of the same work, the
question arises which of the two versions is earlier. In some cases, such as Exodus 35–40, the two editions differ merely in order. However, in many cases
the most significant difference between the two editions relates to their
length. For example, a statistical comparison between the MT and LXX editions of Jeremiah indicates that the shorter (LXX, 4QJer[b,d]) version of the
book is at least one-sixth shorter than the MT version.[31] Although the deci-
sion regarding which of the two precedes the other is by definition subjective,

28. For example, the author skips over the dialogue between God and humans
found in Gen. 3:8-13 and 4:8-12.

29. The most obvious example is the Angel of the Presence as the intermediary at Sinai. Other instances include 3:1, 9, 12, 15; 4:2; 16:1; 18:9-11; etc.

30. For a discussion of the pseudepigraphical aspects of the *Temple Scroll*, see L. H.
Schiffman, "The Temple Scroll and the Halakhic Pseudepigrapha of the Second Temple
Period," in *Pseudepigraphic Perspectives: The Apocrypha and Pseudepigrapha in Light of the
Dead Sea Scrolls. Proceedings of the Second International Symposium of the Orion Center for
the Study of the Dead Sea Scrolls and Associated Literature, 12-14 January 1997*, ed. E. Chazon
and M. E. Stone (Leiden: Brill, 1999), 121-31.

31. Tov, *Textual Criticism*, 320-27.

the overwhelming impression from the study of that book is that the shorter version was later expanded into the longer edition. The same argument can be used with reference to other books such as Esther and Daniel, and to shorter passages such as the opening of 1 Samuel 11[32] and the two editions of Psalm 151 (LXX and 11QPs[a]).[33] Scribes in the ancient world were not merely copyists, but allowed themselves the liberty of adding to their biblical sources. Interestingly, the number of instances in which one can identify abridgment or reduction by such scribes of their sources is somewhat rare. The tendency to refrain from deleting material can be understood against the religious backdrop of the scribes. Although they felt enough freedom to change their texts, such alterations did not do away with any of the material found in their *Vorlagen*. The texts they revised and rewrote were holy in their eyes, and thus needed to be preserved. From their perspective, the addition of material to improve their texts preserved the original text they were revising, and this revised copy continued to be treated as the same composition as its source. Once a scribe removed material, he could no longer claim he was preserving the same composition, because one can no longer identify the source within the revision.

In rewritten biblical compositions one finds both phenomena, expansion and abridgment, side by side. Sometimes the rewriter adds to his source, and at other times he shortens the biblical stories. At times he skips over entire passages and chooses not to refer to them in his new composition. By definition, after a reviser has abridged, deleted, or disregarded entire sections, his new composition no longer contains the biblical source he reworked. In contrast to another edition of the same composition, a scribe who reduces his source makes no pretense of producing a text identified with or equal to it. Thus by changing it, he has not corrupted his biblical source, for he never intended to produce another edition of that work.

---

32. As argued by A. Rofé, "The Acts of Nahash according to 4QSam[a]," *IEJ* 32 (1982): 129-33; against F. M. Cross, "The Ammonite Oppression of the Tribes of Gad and Reuben: Missing Verses from 1 Samuel 11 Found in 4QSamuel[a]," in *The Hebrew and Greek Texts of Samuel*, ed. E. Tov (Jerusalem: Academon, 1980), 105-20, reprinted in H. Tadmor and M. Weinfeld, eds., *History, Historiography, and Interpretation* (Jerusalem: Magnes Press, 1983), 148-58; P. K. McCarter Jr., *I Samuel*, AB 8 (Garden City, N.Y.: Doubleday, 1980), 198-207; Tov, *Textual Criticism*, 342-44. Even those scholars who posit that these verses are original to 1 Sam. 11 suggest that they were omitted by accident.

33. See my discussion, "The Literary Development of Psalm 151: A New Look at the Septuagint," *Textus* 21 (2002): 139-58.

Tendentious Editorial Layer

According to the formulation of the question raised earlier in the article, both biblical manuscripts and rewritten biblical compositions attest to scribal intervention in their sources. But it is important to stress that the alterations in each category differ in both content and thoroughness. Regarding the content, the differences between two editions of the same biblical composition do not change the basic ideological framework of the book. For example, Tov described the ideational and editorial nature of the additional layer found in the MT of Jeremiah as consisting of the following elements: emphasis upon the guilt of the nation, emphasis upon the centrality of God, actualization, possible priestly emphases, fulfillment of prophecies, exile of the residents of Jerusalem who survived the destruction, and a reference to the Covenant between the Pieces in 34:18-19.[34] None of these differences changes the message of this work or the totality of ideas preserved in the shorter edition. 4Q365 (labeled 4QRP^c), fragments 6a column ii and 6c, preserves an expanded form of the Song of Miriam, which consists of only one verse (Exod. 15:21) in all other textual witnesses. This expansion does not alter the narrative context of the crossing of the sea in any way, and was apparently intended to create symmetry between the shorter Song of Miriam and the longer Song of the Sea sung by Moses and the people of Israel.[35] Even in the book of Daniel, where entire stories such as Susanna and Bel and the Dragon were added in the longer edition, as attested in the LXX version of the book, those additions blend into the general spirit of the book.[36]

In contrast, regarding rewritten biblical compositions, it is possible in almost every case to identify and describe the fundamental beliefs and concepts of the rewritten works. In many cases these beliefs differ from those found in the biblical source undergoing revision. For example, concerning Chronicles, Japhet identified differences between this later biblical book and its sources regarding fundamental beliefs and concepts such as: perception of God, the relationship between Israel and the Lord, and the essence of Israel itself.[37] Similarly, in *Jubilees* one can identify clear tendencies that influenced

---

34. E. Tov, "The Characterization of the Additional Layer of the Masoretic Text of Jeremiah," *ErIsr* 26 (1999): 55-63 (in Hebrew).

35. Tov and White, "Reworked Pentateuch," 269-72.

36. A possible exception to this phenomenon can be found in Esther, where the additions to the book preserved in the LXX do change the ideational framework of the story, specifically by inserting God, who is absent in the MT, into the narrative.

37. S. Japhet, *The Ideology of the Book of Chronicles and Its Place in Biblical Thought*, BEATAJ 9 (New York: Peter Lang, 1997).

the rewriting of the Pentateuch, concerning eschatology, calendar and chronology, angels, and the origin of law in the patriarchal period. These beliefs certainly have roots in the Bible itself, but these ideas serve as a basis for further development in the rewritten compositions. Despite the literary dependence upon their sources, the rewritten compositions differ in their ideas and spirit from the compositions upon which the new texts are based.

Among textual witnesses of the Bible, one can identify variants that are the result of ideological or theological considerations. Thus, for example, the MT of Deuteronomy 32:8 preserves the well-known theological correction, למספר בני ישראל, "according to the number of the children of Israel," instead of the original reading found in the LXX and 4QDeutʲ, למספר בני אלהים, "according to the number of the children of God." The MT version of this verse attests to an attempt to remove a possible polytheistic reference from the Song of Moses.[38] But the difference between this variant and the tendencies that appear in the rewritten compositions pertains to the scope of such changes. A tendentious editorial layer includes scribal intervention not merely in specific verses but throughout the entire composition. This editorial process, which as suggested above is the primary motivation behind the rewriting of biblical texts, presents the innovation of the revised composition.

Explicit References to the Source Composition

In at least one composition one finds an explicit reference to the source composition upon which the rewritten composition is based. *Jubilees* 6:22, describing the Feast of Weeks, comments that the laws of this festival will not be quoted in *Jubilees* itself, for they are already found in *maṣḥafa ḥagg za-qadāmi*, "the book of the first Law." This presumably refers to the Pentateuch itself, which includes the laws of all the festivals. *Jubilees* itself would thus be "the book of the second Law," a title which is appropriate for the description above of *Jubilees* as the object of the revelation on Moses' second ascent to Sinai. This reference to the Torah with a specific title indicates that the author perceived his work to be separate from his source. Information included in his source need not be repeated in his new composition. In contrast, biblical

---

38. Compare the similar correction in the two parallel verses, Pss. 29:1 and 96:7. The use of the Greek word ἄγγελος, "angel," to translate בן, "son," in the phrase "sons of God" in Gen. 6:2; Deut. 32:8; Job 1:6; 2:1; 38:7 is also an attempt to mitigate any suggestion of divine offspring.

manuscripts cannot offer any such references, for they are intended to present a copy of the same work, and therefore cannot refer to their source as a different text.

Proliferation of Rewritten Biblical Compositions in the Second Temple Period

This study relates to the phenomenon of Rewritten Bible specifically in the Second Temple period, for the vast majority of compositions belonging to this genre originated during this time. A comparison with the reuse of biblical literature in earlier periods will perhaps shed light on the proliferation of such works in this era.

Numerous scholars have recognized that the Bible itself attests to the earliest stages of biblical interpretation. Thus, for example, certain laws in Deuteronomy present reinterpretations of those found in the Book of the Covenant. Most significantly, it can be shown that this later revision adopts the language and formulations found in the legal passages in Exodus, altering the earlier material according to a new perspective.[39] This process is essentially the same as found in later rewritten compositions, but on a smaller scale. This process of rewriting is found in other genres of biblical literature as well. Micah 4:1-5 quotes Isaiah 2:2-4 (with minor variations), and then proceeds to overturn Isaiah's universalistic message through the addition of verse 5, "for all the nations will go each in the name of his god, and we will go in the name of YHWH our God forever and ever."[40]

In light of the vast collection of such examples amassed in studies of inner-biblical interpretation,[41] it is possible to posit that the genre of Rewritten Bible is not unique to the Second Temple period, but rather can be identified in earlier stages of biblical literature. The motivation behind this reuse in earlier literature is presumably the same as that suggested above for the phenomenon of rewriting in the Second Temple period: the reuse of the earlier, authoritative texts automatically ascribes that authority to the new composition that contains the source. If so, the importance of the Rewritten

39. Cf. B. M. Levinson, *Deuteronomy and the Hermeneutics of Legal Innovation* (New York: Oxford University Press, 1997).

40. Y. Zakovitch, *An Introduction to Inner-Biblical Interpretation* (Even Yehuda: Rekhes, 1992), 81 (in Hebrew).

41. Major studies of this phenomenon include M. Fishbane, *Biblical Interpretation in Ancient Israel* (Oxford: Oxford University Press, 1985); Zakovitch, *An Introduction to Inner-Biblical Interpretation*.

Bible compositions in the Second Temple period should not be exaggerated. The later rewritings essentially follow the patterns and processes present in the creation of compositions from the First Temple period and on. Rewriting, as opposed to creative composition, is characteristic of this corpus of religious literature in which later writers always looked to the past to suggest new ideas in the present and for the future. Rewriting was thus the rule and not the exception.

At the same time, one cannot ignore the pronounced proliferation of rewritten compositions in the Second Temple period. The primary difference between these texts and the examples of inner-biblical rewritings described above is the scope of the compositions being rewritten. In the earlier examples one can identify individual laws, prophecies, or narrative passages undergoing a process of adoption and revision in other biblical books. In the Second Temple period, this technique of rewriting was expanded and applied to entire compositions. Chronicles, *Jubilees*, the *Temple Scroll*, and 1 Esdras all rewrote complete crystallized literary works. Perhaps this profusion of such works can be related to the development of biblical literature as a whole. Today the vast majority of scholars has accepted that most of the biblical books reached their final literary form only in the exilic and postexilic periods. Only then did they crystallize into extensive literary units. The process of rewriting these lengthy compositions could thus begin only in the Second Temple period when such works were in circulation.

The process of using earlier material, creating new compositions by using the building blocks of the past, continued until the rabbinic period, following the destruction of the temple, in which the process of rewriting older material appears to have ceased. In its place one finds almost exclusively the quotation of a lemma followed by interpretation.[42] Thus in the area of literary composition, the authors of the Second Temple period can be located in the world of biblical writers and not alongside rabbinic interpreters.[43]

---

42. The Qumran scrolls provide examples of a lemma followed by exegesis, for example in the *pesher* literature. M. J. Bernstein, "4Q252: From Rewritten Bible to Bible Commentary," *JJS* 45 (1994): 1-27, has also demonstrated the beginnings of this form in 4Q252, a composite, exegetical commentary on Genesis.

43. S. Talmon, "The Textual Study of the Bible: A New Outlook," in *Qumran and the History of the Biblical Text*, 321-400, on pp. 378-81 stresses this point specifically regarding the Qumran sect. His remarks can be extended to include other Jewish groups in the Second Temple period as well.

Interpretations of the Creation of Humanity in the Dead Sea Scrolls

JOHN J. COLLINS

The Dead Sea Scrolls are what the literary critic Harold Bloom would call "belated literature" in the sense that they are, and explicitly claim to be, largely derivative from an older corpus of writings that is recognized as authoritative.[1] By the Hellenistic age, the books of the Torah and the prophets had acquired what would later be called "canonical" status,[2] and new teachings were often presented as interpretations of the sacred texts. (An early example of explicit biblical interpretation can be seen in Daniel 9, where Jeremiah's prophecy that Jerusalem would be desolate for seventy years is reinterpreted as meaning seventy weeks of years.) This reliance on older scriptures is especially evident in the Dead Sea Scrolls. According to the *Damascus Document,* the "converts of Judah" dug the "well" of the Torah with the implements provided by the Interpreter of the Law (CD 6), who was presumably identical with the Teacher of Righteousness, "to whom God made known all the mysteries of the words of his servants the Prophets" (1QpHab 7).

Biblical interpretation takes many forms in the Dead Sea Scrolls, and is found in a wide range of literary genres.[3] These include the explicit bibli-

---

1. Harold Bloom, *The Anxiety of Influence* (New York: Oxford University Press, 1975), passim.

2. On the formation of the canon, see J. J. Collins, "Before the Canon: Scriptures in Second Temple Judaism," in Collins, *Seers, Sibyls, and Sages in Hellenistic-Roman Judaism* (Leiden: Brill, 1997), 3-21; Lee McDonald and James A. Sanders, eds., *The Canon Debate* (Peabody, Mass.: Hendrickson, 2002).

3. For an overview see M. J. Bernstein, "Interpretation of Scriptures," in *Encyclope-*

cal commentaries on prophetic texts, known as *pesharim*,[4] but also narrative and legal texts that weave biblical allusions into their fabric. The examples I want to consider here are found primarily in wisdom texts. They are not formal interpretations, where a passage is cited and then explained. Rather they allude to the biblical text in the process of expounding their teaching. Nonetheless, they imply an exegetical understanding of the texts in question, and at least in some cases we can reconstruct the reasoning that is involved.

Adam and Eve

The passages that I will consider relate to the creation of humanity, and involve the interpretation of Genesis 1–3. Few if any passages in Scripture are better known than the story of Adam and Eve, and few have had such a profound influence on the understanding of human nature in the Western world. It may come as a surprise, then, to find that this story is hardly reflected at all in the rest of the Hebrew Bible. The prophet Ezekiel taunts the king of Tyre by saying that he was in "Eden the garden of God" after he was created, and was subsequently driven out by a cherub (Ezek. 28:13-16), and so he presumably knew a story about the primal man. Ezekiel's story is somewhat different from what we find in Genesis, however. His Eden is "on the mountain of God" and the primal man is covered with precious stones. There is no mention of Eve. Ezekiel may have known a different story about the primal man and Eden, even if it overlapped with the Genesis narrative in some details.[5] There is in fact no clear reference to the story of Adam and Eve in the Hebrew Bible. In view of the importance of the story in later tradition, this fact is quite amazing. Apparently, the question of the origin of sin, and of what we know as the fallen human condition, was not felt to be as pressing by the biblical writers as by later theologians.

That situation changed, however, in the early second century B.C.E.,

---

dia of the Dead Sea Scrolls, ed. L. H. Schiffman and J. C. VanderKam, 2 vols. (New York: Oxford University Press, 2000), 376-83.

4. See most recently J. H. Charlesworth, ed., *The Dead Sea Scrolls. Hebrew, Aramaic, and Greek Texts with English Translations*, 6B. *Pesharim, Other Commentaries, and Related Documents* (Tübingen: Mohr Siebeck; Louisville: Westminster John Knox, 2002); D. W. Parry and E. Tov, eds., *Exegetical Texts* (Leiden: Brill, 2004). There are also *pesharim* on Genesis and Psalms, and thematic *pesharim* that weave together passages from various books.

5. The myth to which Ezekiel alludes remains elusive. See M. Greenberg, *Ezekiel 21–37*, AB 22A (New York: Doubleday, 1997), 592-93.

when there seems to have been a lively debate about the origin of sin.[6] One colorful explanation, the myth of the fallen angels, which is propounded at length in the Book of the Watchers in *1 Enoch* 1–36, took as its point of departure the story in Genesis 6 of the "sons of God" who were attracted to the daughters of men. It is at this time too that we begin to find reflection on Genesis 2–3. Some of the earliest examples of such reflection are found in the book of Ben Sira, or Ecclesiasticus, and the tradition is carried on in the Dead Sea Scrolls.[7] Here I want to begin with Ben Sira in order to illustrate the context in which interpretations found in the scrolls developed.[8]

Ben Sira

Ben Sira's best-known allusion to Genesis 2–3 is a rather unfortunate one: "From a woman sin had its beginning, and because of her we all die" (Sir. 25:24). This reading of Genesis, placing the primary blame and responsibility on Eve, became very common in antiquity. It was enshrined in the canonical New Testament in 1 Timothy 2:13-14, which forbade women to teach or have authority over men, since "Adam was not deceived, but the woman was deceived and became a transgressor." This line of interpretation, however, becomes common only in the first century of the common era. Even in Ben Sira, as we shall see, it is somewhat anomalous, as it does not occur in the passages where he discusses the Genesis account of creation. In fact, it has been suggested that he was not referring to Eve at all when he said that sin had its beginning from a woman, although the suggestion is not persuasive.[9] There is only one comparable text in

6. See J. J. Collins, *Apocalypticism in the Dead Sea Scrolls* (London: Routledge, 1997), 30-35.

7. An extensive sampling of passages treating Adam and Eve in early Jewish and Christian literature, including Ben Sira, can be found in J. L. Kugel, *Traditions of the Bible: A Guide to the Bible as It Was at the Start of the Common Era* (Cambridge: Harvard University Press, 1998), 93-144. The wisdom texts from the Dead Sea Scrolls, which were edited only in recent years, are not included in Kugel's survey. G. A. Anderson, *The Genesis of Perfection: Adam and Eve in Jewish and Christian Imagination* (Louisville: Westminster John Knox, 2001), provides a rich survey of traditions but refers neither to Ben Sira nor to the Dead Sea Scrolls. Other early reflections on Gen. 2–3 are found in *1 Enoch* 32:6; 85:3-10; *Jub.* 2–3. See further my essay "Before the Fall: The Earliest Interpretations of Adam and Eve," in *The Idea of Biblical Interpretation: Essays in Honor of James L. Kugel,* ed. H. Najman and J. H. Newman (Leiden: Brill, 2004), 293-308.

8. For a fuller treatment of Ben Sira's interpretation of Genesis see J. J. Collins, *Jewish Wisdom in the Hellenistic Age* (Louisville: Westminster John Knox, 1997), 80-84.

9. J. R. Levison, "Is Eve to Blame? A Contextual Analysis of Sirach 25:24," *CBQ* 47 (1985): 617-23.

the Dead Sea Scrolls. This is a rather notorious fragment that was published by John Allegro under the title "The Wiles of the Wicked Woman" (4Q184).[10] This text describes a seductress, of whom it says: "She is the beginning of all the ways of iniquity . . . for her ways are ways of death." The Qumran text is not alluding to Genesis, but rather to the description of the "strange woman" (אשה זרה) in Proverbs 7. In Proverbs, this evil woman is the antitype of Wisdom, who is also portrayed as a female figure, and who is created as the beginning of the ways of God. The same Hebrew word (ראשית) is used for "beginning" in Proverbs and in 4Q184, whereas Sirach uses a different word (תחלה). In the Qumran text (as in Proverbs) the ways of death refer to spiritual death, which can be avoided. In contrast, Sirach says that "because of her we all die," and this is surely an allusion to Genesis. The point I would like to emphasize, however, is that this reading of Genesis was exceptional in the pre-Christian period, although later it was espoused by Jews and Christians alike.[11]

Ben Sira draws directly on Genesis in an account of creation in chapter 17:

> The Lord created human beings out of earth,
>   and makes them return to it again.
> He gave them a fixed number of days,
>   but granted them authority over everything on the earth.
> He endowed them with strength like his own,
>   and made them in his own image.
> He put the fear of them in all living beings,
>   and gave them dominion over beasts and birds. . . .
> He filled them with knowledge and understanding,
>   and showed them good and evil. . . .
> He bestowed knowledge upon them,
>   and allotted to them the law of life.
> He established with them an eternal covenant,
>   and revealed to them his decrees. (Sir. 17:1-12)

Several points should be noted about this passage. First, Ben Sira makes no distinction between the account of creation in Genesis 1 and that in Genesis

---

10. J. M. Allegro, "The Wiles of the Wicked Woman: A Sapiential Work from Qumran's Fourth Cave," *PEQ* 96 (1964): 53-55; *Qumrân Cave 4.I (4Q158-4Q186)*, DJD 5 (Oxford: Clarendon, 1968), 82-85. Note the corrections of Allegro's edition by John Strugnell, "Notes en marge du volume V des 'Discoveries in the Judaean Desert of Jordan,'" *RevQ* 7 (1970): 263-68. See also D. J. Harrington, *Wisdom Texts from Qumran* (London: Routledge, 1996), 31-35.

11. For further examples of this line of interpretation see Kugel, *Traditions of the Bible*, 100-102 and 128-29; Anderson, *The Genesis of Perfection*, 99-116.

2–3. The idea that human beings are taken from the earth is derived from Genesis 2, while the statements that God made them in his own image and gave them dominion over the beasts come from Genesis 1. Ancient exegetes were not unaware of the differences between the two accounts in Genesis, and could exploit them when it suited their purposes, as we shall see, but they did not feel constrained by them, as a modern interpreter might.

A second observation is more significant, as it concerns an apparent discrepancy between Ben Sira and the biblical text. According to Genesis, God explicitly forbade Adam and Eve to eat from the tree of the knowledge of good and evil. Ben Sira records no such prohibition. On the contrary, we are told, God filled them with knowledge and showed them good and evil. This is a bold reinterpretation of what seems to be the perfectly clear meaning of the biblical text. Wisdom and knowledge were unequivocally good things from the point of view of a wisdom teacher like Ben Sira. It was inconceivable that God would have restricted human access to them. So Ben Sira here simply skips the whole unpleasant incident of the fall. There is no original sin here, and mortality is not imposed as a punishment. From the beginning, God intended that people would live a limited number of days. (This point is reiterated later in 41:4, where we are told that death is simply "the decree of the Lord for all flesh.") The situation of Adam is no different from that of his descendants. All alike are given an eternal covenant and told God's decrees. (Here Sirach seems to read the revelation at Sinai back into the account of creation.) Genesis is read in light of Deuteronomy. Everyone has knowledge of the law, and is responsible for his or her own actions. In all of this, Sirach seems to read Genesis in light of everything else he believes to be true. Genesis, as part of the revealed Torah, cannot contradict the truth, even if this means that some parts of the text must be disregarded.

But if God had endowed humanity with wisdom and given them knowledge of good and evil, how is the reality of human sin to be explained? Ben Sira addresses this problem in another passage:

> Do not say, "It was the Lord's doing that I fell away,"
> for he does not do what he hates.
> Do not say, "It was he who led me astray,"
> For he has no need of the sinful. . . .
> God created humankind in the beginning
> and placed him in the power of his inclination.
> If you choose, you can keep the commandments,
> and to act faithfully is a matter of your own choice. (15:11-20)

The idea that it might be the Lord's doing was not altogether far-fetched. The Hebrew Bible had spoken of "an evil spirit from the Lord" that afflicted King Saul (1 Sam. 19:9). Ben Sira himself seems to entertain such a possibility in another passage that refers to Genesis (Sir. 33:10-13): "Every man is a vessel of clay, and Adam was created out of the dust. In the fullness of his knowledge the Lord distinguished them and appointed their different ways. Some he blessed and exalted, and some he made holy and brought near to himself; but some he cursed and brought low, and turned them out of their place. Like clay in the hand of the potter, to be molded as he pleases, so all are in the hand of their Maker, to be given whatever he decides." In chapter 15, however, Ben Sira places the emphasis on human free will rather than on divine determinism. His way of doing this, however, is noteworthy. Human beings are in the power of their inclination. The Hebrew word here, יֵצֶר, comes from the verb meaning "to form" which is used in Genesis 2:7 ("The Lord God formed man out of the dust of the ground"). There is no mention of an inclination in Genesis 2–3, but the word occurs twice in the flood story: "every inclination of their thoughts is evil continually" (Gen. 6:5) and "the inclination of the human heart is evil from youth" (Gen. 8:21). The association of the "inclination" with evil is typical of biblical usage. Only two passages in the Hebrew Bible use the word in a positive sense (Isa. 26:3 and 1 Chron. 29:18). The negative sense of the inclination is attested in the book of 4 Ezra, which was composed about 100 C.E. and attributes the sin of Adam to the fact that he was burdened with "an evil heart." Later, in rabbinic literature there was a developed doctrine of two inclinations.[12] The righteous are ruled by the good inclination, the wicked by the evil inclination, and average people by both. The idea of two inclinations was derived from Genesis by a typical piece of rabbinic exegesis. The Hebrew word for "formed" in the phrase "the Lord God formed man" (וַיִּיצֶר) has the letter *yod* twice, and this was taken to indicate that there were two inclinations.[13] This distinction between good and bad inclinations is not yet found in Ben Sira, at least not clearly, but we can see that he is using the Genesis text to wrestle with the problem of the origin of evil. It should be noted that Ben Sira has no place for a devil, and that he ignores the snake of Genesis.[14]

12. See G. F. Moore, *Judaism in the First Centuries of the Christian Era* (New York: Schocken, 1975), 1:474-96; E. E. Urbach, *The Sages: Their Concepts and Beliefs* (Jerusalem: Magnes, 1975), 1:471-83; G. H. Cohen Stuart, *The Struggle in Man between Good and Evil: An Inquiry into the Origin of the Rabbinic Concept of Yeṣer Hara'* (Kampen: Kok, 1984).

13. *Gen. Rab.* 14:4.

14. The Hebrew text of Sir. 15:14 adds "and placed him in the power of his spoiler," but this statement is not found in the ancient translations and is evidently a late addition to the text. The snake in Genesis is clearly identified as the devil in Rev. 12:9. The Wisdom

Wisdom Texts in the Scrolls

The idea that God endowed humanity with knowledge and wisdom from the beginning, which we have seen in Sirach 17, is also found in several texts from Qumran. In 4QWords of the Heavenly Luminaries (4Q504) we read that God fashioned Adam in the image of his glory: "the breath of life you blew into his nostril, and intelligence and knowledge."[15] This understanding of Genesis is also reflected in the fragmentary 4QMeditation on Creation (4Q303), which mentions "the knowledge of good and evil" before the creation of Eve.[16] Like Ben Sira, some of these texts telescope Genesis 1 and Genesis 2–3 into a single account. This appears to be the case in the Words of the Heavenly Luminaries, and also in 4QParaphrase of Genesis and Exodus (4Q422).[17] The latter two texts explicitly refer to the prohibition, which led to the fall.[18] This is not the case, however, in all texts from Qumran that discuss the story of creation.

The most important of the wisdom texts found at Qumran is a long composition now known as 4QInstruction (formerly 4QSapiential Work A).[19] This text touches on the interpretation of Genesis at a number of points. One of the relevant passages is found in the fragmentary 4Q423: "and every fruit that is produced and every tree which is good, pleasing to give knowledge. Is [it] not a ga[rden of pastu]re [and pleasant] to [gi]ve great knowledge? He set you in charge of it to till it and guard it . . . thorns and thistles it will sprout forth for you, and its strength it will not yield to you . . . in your being unfaithful."[20] While much is unclear in this passage, it appears that the Genesis story is taken as a metaphor for the situation of the person addressed in the text. Most

---

of Solomon, which was composed in the early first century c.e., says death entered the world through "the envy of the devil" (Wis. 2:24). This is probably an allusion to the snake of Genesis.

15. E. G. Chazon, "The Creation and Fall of Adam in the Dead Sea Scrolls," in *The Book of Genesis in Jewish and Oriental Christian Interpretation,* ed. J. Frishman and L. van Rompay (Leuven: Peeters, 1997), 15.

16. T. H. Lim, "303. 4QMeditation on Creation A," in *Qumran Cave 4. XXV: Sapiential Texts, Part 1,* ed. T. Elgvin et al., DJD 20 (Oxford: Clarendon, 1997), 152-53.

17. T. Elgvin and E. Tov, "Paraphrase of Genesis and Exodus," in *Qumran Cave 4. VIII: Parabiblical Texts, Part I,* ed. H. Attridge et al., DJD 13 (Oxford: Clarendon, 1994), 421-22.

18. Chazon, "The Creation and Fall," 16-17; T. Elgvin, "The Genesis Section of 4Q422 (4QparaGenExod)," *DSD* 1 (1994): 185.

19. J. Strugnell and D. J. Harrington, *Qumran Cave 4. XXIV: Sapiential Texts, Part 2. 4QInstruction (Mūsār lĕMēvîn),* DJD 34 (Oxford: Clarendon, 1999).

20. The edition of 4Q423 in DJD 34 is by Torleif Elgvin. Elgvin's dissertation, *An Analysis of 4QInstruction,* is forthcoming from Brill.

noteworthy is the interpretation of the trees. According to Genesis 2:9: "Out of the ground the Lord God made to grow every tree that is pleasant to the sight and good for food, the tree of life also in the midst of the garden, and the tree of the knowledge of good and evil." Again in 3:6: "the woman saw that the tree was good for food, and that it was a delight to the eyes, and that the tree was to be desired to make one wise." The Qumran text picks up the idea that the trees are symbolic sources of wisdom and knowledge. It does not, however, seem to pick up the prohibition against eating from the tree of the knowledge of good and evil. Rather, it would seem, the garden is ambiguous. It gives knowledge and wisdom to the good, but thorns and thistles to those who are unfaithful. If this is correct (the text is too fragmentary to permit certainty), then the Qumran text is taking a position similar to what we found in Ben Sira: there is no prohibition of the knowledge of good and evil, and consequently no "fall," but people may still choose to do wrong. If the earth produces thistles and brambles, this is not the fault of a primeval Adam but of each generation of human beings. The idea that nature responds differently to the righteous and to the wicked is found explicitly in Ben Sira 39:27: "All these are good for the godly, but for sinners they turn into evils." The precise interpretation of 4Q423, however, depends on what is meant by "being unfaithful," which is difficult to assess with certainty because of the fragmentary state of the text.

Also like Ben Sira, the Qumran text posits a role for the human "inclination."[21] "Let not the thought of the evil inclination seduce you," the reader is told (4Q417 2 ii 12-13). Another passage speaks of "the inclination of the flesh" in the context of the need to distinguish between good and evil (4Q416 1 i 15-16). Yet another passage uses "inclination" in a positive sense, "to walk in the inclination of his understanding" (4Q417 1 i 11). It appears, then, that the human inclination may be either good or bad in this text.

The most important discussion of Genesis in the Qumran wisdom texts is found in 4QInstruction in 4Q417 1 i 16-18.[22] The passage speaks of an engraved law that is decreed by God for all the wickedness of the sons of Seth (or Sheth), and a book of remembrance that is written before him for those

21. See J. J. Collins, "Wisdom, Apocalypticism and the Dead Sea Scrolls," in Collins, *Seers, Sibyls, and Sages,* 369-83.

22. Strugnell and Harrington, *Qumran Cave 4. XXIV,* 151-66. For more detailed analysis see J. J. Collins, "In the Likeness of the Holy Ones: The Creation of Humankind in a Wisdom Text from Qumran," in *The Provo International Conference on the Dead Sea Scrolls,* ed. D. W. Parry and E. Ulrich (Leiden: Brill, 1999), 609-18. See now also C. H. T. Fletcher-Louis, *All the Glory of Adam: Liturgical Anthropology in the Dead Sea Scrolls* (Leiden: Brill, 2002), 113-18. M. J. Goff, *The Worldly and Heavenly Wisdom of 4QInstruction* (Leiden: Brill, 2003), 80-126.

who keep his word. This is also called "the Vision of Hagu" or Meditation. The book of Meditation is mentioned elsewhere in the scrolls. Youths are supposed to be educated in it (1QSa 1:6-8) and judges are supposed to study it (CD 10:6; 13:2). It was obviously an important revelation of wisdom, but we cannot identify it with confidence with any extant writing. While the Vision of Hagu in this passage is surely related to the book mentioned elsewhere, the two are not necessarily identical. Then the passage continues: "and he gave it as an inheritance to Enosh (Man?) for according to the likeness of the Holy Ones is his inclination (or: he formed him). But the Hagu (Meditation) was not given to the spirit of flesh, for it did not know the difference between good and evil according to the judgment of its spirit."

This passage bristles with difficulties, and every phrase in it has been interpreted in several ways. One clear point of entry, however, is provided by the statement that the spirit of flesh did not distinguish between good and evil. Here, it seems to me, we have a clear allusion to Genesis 2–3. God did not forbid humanity to eat of the tree of the knowledge of good and evil, according to this text, but some human beings, those who had a "spirit of flesh," failed to grasp the distinction. The spirit of flesh, however, stands in contrast to a "spiritual people," associated with "Enosh," who was deemed worthy to receive the revelation and presumably recognized the difference between good and evil. The reference to "Enosh" has confused modern interpreters, because the word is ambiguous. It can be read as a proper name, referring to the son of Seth, grandson of Adam, who is mentioned in Genesis 4:26; 5:6-7, 9-11.[23] In his time, people began to call on the name of the Lord, and the book of *Jubilees* says he was the first to do so. A reference to Enosh, then, is not implausible here. But neither is it necessary. The Hebrew word אנוש (’ĕnōš) occurs numerous times in the *Thanksgiving Hymns* or *Hodayot* as a generic term for humanity.[24] "How will a man (אנוש) recount his sins?" asks the psalmist in 1QH 9:25. This usage would be problematic in the wisdom text, which distinguishes two kinds of human beings, a spiritual people and a spirit of flesh, and Enosh is associated only with the spiritual people. The word, then, cannot refer here to humanity at large. There is another use of the word, however, that has often been overlooked. The Instruction on the Two Spirits in the *Community Rule* says God "created אנוש to rule the world." In this case אנוש (’ĕnōš) is clearly Adam, the prototypical human being.

23. So A. Lange, *Weisheit und Prädestination. Weisheitliche Urordnung und Prädestination in den Textfunden von Qumran* (Leiden: Brill, 1995), 87.

24. Strugnell and Harrington entertain the possibility both of a general reference and of a reference to Enosh (DJD 34, 164).

The relevance of Adam to the passage from 4QInstruction is shown by the qualifying phrase: "for according to the likeness of the Holy Ones is his inclination" (or, he formed him). The Holy Ones in the Dead Sea Scrolls and contemporary texts are heavenly beings, or angels. The scrolls sometimes call these beings אלהים (*ĕlōhîm*), which can mean either gods, in the plural, or God in the singular. The Hebrew phrase "according to the likeness of the Holy Ones" is in fact a paraphrase of Genesis 1:27, which says God created Adam (or humankind) "in the image of God." The Qumran text understands this as in the image of the Holy Ones or angels, rather than in the image of the Most High. Enosh is Adam, formed in the likeness of the heavenly beings.

But then where does the "spirit of flesh" come from? The simplest answer, perhaps, is from Genesis 2. We have seen that Ben Sira harmonized the two accounts in Genesis, and read them as one. 4QInstruction, if I read it correctly, uses the two accounts in order to distinguish two kinds of human being, the spiritual kind, whose creation is reported in Genesis 1, and the fleshly kind described in Genesis 2–3.[25] Only the fleshly kind fails to recognize the difference between good and evil, in accordance with the story in Genesis 2–3. This kind of interpretation of Genesis, which explains the two creation stories as a double creation, is rare in antiquity but not unique. Philo of Alexandria wrote in his *Allegorical Interpretation:* "There are two types of men; the one a heavenly man, the other an earthly. The heavenly man, being made after the image of God, is altogether without part or lot in corruptible and terrestrial substance; but the earthly one was compacted out of the matter scattered here and there, which Moses calls clay."[26] Philo interprets the two Adams in a framework derived from Greek philosophy, and this is very different from anything we find in the Dead Sea Scrolls. What he has in common with the Qumran wisdom text is the idea that the two accounts of creation in Genesis describe the creation of two different kinds of human being. Philo was apparently aware of other interpretations along the same lines.[27] The Qumran texts

25. Against this interpretation, Elgvin has argued that the use of the word יצר (*yṣr*), "to fashion," in connection with creation after the pattern of the holy ones, shows that the two accounts are conflated, since this is the verb used in Gen. 2:7. On his interpretation, the contrast is between Adam before and after the fall. This may read too much, however, into the use of the word יצר (*yṣr*). It is not apparent to me that the man who is made in the likeness of the holy ones is thought to sin or fall at all.

26. Philo, *Allegorical Interpretation* 31; cf. *De Opificio Mundi* 134-35. See T. H. Tobin, *The Creation of Man: Philo and the History of Interpretation* (Washington, D.C.: Catholic Biblical Association, 1983), 108.

27. Philo, *Questions on Genesis* 1.8, reports various answers that were given to the question "why does He place the moulded man in Paradise, but not the man who was made in his image?"

suggest there may have been a wider tradition of interpretation, found also in Hebrew in the land of Israel, that distinguished between the two creation accounts in Genesis.

The later rabbis were also aware of the duplication of creation. According to *Genesis Rabbah* 14:

> There were two formations [one partaking of the nature] of the celestial beings, [the other] of earthly creatures. . . . He created him with four attributes of the higher beings [i.e. the angels] and four of the lower creatures [i.e. the beasts]. . . . R. Tifdai said in R. Aḥa's name: The celestial beings were created in the image and likeness [of God] and do not procreate, while the terrestrial creatures procreate but were not created in [His] image and likeness. Said the Holy One, blessed be He: "Behold, I will create him [man] in [My] image and likeness; [thus he will partake] of the [character of the] celestial beings, while he will procreate [as is the nature] of the terrestrial beings." R. Tifdai [also] said in R. Aḥa's name: The Lord reasoned: "If I create him of the celestial elements he will live [for ever] and not die; while if I create him of the terrestrial elements, he will die and not live. Therefore I will create him of the upper and lower elements; if he sins he will die, and if he dies he will live [in the future life]."[28]

The midrash, however, differs from the Qumran text insofar as it combines the celestial and terrestrial elements in all human beings, whereas the Qumran text distinguishes two distinct types.

The Instruction on the Two Spirits

The distinction between two types, each indicated by the word "spirit" ("people of spirit," "spirit of flesh"), points us to another account of creation in the Dead Sea Scrolls, where the human being is also called אנוש. This is the Instruction on the Two Spirits in the *Community Rule*. According to that passage:

> From the God of Knowledge comes all that is and shall be. Before ever they existed He established their whole design. . . . He has created man (אנוש) to govern the world, and has appointed for him two spirits in which to walk until the time of His visitation: the spirits of truth and injustice. Those born of truth spring from a fountain of light, but those born of injustice spring from a source of darkness. All the children of righteousness are

28. *Gen. Rab.* 14:3; trans. and ed. H. Freedman and M. Simon (New York: Soncino, 1983), 112.

ruled by the Prince of Light, and walk in the ways of light, but all the children of injustice are ruled by the Angel of Darkness and walk in the ways of darkness. . . . (1QS 3:15-21)

This remarkable passage has often been taken as the quintessence of the distinctive theology of the sectarian scrolls. There is no precedent for warring spirits of light and darkness in the Jewish tradition. On the contrary, this concept has its closest parallel in Persian dualism, as has often been noted.[29] While the Jewish author certainly adapts the Persian myth for his purpose, the influence of that myth in shaping the idea of conflicting spirits of light and darkness cannot be doubted. And yet the passage is also an interpretation of Genesis, as we might expect in an account of the creation of humanity. Dependence on Genesis is signaled most clearly in the statement that God created man to rule the world — compare Genesis 1:26. I would argue, however, that even the doctrine of the two spirits should be understood in the context of the ongoing debate about the meaning of Genesis 1–3 and the origin of evil that we have seen in Ben Sira and in the wisdom texts from Qumran.

The insistence that "from the God of knowledge comes all that is" is at odds with at least one strand of Ben Sira's thought, which denied that sin comes from God (although we have seen that Ben Sira was not fully consistent on the subject). If everything comes from God, then sin must come from God too, even if indirectly. The text gives no exegetical justification for the statement that God created two spirits. A possible source may be suggested in Genesis 2:7, which says God breathed into his nostrils the breath of life (נשמת חיים) and he became a living being (נפש חיה); both the breath and the נפש (nepeš) could be understood as spirits. The distinction could also be a development of the distinction between good and bad inclinations.[30] One of the earlier commentators on the passage, P. Wernberg-Moeller, argued that "it is significant that our author regards the two 'spirits' as created by God, and that according to IV,23 and our passage both 'spirits' dwell in man as created by God. We are therefore not dealing here with a kind of metaphysical, cosmic dualism represented by the two 'spirits,' but with the idea that man was created by God with two 'spirits' — the Old Testament term for 'mood' or 'disposition.' . . . We have thus arrived at the rab-

29. See Collins, *Apocalypticism*, 41-43; Collins, *Seers, Sibyls, and Sages*, 287-99; M. Philonenko, "La Doctrine Qoumrânienne de Deux Esprits," in *Apocalyptique Iranienne et Dualisme Qoumrânien*, ed. G. Widengren, A. Hultgård, and M. Philonenko (Paris: Maisonneuve, 1995), 163-211.

30. The term יצר (yṣr) is used in a positive sense in 1QS 4:5 and 8:3, and in a negative sense in 1QS 5:5, but it does not appear in the account of creation.

binic distinction between the evil and the good inclination."[31] The attempt to deny any reference to metaphysical, cosmic dualism in the text is not convincing; the text clearly refers to Angels of Light and Darkness, and these are Spirits in one sense of the word. But the spirits also have a psychological dimension, and here Wernberg-Moeller was right to note the affinity of this distinction with that between the good and evil inclinations. The Persian myth provided the author of this Qumran passage with new language and a new concept to address an old problem — how could the creation of one omnipotent God have yielded evil as well as good? Here again nothing is said about a fall; the assumption is that creation has continued in accordance with God's design. The Instruction concludes with a statement that God has allotted the two spirits to the children of men "that they may know good and evil," another clear allusion to Genesis. Like Ben Sira and 4QInstruction, this text denies that God had ever forbidden humanity to know good and evil. Quite the contrary. Recognition of the distinction might be said to be one of the goals of creation.

Conclusion

What light does this discussion shed on biblical interpretation in the Dead Sea Scrolls?

The first point I would emphasize is that the people who wrote these scrolls were not isolated from the intellectual debates going in Judaism at the time. Of course, it is not certain that the wisdom texts were sectarian in origin. They may have been part of the wider literature preserved at Qumran (like the biblical books, or the books of Enoch). Some scholars even argue that the Instruction on the Two Spirits was composed before the Dead Sea sect separated from the rest of Judaism.[32] Nonetheless, both 4QInstruction and the Instruction on the Two Spirits distinguish two types within humanity, and this kind of distinction was foundational for the self-understanding of the text. Yet we can see the beginnings of this kind of distinction in Ben Sira, who taught that all the works of the Lord come in pairs, one opposite the other (Sir. 33:15), and that God blessed some people and cursed others (33:12). To be sure, the Dead Sea sect did not secede from the rest of Judaism because

31. P. Wernberg-Moeller, "A Reconsideration of the Two Spirits in the Rule of the Community (1Q Serek III,13–IV,26)," *RevQ* 3 (1961): 422.

32. So Lange, *Weisheit und Prädestination,* 126-28; H. Stegemann, *The Library of Qumran* (Grand Rapids: Eerdmans, 1998), 110.

of their understanding of creation or their interpretation of Genesis, but these issues were part of the complex web of factors that shaped the distinctive self-understanding of the sect.

A second issue concerns the variety of biblical interpretation in the scrolls. When we speak of biblical interpretation at Qumran, we most often think of the *pesharim,* which interpreted the prophetic texts as predictions of events in the Hellenistic and Roman periods. But this was not the only kind of biblical interpretation practiced at Qumran. The readings of Genesis 1–3 implied in the texts we have considered resemble the *pesharim* insofar as they typically argue that the biblical texts describe the situation in which the sectarians found themselves. Adam was not a figure of ancient history, but a paradigmatic case with which the reader can identify. In the words of a later apocalypse, each of us is his own Adam (*2 Bar.* 48:42). But we have found no readings of Genesis 2–3 that engage in one-to-one interpretations of elements in the text, such as "the snake is the devil." The interpretations are more subtle than that, and less atomistic. They involve interpretations of creation, not just of the words of Genesis, although verbal interpretation also plays a part.

A third conclusion concerns the freedom of interpretation that we find in these texts. For the modern interpreter it is difficult to understand how someone could ignore the divine commandment to Adam and Eve that they not eat from the tree of good and evil. But all interpretation involves a correlation of what we find in the text with what we hold as true from other sources. For Ben Sira and the wisdom teachers whose work is preserved in the scrolls, it was inconceivable that God would have forbidden people to acquire the knowledge of good and evil. Rather, we are told, people who had a "spirit of flesh" could not grasp the distinction, or the entire creation story unfolded in accordance with a divine plan, so that people would come to understand good and evil and their own mortality. The principle of correlation is also in evidence in the Instruction on the Two Spirits, which seems at first glance to be wildly at variance with the biblical account of creation. The author found in the Persian myth of Light and Darkness apt language to describe his experience of the universe. He then assumed that this must be a fair reflection of the process of creation described in Genesis. We would have appreciated a closer exegetical argument, such as we find later in the midrash, but the author provides sufficient allusions to Genesis to indicate that the two accounts were thought to correspond.

The last point raises a question about the nature of interpretation. Modern theorists have repeatedly emphasized that interpretation is never a neutral matter, that it always depends on the presuppositions we bring to the text. This is as true of modern critical interpretation as it is of interpretation in the Dead Sea Scrolls. Of course, the presuppositions of the authors of the scrolls are generally untenable in the modern world, because of the vast changes in science and philosophy over the last two thousand years. But the transparency of presuppositions in ancient interpretation can carry a salutary lesson for modern critics. If anyone still reads Genesis two thousand years from now, our own interpretations will undoubtedly seem as dated and time-conditioned to those future interpreters as those of the scrolls do to us.

Sinai Revisited

JAMES C. VANDERKAM

The copy of the *Community Rule* from Cave 1 (formerly called the *Manual of Discipline*) was among the first Qumran manuscripts to be found, photographed, and published. It proved to be a rare phenomenon: a Qumran scroll that, apart from a few words here and there, is completely preserved. The added bonus that it presents detailed information about the way a group lived has made it for the last fifty years a central document in scholarship on the nature and identity of the community that resided in the area of Qumran. One of the first and finest commentators on the scroll, J. Licht, wrote that from the *Community Rule,*

> the members of the Qumran community learned how to act and what to believe. Their way of life is defined in it through precise laws and rules that are accompanied by stern warnings directed towards those who transgress the law. Thus they had in this composition the principles of their faith in their explicit formulation. As a result, in this composition the sect describes itself, or — to put it more precisely — through it it presents to the reader the desired, the ideal image, that is, the unique organization and its communal and religious aspirations. The person who approaches the Dead Sea Scrolls to learn from them the nature of the social phenomenon and the religious movement that led to their being written, the one interested in the sect itself (and not in its history or in its literary output) will find precisely in the Community Rule most of the information he desires.[1]

---

1. J. Licht, *The Rule Scroll: A Scroll from the Wilderness of Judea 1QS 1QSa 1QSb* (Jerusalem: Bialik Institute, 1965 [reprint 1996]), 8 (Hebrew; my translation).

Ten additional but fragmentary copies from Cave 4 have allowed us an opportunity not only to observe how important the work was but also to glimpse the evolution of the text, apparently from a shorter early form to a fuller version at a later time. Ironically, the Cave 1 copy, the best-preserved one, although it contains a late form of the text, is one of our most ancient copies.[2]

Although we should grant that a history of writing and editing lies behind the text of 1QS, we may still say that this evolved form of the work, complete with the contents of columns 1-4 (thought to be missing from 4Q258), dates from an early phase of the community's existence. The paleographically determined date of the Cave 1 manuscript is 100-75 B.C.E.[3] and the AMS date is 164-144 B.C.E. or 116 B.C.E.–50 C.E.;[4] thus the text may well offer us data about the community's self-image around or earlier than 100 B.C.E. The self-image of the community as presented in 1QS and the scriptural sources for it are the subject of this paper.

Elements of the Community's Self-Image in 1QS

First we should gather data about the contours of the community that the text depicts. The community behind the text designated itself a יחד *(yaḥad)*, a unity or community (1:1, the noun appears sixty-three times). The term points to the fact that the group formed a unit, a cohesive whole — a feature which comes to visible expression in shared activities such as eating, studying, and praying (cf. 5:2; 6:2-3, 7-8). "As a term for a community it appears only in the Qumran scrolls. The diffusion of the term in the literature of the sect is comparable to that of the parallel Greek term κοινόν or κοινωνία among terms for associations in the Hellenistic period."[5] They were people

---

2. On the development of the text and the relations between the copies, see S. Metso, *The Textual Development of the Community Rule*, STDJ 21 (Leiden: Brill, 1997); and the summary of M. Knibb, "Rule of the Community," in *Encyclopedia of the Dead Sea Scrolls*, ed. L. H. Schiffman and J. C. VanderKam, 2 vols. (New York: Oxford University Press, 2000), 793-97. The official publication of the Cave 4 copies is P. Alexander and G. Vermes, *Qumran Cave 4. XIX: Serekh Ha-Yaḥad and Two Related Texts*, DJD 26 (Oxford: Clarendon, 1998).

3. F. M. Cross, *The Ancient Library of Qumran and Modern Biblical Studies* (Garden City, N.Y.: Anchor Books, 1958), 58.

4. See most recently G. Doudna, "Dating the Scrolls on the Basis of Radiocarbon Analysis," in *The Dead Sea Scrolls after Fifty Years: A Comprehensive Assessment*, ed. P. W. Flint and J. C. VanderKam, 2 vols. (Leiden: Brill, 1998, 1999), 1:469 (one sigma).

5. M. Weinfeld, *The Organizational Pattern and Penal Code of the Qumran Sect: Comparison with Guilds and Religious Associations of the Hellenistic-Roman Period*, NTOA 2 (Fribourg: Éditions Universitaires; Göttingen: Vandenhoeck & Ruprecht, 1986), 13.

who pledged to seek God with their entire heart and soul and to do what God considered good and upright "as He commanded by the hand of Moses and all His servants the Prophets" (1:2-3).[6] Near the beginning of the text one finds an important statement defining the duties of members: "All those who freely devote themselves to His truth shall bring all their knowledge, powers and possessions into the Community [ביחד] of God, that they may purify their knowledge in the truth of God's precepts and order their powers according to His ways of perfection and all their possessions according to His righteous counsel" (1:11-13). Indeed, anyone who "crossed over" (1:16, 18, 20, 24; 2:10) into this covenant fellowship took it upon himself to do all that God had commanded (1:16-17).

Once it has introduced the idea and basic requirements of the covenantal community, the text next depicts various stages in a ceremony for the confirmation and reconfirmation of that covenantal agreement which was the basis of their corporate life (1:18-19). The ceremony, led by priests and levites, involved a confession of sins, blessings recited by the priests, and curses intoned by the levites (as in Deuteronomy 27). The priestly blessing is a reworking of Aaron's benediction in Numbers 6:24-26, while the curse is a negative paraphrase of it (2:2-9). The ceremony is to take place annually, although no date is given (2:19; cf. 5:24).[7] The arrangement of the community members at the ceremony is interesting when we keep in mind that a small group of no more than two hundred members may have lived at Qumran (though they may have been joined by others from different camps): first are the priests, then the levites, and finally the people enter in order "in their Thousands, Hundreds, Fifties, and Tens, that every Israelite may know his place in the Community of God according to the everlasting design" (2:21-23).

Both directly after this description and later in the text we encounter a set of statements about the type of fellowship the covenantal community was meant to practice. Among the statements, these should be highlighted:

---

6. Quotations from the scrolls are taken from G. Vermes, *The Complete Dead Sea Scrolls in English* (New York: Penguin Books, 1997).

7. On the covenantal ceremony section, see M. Weise, *Kultzeiten und kultischer Bundesschluss in der "Ordensregel" vom Toten Meer,* SPB 3 (Leiden: Brill, 1961), 61-112. In the older literature about this section of the *Rule of the Community,* the date on which the ceremony took place was often thought to have been the Day of Atonement. Cf., for example, P. Wernberg-Møller, *The Manual of Discipline,* STDJ 1 (Leiden: Brill, 1957), 14. Weise discusses the matter carefully and concludes that only a special day of confession of sins is entailed (*Kultzeiten,* 79-82, 111).

1. "For according to the holy design, they shall all of them be in a community of truth [ביחד אמת] and virtuous humility, of loving-kindness and good intent one towards the other, and (they shall all of them be) sons of the everlasting Company" (2:24-25).

2. "*This is the Rule for the men of the Community* [היחד] *who have freely devoted themselves* [המתנדבים] *to be converted from all evil and to cling to all His commandments according to His will.* They shall separate from the congregation of the men of injustice and shall unite, with respect to the Law and possessions, under the authority of the sons of Zadok, the Priests who keep the Covenant, and of the multitude of the men of the Community who hold fast to the Covenant" (5:1-3).

3. "Whoever approaches the Council of the Community shall enter the Covenant of God in the presence of all who have freely pledged themselves. He shall undertake by a binding oath to return with all his heart and soul to every commandment of the Law of Moses in accordance with all that has been revealed of it to the sons of Zadok, the Priests, Keepers of the Covenant and Seekers of His will, and to the multitude of the men of their Covenant who together have freely pledged themselves to His truth [המתנדבים יחד לאמתו] and to walking in the way of His delight" (5:7-10).

4. "They shall eat in common and bless in common and deliberate in common" (6:2-3; the word יחד is used for the three instances of "in common").

The procedure for admission into this ideal society, a process that lasted more than two years and apparently culminated in the ceremony described above, involved several stages. One way this gradual admission to full membership comes to expression is evident in the treatment of the candidate's possessions. Upon being admitted to the council of the community after a one-year trial period, "his property and his earnings shall be handed over to the Bursar of the Congregation who shall register it to his account and shall not spend it for the Congregation" (6:19-20). Once he has satisfactorily completed a second year of testing, "his property shall be merged" (6:22) and he begins enjoying full membership in the group.

We could summarize several highlights from these passages as follows:

1. The members of the community considered themselves entrants into a covenant which required that they pledge themselves to obeying all of the law of Moses; they confirmed or reconfirmed the covenant through an annual ceremony.

2. They called themselves a יחד, a unity, and spoke of themselves as ones who had freely pledged loyalty to the covenant. They lived in ideal harmony organized as priests, levites, and people who were further subdivided into units of thousands, hundreds, fifties, and tens.

3. Their community involved extensive sharing, including a community of goods.

4. The *Community Rule* legislates for males, never mentioning women members. Here we should keep in mind the external testimony of Pliny the Elder, who wrote that Essenes living along the shore of the Dead Sea were "without women" (*Natural History* 5.73), and that, according to Josephus, most Essenes did not marry (*War* 2.120-21; *Ant.* 18.21; see Philo, *Apol.* 11.14-17).

Sources for the Group's Self-Image in 1QS

Why did the Qumran community as described in the Cave 1 copy of the *Community Rule* adopt this structure and present itself in these terms? What were the sources, the causes, for these aspects of its self-understanding? I propose that we can explain the situation in good part by seeing the Qumran community as modeling itself after the Israel of the wilderness period, and more particularly after the likeness of Israel as it encamped at the foot of Mount Sinai, with Exodus 19–20 and 24 being the key scriptural foundations. Although, as M. Weinfeld and others have shown, the Qumran community shares a whole series of traits with Hellenistic associations,[8] it is clear that it placed a special stamp on those shared characteristics, a stamp thoroughly influenced by biblical and later Jewish traditions. There are clues enough in the text of Exodus 19–24, especially as that passage was understood by ancient Jewish exegetes, to conclude that Israel at Sinai was the template for the Qumran fellowship. We should survey the evidence under the four points enumerated above.

1. The members of the community considered themselves entrants into a covenant which required that they pledge themselves to obeying all of the law of Moses; they confirmed or reconfirmed the covenant through an annual ceremony.

---

8. Weinfeld, *The Organizational Pattern and Penal Code of the Qumran Sect.* See also M. Klinghardt, "The Manual of Discipline in the Light of Statutes of Hellenistic Associations," in *Methods of Investigation of the Dead Sea Scrolls and the Khirbet Qumran Site: Present Realities and Future Prospects,* ed. M. Wise, N. Golb, J. Collins, and D. Pardee, Annals of the New York Academy of Sciences 722 (New York: New York Academy of Sciences, 1994), 251-67.

The word for "covenant" (ברית) occurs often in 1QS — some thirty-two times in its eleven columns; the high frequency of the word furnishes a clear indication of its importance. The people of Qumran apparently considered themselves and like-minded individuals *the* members of God's covenant with Israel. The notion of covenant could lead us back to several texts in the Hebrew Bible where it is a central concept, but the word draws us primarily to the agreement made and ratified under Moses' leadership at Mount Sinai. Israel's experience at that mountain takes up the equivalent of about two books in the Pentateuch (Exod. 19:1–Leviticus–Num. 10:11), and it plays a significant role elsewhere in the Bible. That the Sinai covenant was on the minds of the Qumran community is evident from the fact that they swore obedience to the entire law of Moses (1QS 1:8-9, 13-15, 16-17, etc.). The book of Exodus, of course, identifies the agreement made at Sinai as a covenant. At the beginning of the story, the Lord says: "if you obey my voice and keep my covenant" (19:5),[9] and, later, after the people promised to obey the Lord's words, "Moses took the blood and dashed it on the people, and said, 'See the blood of the covenant that the LORD has made with you in accordance with all these words'" (24:8).

The dating of the yearly reenactment of the covenantal ceremony (apparently at Qumran) probably also points to a background in the Sinai stories. That the renewal occurred annually (1QS 2:19; 5:24) is related to the fact that the covenant made at Mount Sinai came over time to be associated with the Festival of Weeks, a biblical pilgrimage festival celebrated every year. According to the legislation in Leviticus 23:9-21, that holiday was to be observed fifty days after the ceremonial waving of the barley omer that took place in the first month, a short time after Passover. Leviticus is uncharacteristically vague about the date for the Festival of Weeks, but on any calculation the holiday would have to be celebrated at some time in the third month, and it is this fact that caused it to be associated with the covenant at Mount Sinai. As Exodus 19:1 says, "On the third new moon [= month] after the Israelites had gone out of the land of Egypt, on that very day, they came into the wilderness of Sinai." Because the Festival of Weeks was the religious festival nearest the time of the year when the covenant was made in the wilderness, the two were connected and the Festival of Weeks became the holiday of the Sinaitic covenant.

While it was natural to associate a festival of the third month with the covenant made in the third month at Mount Sinai, the earliest surviving source for the association is the book of *Jubilees,* which was written around 160 B.C.E. and was considered an authoritative work by the people of Qum-

---

9. Biblical citations are from the NRSV.

ran. In *Jubilees* all the covenants of Genesis and Exodus are assigned to the third month, and it says almost all of them were made in the middle of the third month — a date that turns out to be the fifteenth of the third month.[10] The precise date for the festival was a disputed matter during and after the Second Temple period, but the writer of *Jubilees* seems to have arrived at 3/15 as the correct time for the holiday through exegesis of the way the date in Exodus 19:1 is worded. That verse, as we have seen, places the Israelites' arrival in the Sinai wilderness in the third month, with the covenant following a few days after. The verse does not, however, specify a date in the month when they entered the region of Sinai; rather, it says "on that very day." The natural question to ask is: Which day? The expression "on that very day" is pointless in a context where no definite date has been mentioned.[11] In order to deal with this difficulty, the writer of *Jubilees* employed an exegetical device that would later be called *gematria*, that is, adding up the numerical value of the letters in a word in order to derive added meaning from it. In this case the problematic word so treated is the one translated "that" in the expression "on that very day." The letters of the word (זה) add up to 12 (ז = 7, ה = 5), so the author of *Jubilees* read the phrase to mean that the Israelites reached the Sinai wilderness in the third month on the twelfth day. Then Moses is told to prepare the people for an appearance by God on the third day (Exod. 19:10-11, 15). The author of *Jubilees* took those three days to be 3/13-15, with the covenant being made on the last of them.[12]

The people of Qumran accepted the same date — 3/15 — for the Festival of Weeks, as we know from some of the calendar texts from Cave 4 (e.g., 4Q320 frg. 4 iii 1-5; 321 2 ii 4-5).[13] If they accepted this date for the Festival of Weeks and reconfirmed the Sinaitic covenant every year, it would be reasonable to infer that they did so on 3/15. Yet, as we have seen, the text of the *Community Rule* does not date the ceremony and, until recently, we lacked the evi-

10. For the relevant information about the date of the book and its dating of the covenant, see, e.g., J. C. VanderKam, "Jubilees, Book of," in *Encyclopedia of the Dead Sea Scrolls*, 434-36.

11. See the analysis and summary of views in C. Houtman, *Exodus*, 3 vols., Historical Commentary on the Old Testament (Kampen: Kok, 1993, 1996; Leuven: Peeters, 2000), 2:439-40. He thinks the most likely reading of the phrase is that it "denotes the very day of the exodus (cf. 12:14, 17, 41, 51); hence, two months after the departure from Egypt on the fifteenth of the first month and one month after entering the Desert of Sin (16:1), Israel arrives at Sinai on the fifteenth of the third month" (440).

12. VanderKam, "Studies on the Prologue and Jubilees 1," in *For a Later Generation: The Transformation of Tradition in Israel, Early Judaism and Early Christianity*, ed. R. Argall, B. Bow, and R. Werline (Harrisburg, Pa.: Trinity, 2000), 273-79.

13. See J. C. VanderKam, "Shavu'ot," in *Encyclopedia of the Dead Sea Scrolls*, 871-72.

dence for demonstrating it took place in the third month; now, however, the desired information is probably available in the last part of the *Damascus Document* as it appears in some of the Cave 4 copies. The *Damascus Document* is closely related to the *Community Rule* in a number of ways but seems to legislate for a different kind of community. The last part of the text locates an expulsion ceremony in the third month, a ceremony replete with curses reminiscent of those mentioned in the annual covenantal renewal in the *Community Rule*. It stipulates, after describing the procedure, that "[the inhabitants of] the camps shall assemble in the third month and curse the one who turns aside to the right [or to the left from the] law." J. T. Milik had noted the similarities in language between the end of the *Damascus Document* and 1QS 2:25–3:6, and thought both texts should be related to the annual renewal ritual set forth in 1QS 1:16–3:12.[14] In her study of the laws in the *Damascus Document*, C. Hempel agrees with his assessment.[15] The result is that there is now good reason for believing that the annual covenantal ceremony of the *Community Rule* was conducted on the Festival of Weeks and therefore, quite logically, as a commemoration of the Sinai covenant. Hence the early hypothesis that the yearly ceremony took place on the Day of Atonement (7/10) now seems highly unlikely.

It is possible that there is other evidence for this ceremony of the third month in 4Q275, a fragmentary text that goes under the name 4QCommunal Ceremony. Fragment 1:3 mentions the third month; fragment 2 refers to disciplining oneself, possibly to the seventh week; and fragment 3 seems to reflect a gathering of the community, with fragment 3:4 perhaps containing the beginning of a curse formula. The editors conclude from these broken pieces of information that, "[t]aken together, these indicators suggest that 4Q275 may be the remains of a Rule which described the order of service for the annual festival for the renewal of the covenant."[16]

2. They called themselves a יחד, a unity, and spoke of themselves as ones who had freely pledged loyalty to the covenant. They lived in ideal harmony organized as priests, levites, and people who were further subdivided into units of thousands, hundreds, fifties, and tens.

---

14. J. T. Milik, "Milkî-ṣedeq et Milkî-rešaʿ dans les anciens écrits juifs et chrétiens," *JJS* 23 (1972): 136.

15. C. Hempel, *The Laws of the Damascus Document: Sources, Traditions, and Redaction*, STDJ 29 (Leiden: Brill, 1998), 183-85. The translation of the lines just quoted comes from her book, p. 176, lines 17-18a. See also M. Knibb, *The Qumran Community*, Cambridge Commentaries on Writings of the Jewish and Christian World, 200 BC to AD 200 (Cambridge: Cambridge University Press, 1987), 88-89.

16. Alexander and Vermes, DJD 26, 211.

If the community annually renewed the covenant made with Israel at Sinai and did so on a date related to the Sinai stories, we are justified in looking for more clues that Israel at Sinai provided elements of the Qumran association's self-understanding.

It will be recalled that the group behind the *Community Rule* employs the term יחד for itself; that is, they were a unit, a unity which the repentant pledged to enter. In view of the importance of the Sinai narratives to the group, it would not be surprising if they found a basis for it in these chapters. In fact, it may have been derived from Exodus 19:8. There, after the Lord spoke to Moses the rich covenantal lines of verses 3-6 and Moses had relayed these words to the people in verse 7, "The people all answered as one [יחדו]: 'Everything that the LORD has spoken we will do'" (see 24:3, where קול אחד is the parallel expression). The word יחדו occurs 96 times in the Hebrew Bible, and related terms are also found (the total is 154),[17] but this context in Exodus with which the *Community Rule* has other close associations is a very plausible source for יחד as a name for the fellowship of the Qumran covenanters who were also living together in the wilderness and who solemnly pledged the same loyalty to the entire Mosaic law. This may be asserted, even though, as Weinfeld argues, "[i]t seems that the term יחד was adopted by the sect under the influence of the Greek term κοινόν, κοινωνία which was commonly used at that time. Indeed, both Philo and Josephus speak of κοινόν and κοινωνία in the course of their descriptions of the life of the Essenes."[18] The choice of the term may well owe something to the character of Hellenistic guilds, but the specific impetus for employing the word may have arisen from Exodus 19:8.

Further evidence that the Sinai pericope is the principal source of the communal self-portrait in the *Community Rule* comes from some unusual features in the biblical text and the ways they were interpreted by ancient experts. The first of these is the passage just cited, Exodus 19:8. The peculiar feature here is that the people of Israel are presented in an astonishingly positive light. Judging from the previous sections in the book of Exodus, we are not prepared to be very optimistic about the people of Israel. In the short time between leaving Egypt and arriving at Sinai, they complained several times about Moses' leadership (15:24; 16:2-12; cf. 14:10-12) and quarreled with him (17:2-7). Indeed, in 17:4 Moses cries to the Lord: "What shall I do with this people? They are al-

---

17. These numbers are from H.-J. Fabry, "יחד," in *TDOT*, 6:40-48. For the word in the Hebrew Bible, see the interesting proposals in S. Talmon, "The Sectarian יחד — a Biblical Noun," *VT* 3 (1953): 133-40.

18. Weinfeld, *Organizational Pattern*, 13-14.

most ready to stone me." Yet this contentious nation, the famous murmurers of the Pentateuchal stories, declare as one almost immediately upon reaching Sinai: "Everything that the Lord has spoken we will do."

Furthermore, the astonishing, all-encompassing affirmation is uttered even before the deity has issued any commands (the first ones do not come until later in this chapter and especially in chaps. 20–23); it appears to be an open-ended acceptance of anything God might choose to dictate. And, even more remarkably, this was not the only time Israel responded so nobly. Twice more after the commands and statutes of Exodus 20–23 were revealed the people respond with similar declarations (24:3, 7). So they unanimously accepted everything in faith the first time and then reaffirmed it twice, once they understood what the laws of the covenant involved.

These remarkable and admirable assertions by Israel at Sinai seem to have been the triggers that led early expositors to the conclusion that the people on this occasion constituted an ideal society. Of course, that ideal would be shattered a short forty days later with the incident of the golden calf (Exod. 32), but at first they were an unparalleled unity. Commentators searched the text for other hints of this virtuous harmony and resolve. One seemingly unlikely place for spotting a clue was Exodus 19:2: "They had journeyed [וַיִּסְעוּ] from Rephidim, entered [וַיָּבֹאוּ] the wilderness of Sinai, and camped [וַיַּחֲנוּ] in the wilderness; Israel camped [וַיִּחַן] there in front of the mountain." An odd fact about the four verbs in verse 2 was what caught the eye of careful readers: the first three are plural in form, but the fourth is singular. A tedious grammarian might point out that the difference in number of the verbs was conditioned by the switch in subject from the pronoun "they" (representing "the sons of Israel" from v. 1) to the singular "Israel," but that seems not to have satisfied some ancient exegetes. The change in verbal form must have some significance in Scripture. As a result, when we read Exodus 19:2 in *Targum Pseudo-Jonathan,* we find: "They set out from Rephidim, and coming to the wilderness of Sinai, they encamped in the wilderness. Israel encamped there, united in heart, in front of the mountain."[19] The same understanding of the singular form of the verb comes to expression in two midrashic works: the *Mekhilta* of Rabbi Ishmael and *Pirke de Rabbi Eliezer.* In the *Mekhilta,*[20] with reference to

19. The translation is from M. Maher, *Targum Pseudo-Jonathan: Exodus,* Aramaic Bible 2 (Collegeville, Minn.: Liturgical Press, 1994), 214. The same idea is present in *Targum Neophyti* but is attached to Exod. 19:8: "And all the people answered together *in a perfect heart . . ."* (M. McNamara, *Targum Neofiti 1: Exodus* [in the same volume], 81). See also *Lev. Rab.* 9:9.

20. This *Mekhilta,* which contains commentary on Exod. 12:1–23:19; 31:12-17; 35:1-3, may have a Tannaitic base, but it appears to have been edited several times afterward. In its

this passage, the text explains: "In every passage in which Scripture says, '. . . and they journeyed . . . and they encamped . . . ,' it was in dissension that they journeyed, and it was in dissension that they encamped. But here it says, 'And there Israel encamped,' meaning that all were of a single mind about the matter" (*Baḥodesh* 1.3).[21] Virtually the same words may be read in *Pirke de Rabbi Eliezer* 41, where they are also connected with the Israelite people's declaration in Exodus 24:7: ". . . until they all came to Mount Sinai, and they all encamped opposite the mountain, like one man with one heart, as it is said, 'And there Israel encamped before the Mount.' The Holy One, blessed be He, spoke to them: Will ye receive for yourselves the Torah? Whilst the Torah had not yet been heard they said to him: We will keep and observe all the precepts which are in the Torah, as it is said [Exod. 24:7 is quoted]."[22]

God himself uses some remarkable language about the Israelites encamped at the mountain. He promised that they would be his "treasured possession out of all the peoples" (19:5) and "a priestly kingdom and a holy nation" (v. 6). For *Pirke de Rabbi Eliezer* 41, this holiness consisted in the avoidance of sex,[23] but it meant more. The *Mekhilta* reports that the sages said about these words: "The Israelites were worthy of eating food in the status of holy things before they made the golden calf" (*Baḥodesh* 2.19). That is, they were permitted to eat those parts of sacrificial animals set aside for priests. Also, they were holy in the sense of being "consecrated, separate from the nations of the earth and their abominations" (2.21). It was thought that they were given an extraordinary ability not only to hear the divine word but also to understand and explain it (9.5).

More specifically, commentators inferred from several verbs employed in the context that there were no handicapped individuals among the Israelites at Sinai. From Exodus 20:18 ("all the people witnessed [literally: saw] the thunder and lightning"), it could be concluded that there were no blind persons (*Baḥodesh* 9.6); the statement that all heard meant there were no deaf Is-

---

final form it may date from the later third century c.e. (see H. Strack and G. Stemberger, *Introduction to the Talmud and Midrash* [Edinburgh: Clark, 1991], 274-80). The tractate that includes the Sinai chapters is called *Baḥodesh*.

21. J. Neusner, *Mekhilta according to Rabbi Ishmael: An Analytical Translation*, vol. 2, BJS 154 (Atlanta: Scholars Press, 1988), 45. See also 5.2: "For when all of them stood before Mount Sinai to receive the Torah, they were unanimous in receiving the dominion of God with a whole heart" (p. 66).

22. Translation of G. Friedlander, *Pirkê de Rabbi Eliezer* (reprint, New York: Hermon, 1970 [London, 1916]), 321. The work in its present form may be as late as the eighth or ninth century c.e. (Strack and Stemberger, *Introduction*, 356-58).

23. Friedlander, *Pirkê de Rabbi Eliezer*, 323.

raelites (24:7); that all answered (19:8) implied there was no one who was dumb; and the fact that all stood at the foot of the mountain (19:17) entailed there were no lame people (*Baḥodesh* 9.6-10). Here it is worthwhile to recall that in 1QSa 2:3-9 we find a list of people with such handicaps and other defects; there they are excluded from the community. The explanation consistently given at Qumran for such exclusions is that the holy angels were among them. Such defects were thought to compromise holiness (see also 1QM 7:4-7; CD 15:15-18 [with 4Q268 6 2]; cf. 4QFlor 1:3-5).[24]

Pirke de Rabbi Eliezer 41 offers these comments about Israel's sanctity: it not only mentions abstinence from sex but also that "[t]here were no uncircumcised people in their midst; the manna descended from heaven for them; they drank water out of the Well; clouds of glory surrounded them."[25] Also, "Rabbi Phineas said: All that generation who heard the voice of the Holy One, blessed be He, on Mt. Sinai, were worthy to be like the ministering angels, so that insects had no power over them. They did not experience pollution in their lifetime, and at their death neither worm nor insect prevailed over them. Happy were they in this world and happy will they be in the world to come" (cf. *b. B. Bat.* 15a; Ezek. 34:25; Prov. 1:33).[26]

Perhaps as another hint toward this biblical background, the *Community Rule* uses language that was employed for Israel in the wilderness, including terms such as "freely devoted themselves" and the organization of the people into thousands, hundreds, fifties, and tens. That is, at least for the covenantal ceremony, the people (possibly including more than the fixed residents of Qumran) are said to be arranged in military formation — thousands, hundreds, fifties, and tens. That members freely devoted themselves reminds one of some passages in Exodus that have to do with Israel's making voluntary contributions to the construction and furnishing of the tabernacle, the wilderness sanctuary. In Exodus 25:2 the Lord says to Moses: "Tell the Israelites to take for me an offering; from all whose hearts prompt them [אשר ידבנו לבו] to give you shall receive the offering for me." That command finds its response in 35:20-21, where all the Israelites "came, everyone whose heart was stirred, and everyone whose spirit was willing [וכל אשר נדבה רוחו אתו], and brought the Lord's offering to be used for the tent of meeting, and for all its service, and for the sacred vestments." As Catherine Murphy writes regarding the use of the same terms in the *Community Rule* and Exodus:

24. See A. Shemesh, "'The Holy Angels Are in Their Council': The Exclusion of Deformed Persons from Holy Places in Qumranic and Rabbinic Literature," *DSD* 4 (1997): 179-206.

25. Friedlander, *Pirkê de Rabbi Eliezer,* 323.

26. Friedlander, *Pirkê de Rabbi Eliezer,* 327.

First, both passages mark the commitment to community with the transfer of material possessions from the donor's private reserves to a communal pool. Second, both passages depict the disposition of material goods as a voluntary act, thus highlighting the willful adherence of participants. Third, the terminology used for the community in the Exodus account, "congregation" (עדה), occurs only once in 1QS (V 20) but regularly in 1QSa, the first appendix to 1QS. There, the word is used somewhat interchangeably with the appellation for the group most common in 1QS, "community" (יחד). Fourth, the purpose to which the donated resources are put is connected in both documents to the construction of a wilderness sanctuary.[27]

As for the thousands, hundreds, fifties, and tens (1QS 2:21-22), the phrase is familiar from various passages in the Hebrew Bible where it occurs in military contexts. It may not be a coincidence, however, that it is introduced immediately before the Sinai pericope. In Exodus 18 Moses received advice from his father-in-law Jethro regarding the organization of a judicial system to give some relief to the badly overburdened leader. "You should also look for able men among all the people, men who fear God, are trustworthy, and hate dishonest gain; set such men over them as officers over thousands, hundreds, fifties and tens" (18:21; see v. 25, where Moses appoints them; Deut. 1:15).[28]

3. Their community involved extensive sharing, including a community of goods.

That the Qumran fellowship practiced a community of goods is clear, even if we are not able to discover exactly how it functioned. This is a trait echoed not only in the *Community Rule* but in other texts and in external descriptions of the Essenes. Can this practice also be clarified with reference to the ancient traditions about Israel at Mount Sinai?

It would be possible to view the practice as simply a logical extension of the idea of an ideal community. We could imagine that if ancient exegetes believed Israel was so virtuous when they received the Torah, they might have assumed that the condition extended to property so that no one was in need.

27. C. Murphy, *Wealth in the Dead Sea Scrolls and in the Qumran Community*, STDJ 40 (Leiden: Brill, 2002), 139. Although the topic will not be treated in this paper, one could find a series of parallels between the teachings about the tabernacle in Exodus and the Qumran community's understanding of itself as a sanctuary (see 1QS 8:4-10; 9:3-6).

28. On the phrase, see Y. Yadin, *The Scroll of the War of the Sons of Light against the Sons of Darkness* (Oxford: Oxford University Press, 1962), 59-61, for references in the Bible, in the scrolls, and in other contemporary literature (e.g., 1 Macc. 3:55). Cf. also Knibb, *The Qumran Community*, 89.

An ideal society could not be marred by the distinctions between rich and poor. Also, we have seen above that the designation of the covenanters at Qumran as ones who freely devoted themselves and their goods reminds us of Israel's voluntarily giving their goods for the tabernacle. There is, though, more explicit evidence that even the community of goods at Qumran was related to reflection on Israel at Sinai.

The Qumran practice with regard to the possessions of those who entered the covenantal community is mentioned several times in the *Community Rule,* and in some cases we can detect a scriptural background for it. As the teaching is formulated in 1QS 1:11-12, it is strongly reminiscent of Deuteronomy 6:5 (see the parallels in Deut. 4:29; 10:12; 13:3; 30:10).[29]

1QS 1:11-12	Deut. 6:5
All those who freely devote themselves to His truth shall bring all their *knowledge, powers* and *possessions* into the Community of God.	You shall love the LORD your God with all your *heart,* and with all your *soul,* and with all your *might.*

Though these two passages hardly sound alike and do not employ the same terms, the one in the *Community Rule* is in fact based on the verse in Deuteronomy as early expositors read it. We know that the word "heart" was translated as διάνοια in a number of passages (e.g., Lev. 19:17) so that we could align the terms "heart" and "knowledge," and "powers" may be an attempt at the meaning of "soul." But the key term for our purposes is Deuteronomy's "might" (מאד) where the *Community Rule* has "wealth" or "possessions." In *Targum Pseudo-Jonathan* Deuteronomy 6:5, the word "might" is translated as ממון, and indeed this is a well-attested interpretation of the term in Jewish literature. It appears in *Targum Onqelos* ("with all your possessions [נכסך]")[30] and can be found in several rabbinic texts. *m. Ber.* 9:5 says: "and with all thy might — with all thy wealth [ממונך]."[31] Thus the summary of covenantal obligations in Deuteronomy 6:5 served as the basis for a similar summary in our

29. See Murphy, *Wealth,* 120-25. This point was made early in the study of the *Community Rule.* See M. Black, *The Scrolls and Christian Origins: Studies in the Jewish Background of the New Testament* (reprint, BJS 48, Chico, Calif.: Scholars Press, 1983 [original 1961]), 123; A. Leaney, *The Rule of Qumran and Its Meaning,* NTL (Philadelphia: Westminster, 1966), 122.

30. Quoted from B. Grossfeld, *The Targum Onqelos to Deuteronomy,* Aramaic Bible 9 (Wilmington, Del.: Michael Glazier, 1988), 34. See his n. 2 (pp. 34-35).

31. Cited from H. Danby, *The Mishnah* (Oxford: Oxford University Press, 1933), 10. See also *b. Ber.* 61b; *b. Pes.* 25a; *b. Yoma* 82a; and *b. Sanh.* 74a.

text.[32] The people of Qumran, however, stipulated that possessions were to be brought into the community — an inference that we do not find in these other sources.

Although the summary of obligations does not occur in the book of Exodus, Deuteronomy 6:5 is relevant to the Sinai events. Deuteronomy, which packages itself as Moses' final speech, begins by evoking the previous wilderness experiences and focuses particularly on what happened at Sinai or Horeb. In Deuteronomy 4:9 Moses starts reminding the people of what took place at Sinai/Horeb and of the importance of making no image of the invisible God who spoke to them there (4:9-40). In chapter 5 he resumes the topic of the covenant made at the mountain, repeats the ten commandments, and, among other recollections, cites the people's resolve to do all that the Lord told them. He reminds them that the Lord then announced he would reveal to Moses the commands, statutes, and ordinances they were to do in the land the Lord was giving to them. These are detailed in chapters 6 and following. Hence Deuteronomy 6 belongs to a section that is recalling the Sinai revelation, with 6:5 summarizing Israel's duty to the Lord. We may say that Deuteronomy represents an early stage in reflection on the Sinai event, while the *Community Rule* represents a later one.

4. The *Community Rule* legislates for males, never mentioning women members. Here we should keep in mind the external testimony of Pliny the Elder, who wrote that Essenes living along the shore of the Dead Sea were "without women" (*Natural History* 5.73), and that, according to Josephus, most Essenes did not marry (*War* 2.120-21; *Ant.* 18.21; see Philo, *Apol.* 11.14-17).

Although this should be seen as a kind of appendix to the foregoing sections, it is perhaps worth mentioning that there is a parallel between the Sinai chapters as traditionally read and the all-male character of the Qumran community. That the community was all-male has been a hotly contested thesis, but it is a reasonable position to take and one that may be receiving some archaeological confirmation (or rather, the contrary view is losing its major support).[33]

The sources that emphasize Israel's unity at Mount Sinai also offer an interpretation of the first of God's words to Moses in Exodus 19:3: "Thus you shall say to the house of Jacob, and tell the Israelites [literally: the sons of Is-

---

32. M. Weinfeld, *Deuteronomy 1–11*, AB 5 (New York: Doubleday, 1991), 339-40.

33. See J. Zias, "The Cemeteries of Qumran and Celibacy: Confusion Laid to Rest?" *DSD* 7 (2000): 220-53. He has identified the women's burials at Qumran as much more recent Bedouin graves, not ones contemporaneous with the Qumran community, and thus has removed a crucial plank in the argument against the celibate character of the fellowship there.

rael].″ For the modern reader, the double address is a synonymous pair, a feature common in Hebrew poetry. However, *Targum Pseudo-Jonathan* reads: "Thus you shall say to *the women of* the house of Jacob, and declare to *the house* of Israel" (similarly *Targum Neophyti* [margin]). The *Mekhilta* also takes the first expression as meaning the women and the second as intending the men; in addition, it offers an explanation: "Speak in soft language the main points to the women" and, for the men, "go into details with them" (*Baḥodesh* 2.1).[34] In *Pirke de Rabbi Eliezer* the matter is put this way:

> Rabbi Phineas said: On the eve of the sabbath the Israelites stood at Mount Sinai, arranged with the men apart and the women apart. The Holy One, blessed be He, said to Moses: Go, speak to the daughters of Israel, (asking them) whether they wish to receive the Torah. Why were the women asked (first)? Because the way of men is to follow the opinion of women, as it is said, "Thus shalt thou say to the *house of Jacob*" (Ex. 19:3); these are the women. "And tell the children of Israel" (ibid.); these are the men. (cf. *b. Sukkah* 52a; *b. Šabb.* 87a; *Exod. Rab.* 28:2)[35]

This seemingly arbitrary interpretation may well have followed from the command that Moses gave the people in Exodus 19:15: "Prepare for the third day; do not go near a woman." *Pirke de Rabbi Eliezer* explains that the sanctity of Israel at Sinai "refers to their avoidance of sexual intercourse."[36]

The evidence cited makes it plausible to think that the community reflected in the *Serek* fashioned itself to some extent after the Israelite nation at Sinai as traditionally understood. Like Israel at that time, they, in the wilderness, solemnly agreed to uphold the Sinaitic covenant on the Festival of Weeks and pledged to obey *all* the divine law mediated through Moses. Like ancient Israel, they heard the law and understood it. They too formed a noble unity consisting of those pledged to the covenantal relationship. They organized themselves as ancient Israel had. They established a communal way of life in which much, including property, was shared. They too sanctified themselves, separating men from women, and thus were in the requisite state of purity for God to appear and reveal his will, as ancient Israel had been. All the measures taken by the community seem to aim at establishing a holy entity unlike what the group saw in others. The Qumran community saw itself as re-creating the camp of Israel in the wilderness.

The foregoing analysis has been limited to a small amount of material

34. Neusner, *Mekhilta*, 47.
35. Friedlander, *Pirkê de Rabbi Eliezer*, 321.
36. Friedlander, *Pirkê de Rabbi Eliezer*, 323.

found in one copy of the Qumran *Community Rule.* It could be extended to include several other important motifs in the text. So, for example, the fact that the community considered itself a sanctuary in the wilderness may also be tied to reflection on and intentional modeling after the same biblical base, although we have no reason to think that the Qumran group erected a sacred structure like the tabernacle. Many of the same motifs would emerge from the other copies of the *Community Rule,* but there is reason to believe that the first four columns were lacking from some of them; hence it was more convenient to use the fuller form of 1QS.

Before concluding, we should note that the Qumran community was not the only one in ancient Judaism that allowed its self-image to be shaped by Israel at Mount Sinai. In the New Testament the earliest Jerusalem church, as pictured in Acts, exhibits a number of the same traits. That community was constituted in a new way at the Festival of Pentecost, the Greek term for the Festival of Weeks. On that day many new members were welcomed into the fellowship. Those first followers of Jesus also established a unity, an ideal society in which property was held in common, meals were eaten together, and prayers were offered in community. It too was a community that received revelation in this state in a dramatic divine manifestation. As a matter of fact, an entire series of traits in the Pentecost story (such as the tongues of fire, revelation in the languages of the world) also have their origin in reflection on the Sinai event, an event that was central in the Hebrew Bible and continued to exercise influence for many centuries.

The Interpretation of Biblical Law in the Dead Sea Scrolls: Forms and Methods

MOSHE J. BERNSTEIN *and* SHLOMO A. KOYFMAN

Legal interpretation in the Dead Sea Scrolls, as a subdivision of biblical interpretation at Qumran, has been the subject of academic discourse since even before the Qumran scrolls were discovered. Louis Ginzberg, in his still significant *An Unknown Jewish Sect*, already attempted to characterize the biblical interpretation in the legal portion of the document we now know as CD.[1] To this day, most discussions of biblical interpretation at Qumran focus on nonlegal texts such as the *pesharim*, or the portion of CD called the "Admonition," or the *Genesis Apocryphon*. Legal interpretation nevertheless gets its due, although usually not systematically and often peripherally, in discussions of texts which happen to contain legal material. There is no room, in an essay of this scope, for a review of the scholarship on the subject of legal interpretation, so passing references in the notes will have to suffice. From those allusions, it

---

1. L. Ginzberg, *An Unknown Jewish Sect* (New York: Jewish Theological Seminary of America, 1976); it is the English translation of *Eine Unbekannte Jüdische Sekte*, originally published in 1922. There is no distinct treatment of CD as an exegetical document, but discussions of the interpretations that underlie the laws are pervasive.

Portions of this essay appear in slightly different form in Koyfman's honors thesis at Yeshiva College, "Legal Biblical Exegesis in the Dead Sea Scrolls and Its Implications for Jewish Intellectual History," written under the supervision of Bernstein. We should like to thank Professor Matthias Henze for inviting us to participate in this volume (and for patiently awaiting our contribution), Dr. Shani Berrin, Professor Yaakov Elman, Mr. Aaron Koller, and Dr. Michael Segal for their comments on earlier drafts of this essay, and Mr. Michael S. N. Bernstein for stylistic and editorial remarks.

should be clear to the reader that without the groundbreaking work in this field of scholars like Joseph Baumgarten, Jacob Milgrom, Lawrence Schiffman, and Yigael Yadin our task would have been considerably more difficult.[2]

The text of the Hebrew Bible often does not furnish sufficient detail regarding the ways in which the laws contained in it were to be carried out. Often the mere principles of a law are expressed without any details at all.[3] Any Jew or group of Jews observing Jewish law during the Second Temple era would have needed a way to supplement the legislation of the Hebrew Bible in order to determine how to lead their lives. Scripture did not cover adequately all the issues which arose in everyday life. Changing historical, cultural, and religious situations, furthermore, raised new legal questions which had no explicit answers to be found in the Bible. Even if we grant the existence of older oral interpretive legal traditions which may have pointed the way to clarifying some of them,[4] numerous cases still probably emerged in

2. See for example, J. M. Baumgarten, *Studies in Qumran Law,* SJLA 24 (Leiden: Brill, 1977), and subsequent articles; J. Milgrom, "The Scriptural Foundations and Deviations in the Laws of Purity of the *Temple Scroll,*" in *Archaeology and History in the Dead Sea Scrolls: The New York University Conference in Memory of Yigael Yadin,* ed. L. H. Schiffman, JSOT/ASOR Monographs 2 (Sheffield: JSOT Press, 1990), 83-99; and Milgrom, "The Qumran Cult: Its Exegetical Principles," in *Temple Scroll Studies,* ed. G. J. Brooke, JSPSup 7 (Sheffield: JSOT Press, 1989), 165-80; L. H. Schiffman, *The Halakhah at Qumran* (Leiden: Brill, 1975); Schiffman, *Sectarian Law in the Dead Sea Scrolls: Courts, Testimony, and the Penal Code* (Chico, Calif.: Scholars Press, 1983); Schiffman, *Reclaiming the Dead Sea Scrolls: The History of Judaism, the Background of Christianity, the Lost Library of Qumran,* ABRL (New York: Doubleday, 1994), 218-22, 275-87; and a series of articles on specific laws in the *Temple Scroll;* Y. Yadin, *The Temple Scroll (Megillat haMiqdash),* vols. 1 and 2 (Jerusalem: Israel Exploration Society, 1978 [Hebrew] and 1984 [English]) (all references in this essay to "Yadin" are to this English edition unless specified otherwise). More recently, Steven Fraade, Menahem Kister, and Aharon Shemesh have made significant contributions to the discourse in this area. After this article had been completed and submitted, there appeared two significant contributions to this discussion that could not be taken into consideration in our essay: A. Shemesh and C. Werman, "Halakhah at Qumran: Genre and Authority," and A. Yadin, "4QMMT, Rabbi Ishmael, and the Origins of Legal Midrash," *DSD* 10:1 (2003) 104-29 and 130-49, respectively.

3. Many contemporary students of early biblical interpretation have made this point. For example, G. Vermes employs as his examples of juridical texts which lack sufficient detail "Thou shalt do no work on the Sabbath day" and the law of divorce in Deut. 24:1-4, and discusses the latter in detail ("Bible and Midrash: Early Old Testament Exegesis," in *Cambridge History of the Bible* [Cambridge: Cambridge University Press, 1970], 1:65-67). J. L. Kugel stresses the question in his aptly titled second chapter of *Early Biblical Interpretation,* "The Need for Interpretation" (Philadelphia: Westminster, 1986), 27-39, and discusses Sabbath law and other legal examples on pp. 31-33.

4. For discussion of the history of such traditions, cf. the section on "Legal Exegesis"

the course of time which needed to be resolved. It is clear that by the time of the Second Temple period a variety of traditions and methods had developed for the expansion of scriptural foundations to support novel legislation which had not been explicitly delineated in the Bible.[5] The most fully developed form of such a system is to be found, of course, in later rabbinic literature, but there is little doubt that in this case, as often, the rabbinic system was only one manifestation of broader religious and intellectual currents.

We cannot be certain of how or under what circumstances the Qumran group (or the authors responsible for the production of the Qumran scrolls) produced their various legal interpretations of the biblical texts, nor of the oral traditions which may underlie those readings.[6] Our focus shall be almost ex-

---

in M. Fishbane, *Biblical Interpretation in Ancient Israel* (Oxford: Clarendon, 1985), 91-277, and his conclusions, 525-43.

5. This is not to suggest, of course, that all laws in the Qumran system needed to be derived from the Bible, despite Schiffman's assertion, *The Halakhah at Qumran,* 19, that "we can state with certainty that the Qumran legal traditions are derived exclusively through exegesis." J. Maier, "Early Jewish Biblical Interpretation in the Qumran Literature," in *Hebrew Bible/Old Testament: The History of Its Interpretation. I/1: Antiquity,* ed. M. Sæbø (Göttingen: Vandenhoeck & Ruprecht, 1996), 113, criticizes well such a "biblicist" approach to Qumran law. His remarks, although somewhat overstated, are well taken. Kister's formulation ("Some Aspects of Qumranic Halakhah," in *The Madrid Qumran Congress. Proceedings of the International Congress on the Dead Sea Scrolls, Madrid, 18-21 March 1991,* ed. J. Trebolle Barrera and L. Vegas Montaner, STDJ 11 [Leiden/Madrid: Brill/Editorial Complutense, 1992], 2:575-76) is more nuanced: "The Qumran sect . . . attempted to base all religious observance on the written law, *wherever possible*" (italics ours). In "Nominalism and Realism in Qumranic and Rabbinic Law: A Reassessment," *DSD* 6 (1999): 157-83, a response to D. R. Schwartz's characterization of the dichotomy between Qumranic and rabbinic law, J. L. Rubenstein emphasizes the significance of the exegetical factor in the Qumran legal system, and we believe that further close study of the relationship between Qumran law and Scripture will substantiate that position further. It is certainly clear, nonetheless, that sometimes some other "logic" alone is sufficiently compelling, such as the well-known case of *niṣṣoq* (4QMMT B 55-58), where it is reasoned that a column of liquid joining two vessels unites them for the purpose of transmitting impurity and renders the upper vessel unclean, or the law that grasshoppers must be killed either by water or by fire "for that is the nature of their creation" (CD 12:14-15). In neither of these cases does there seem to be any effort to evoke scriptural support for the law.

6. Cf. S. Fraade, "Looking for Legal Midrash at Qumran," in *Biblical Perspectives: Early Use and Interpretation of the Bible in Light of the Dead Sea Scrolls. Proceedings of the First International Symposium of the Orion Center for the Study of the Dead Sea Scrolls and Associated Literature, 12-14 May 1996,* ed. M. E. Stone and E. G. Chazon, STDJ 28 (Leiden: Brill, 1998), 75 n. 56, who correctly cautions, "we have little way of knowing which of the sectarian laws found in the scrolls were the product of the Qumran community and which had been inherited from previous, pre-Qumranic contexts, or were shared with other Jewish groups." Since in this survey we are examining biblical interpretation as it appears in

clusively on the ways in which the biblical texts appear to have been read and understood by the composers of the documents available to us — a method similar to the one James Kugel has aptly termed "reverse engineering" — and we acknowledge the caveat that we are witnesses only to the final result.[7] We must acknowledge, as well, that this study, as a survey, makes no claim to all-inclusiveness, although we believe it incorporates the major forms and methods which can be observed in the corpus. We shall not, furthermore, treat the significant theme of interpretive authority to the degree it deserves to be treated, attempting to ascertain whence the authors of these texts claimed to derive the right to read the texts in the way they do and to promulgate these readings. In our view, the methods of reading can be, and should be, studied independently of that very central issue in the social and intellectual history of the Qumran group. Finally, we shall also not tackle the somewhat disputed, yet very significant, topic of the interplay between revelation and interpretation within the Qumran community.[8] Such discussions would take us far beyond the boundaries we have set for this essay, and the methodological focus we adopt forces us to leave these important issues for another occasion.

Which Qumran texts are most likely to furnish us with useful data for this endeavor? The most obvious, of course, are texts such as CD (*Damascus Document;* certainly a Qumran text although the MS was not found at Qumran) and its Qumran ancestor 4QD (4Q266-273), 4QMMT (the so-called "Halakhic Letter"; 4Q394-399), and 11QT *(Temple Scroll),* all of which are well-known repositories of Qumran laws.[9] These three texts differ considerably among themselves generically. CD, a combination of legal and nonlegal material often divided into "Admonition" and "Laws," presents in the form of mini-codes much of the legal material it contains, while 4QMMT ap-

---

the texts in their final forms, we shall not distinguish between pre-Qumranic and Qumranic texts. In a more extensive study, such distinction might be a desideratum.

7. Kugel, *In Potiphar's House: The Interpretive Life of Biblical Texts* (San Francisco: Harper and Row, 1990), 251-53. Fraade, "Legal Midrash," 62, demurs from this methodology because of "an uncomfortable circularity in employing rabbinic midrash halakhah to uncover the midrashic methods by which Qumran rules can be said to have been exegetically created, and then to claim from the results proof that these methods were there all along." Fraade's point is valid against the claim that specific rabbinic hermeneutic methods, as such, were available at Qumran, but, in our view, does not carry weight against our proposed methodology.

8. For recent studies of these issues see Fraade's "Looking for Legal Midrash at Qumran" and "Interpretive Authority in the Studying Community at Qumran," *JJS* 44 (1993): 46-69, as well as earlier studies by Baumgarten and Schiffman.

9. Where appropriate, less well-known, more fragmentary legal texts will be introduced where they are particularly germane to our discussion.

pears to be a letter which summarizes a series of sectarian positions regarding halakhic disputes, some, but not all, of which are based on biblical interpretation. The *Temple Scroll,* which is an extended and perhaps unique example of the genre legal "rewritten Bible,"[10] is so biblical in style and formulation that it is easy to forget that it contains interpretation of the Bible as well.[11] The fact that the *Temple Scroll* presents its laws as "Scripture" does not mean that we cannot see pentateuchal interpretation at work in it, even if the author of the scroll did not present it that way and wrote his text employing pseudepigraphic devices.[12] These generic differences among the documents point toward differences in the forms in which interpretation is expressed within them, even when they share an interpretive conclusion.

Forms of Interpretation

Before engaging in the more significant analysis of the *methods* or *types* of legal interpretation found in the scrolls, let us examine briefly some of the variety of *forms* in which exegesis is presented.[13] By form we mean the way the in-

10. We employ the term "rewritten Bible" in the strict sense it had when introduced by G. Vermes, *Scripture and Tradition in Judaism* (Leiden: Brill, 1961), 95, over forty years ago, rather than in the broad sense which has been given to it by many contemporary scholars. Our only departure from Vermes' category is that we acknowledge the existence of a *legal,* as opposed to *narrative,* form of the genre in the case of the *Temple Scroll,* a document then not available to Vermes. The broader usage of the term which includes much Bible-based and para-biblical material under this rubric renders it virtually useless as a meaningful category. At the Thirteenth World Congress of Jewish Studies in Jerusalem in August 2001, we (Bernstein) addressed the issue in "'Rewritten Bible': A Generic Category Which Has Outlived Its Usefulness?" a paper which will appear in *Textus* 22 (2004).

11. Legal interpretation in the Reworked Pentateuch texts (4QRP: 4Q158, 4Q364-367) is virtually nonexistent, and we shall not discuss those texts in our analysis. There is virtually no material included in those documents that is not found in the Pentateuch, although we do find some rearrangement of legal material (e.g., in 4Q366) which is probably interpretive on some level. What should be emphasized is that the example of the non-pentateuchal material on the Wood Festival, including an allusion to the New Oil Festival, in 4Q365 23 4-12, is very much the exception to the handling of legal material in those five texts.

12. Schiffman, *Sectarian Law,* 17, contrasts the *Temple Scroll* and other texts from Qumran, claiming that the latter "see the extrabiblical material as derived from inspired biblical exegesis," while "the author of the *Temple Scroll* sees it as inherent in the biblical text." But those differences have to do with the interpretive stance of the different documents and the way they formulate law, and not with the way their authors read the Pentateuch.

13. Fraade, "Legal Midrash," 60, makes the observation that "for all the midrash and halakhah found within the scrolls, textually they evidence very little *midrash halakhah:* the

terpretation is articulated; by method we mean the way the interpretation is arrived at.[14] Categorizing by form and categorizing by method are not mutually exclusive: different methods of interpretation often share certain forms, while a variety of forms may sometimes express a single method of exegesis; the form of the interpretation, at times, is linked to the form or genre of the document in which it appears. A study of the relationship between form and method is perhaps a desideratum, but goes far beyond the boundaries we have set down for this essay. For our purposes, it is important to bear in mind the fact that the interplay between the two is not clearly defined.

Organization as Interpretation: Internal Interpretation

The stance of an interpreter may be "inside" or "outside" the biblical text, depending upon the genre of interpretation. It is easier to recognize "external" interpretation because the interpreter standing outside the biblical text expresses his understanding of the text in ways that are more overt. But one of the most significant documents of legal interpretation at Qumran, 11QT (*Temple Scroll*), is characterized by what we would call "internal" interpretation because its genre is "rewritten Bible." The author of the *Temple Scroll* is often able to grant his reader access to his understanding of how various legal units of the Bible relate to each other by mere arrangement of the pieces of legal material, without the need to impose his own "extrabiblical locution" onto the original texts. In doing so, he allows the Bible to speak for itself, as it were. It is to this form of interpretation — "interpretation by organization" — that we turn first, for its shape remains closest to that of the biblical texts themselves. We shall examine two categories of this form of interpretation.[15]

---

explicit citation and interpretation of Scripture as a source of or justification for law. Instead, the vast majority of legal texts from Qumran (as elsewhere in Second Temple Judaism) adapt a form of 'rewritten Bible,' or paraphrase." Although, as indicated above, we would disagree strongly with Fraade's characterization of most legal texts from Qumran (with the exception of the *Temple Scroll*) as "rewritten Bible," his remark on the stark formal differences between Qumran "interpretation of biblical law" and rabbinic *midrash halakhah* is fundamentally correct, provided that our focus is only on form. When it comes to the *methods* of reading the biblical text, as we shall see, the dichotomy between Qumran and the rabbis may be much narrower.

14. We acknowledge that "form" is far from a perfect term for that which we intend by it. We employ "form" for all external aspects of the presentation of the interpretation: its shape, its mode of presentation, its arrangement and the disposition of its material; in short, for everything other than the method of interpretation.

15. Our use of the term "interpretation" is consciously quite broad and includes

Collocation/Integration (11QT)[16]

One of the most characteristic ways in which the legal "rewritten Bible" of the *Temple Scroll* sets out its interpretation of the Bible is by collecting within a narrow compass laws which deal with the same or similar topics. On the most basic level, these juxtapositions need not entail any rewriting or modification of the original text; the mere linking together of passages with common themes is an act of interpretation.[17] 11QT 48:7-11 provides an excellent example of this phenomenon in a very brief compass. Into the context of the mourning customs of Deuteronomy 14:1, לא תתגודדו ולא תשימו קרחה בין עיניכם למת ("You must not gash yourselves or shave the front of your heads for the dead"), the scroll introduces a virtual citation of Leviticus 19:28, ושרט

---

even the way the biblical text is handled, arranged, and manipulated, even when no actual interpretive material is added. Cf. G. Vermes, "Bible Interpretation at Qumran," *ErIsr* 20 (1989): *185, ed. A. Ben-Tor et al., who defines the class "implicit exegesis of an editorial type" as consisting of "a rearrangement of biblical texts by means of harmonization, conflation, supplementation, etc., resulting in a clarified, improved or altered meaning, without entailing, as a rule, any added interpretation." The *Temple Scroll* is, of course, the prime example of such interpretation. Vermes' terminology differs somewhat from ours, although we are certainly observing some of the very same phenomena. It should be stressed, however, that our respective usages of the term "implicit" exegesis (see "Implicit Interpretation" below) differ considerably.

16. Since so many other texts containing law from Qumran are fragmentary, it is difficult to ascertain very much about their structure or its logic. It might very well be that if more integral portions of works like 4QD and 4QHalakha A had survived, we might see such collocation in documents of less broad scope than the *Temple Scroll*. In June 2004, Aharon Shemesh presented a convincing paper at the third Annual Meeting of the Haifa Workshop for Research in the Dead Sea Scrolls on "4Q251: Midrash Mishpatim," arguing that this text is systematically based on Exod. 21–23. It will appear in *Meghillot* 3 (2005).

17. Yadin, 1:73-74, distinguishes between "merging commands on the same subject" and "unifying duplicate commands (harmonization)." The former is really part of the author's broad compositional technique and not his exegetical arsenal, if we may distinguish, for the moment, between them. Milgrom, "Exegetical Principles," 170-71, has already faulted Yadin for confusing "unification" (our "collocation") with "harmonization." He concedes that true harmonization is to be found in three cases, two of which (rape/seduction and division of the spoils), following Yadin, we shall discuss under the rubric "Harmonization and Reconciliation," and the third (covering the blood) we shall discuss as an example of *binyan ab* under the subheading "*Binyan Av* (Homogenization)." We feel that the term "harmonization" can be employed even for passages where there is no contradiction between the texts when the author has chosen to integrate the passages literarily. Vermes, "Bible Interpretation," *185-*186, speaks of "grouping and collating parallel texts," with the integration in 11QT 51:19–52:3 of the idolatrous practices prohibited in Deut. 16:21-22 and Lev. 26:1 serving as his example.

67

‏18לנפש לא תתנו בבשרכם וכתבת קעקע לא תתנו בכם ("You shall not make any gashes in your flesh for the dead or make any tattoo marks upon you"), before returning to Deuteronomy 14:2a, ‏כי עם קדוש אתה לה׳ אלהיכה מה [*sic*] ("For you are a people holy to the Lord your God"). The Pentateuch itself presents an integration of the prohibitions of קרחה (baldness) and שרטת (gashes) in Leviticus 21:5, and the author of the scroll (perhaps following that scriptural example) sews together the verses on a single theme from Deuteronomy 14 and Leviticus 19 in the context of the former. The result is (with the section from Leviticus underlined): ‏בנים אתמה לה׳ אלוהיכמה לוא תתגדדו
‏ולוא תשימו קורחה בין עיניכמה למת ושרטת על נפש לוא תתנו בבשרכמה
‏וכתבת קעקע לוא תכתובו בכמה כי עם קדוש אתה לה׳ אלוהיכה מה ("You are children of the Lord your God. You must not gash yourselves or shave the front of your heads for the dead. *You shall not make any gashes in your flesh for the dead or inscribe any tattoo marks upon you.* For you are a people holy to the Lord your God").[19]

The disposition of the laws pertaining to vows furnishes an example on a grander and more complex scale. Taking its cue from Deuteronomy 12:26, the command to bring vows and *sancta* to the "place which the Lord shall choose," 11QT 53:9 proceeds to a discussion of vows on a broader plane, concluding its paraphrase of Deuteronomy 12:26 with ‏או נדרתה בפיכה ("or vowed with your mouth"; 53:10), language borrowed from Deuteronomy 23:24. This enables the scroll to introduce the equivalent of Deuteronomy 23:22-24 (53:11-14), which deals with the gravity of vows and the serious penalties involved in not fulfilling them. From there the scroll moves to Numbers 30, the pentateuchal pericope on personal vows and the rights of fathers and husbands to annul those made by daughters and wives (53:14–54:5). Having integrated the pentateuchal passages on vows, the scroll returns to Deuteronomy 13:1 (54:5), at the approximate point where this large topic began.

Harmonization and Reconciliation

In addition to juxtaposing the various biblical texts that deal with a particular law, the author of the *Temple Scroll* also had to address the problem of vary-

---

18. 11QT reads ‏ושרטת על נפש and ‏לוא תכתובו בכמה ("you shall not inscribe upon yourselves"). See Yadin's commentary *ad loc.* for discussion.

19. Yadin, 1:75, writes that this pericope is "another typical example of harmonizing three similar commands," claiming that it combines Lev. 21:5 pertaining to the priests with Lev. 19:28 and Deut. 14:1-2 which apply to all Israel. But, other than the lexeme שרטת replacing שרט, there is no mark of Lev. 21 on the language of the *Temple Scroll*.

ing, and sometimes contradictory, biblical laws.[20] The Pentateuch contains two similar laws regarding virgins who have been engaged "unwillingly" in sexual activity before marriage. Exodus 22:15-16 employs the word יפתה, "seduce," to describe the action of the male involved, and Deuteronomy 22:28-29 uses ותפשה, "seize (her)." The former passage requires that he pay the bride-price (מהר) for her as a wife, and if her father refuses the marriage, to pay the bride-price for a virgin. The latter text demands that he pay fifty silver pieces to her father and marry the woman with no right to divorce her, without indicating any right of the father to prevent the match. In 11QT's rewriting (66:8-11) of the section of Deuteronomy where the latter law occurs, a single subtle change is made which indicates that the author is treating the two laws as one; the section begins with the language of Exodus, כי יפתה איש ("should a man seduce"), and omits any equivalent of ותפשה ("seize"), the description of the act in Deuteronomy. Beyond that, the passage is completely modeled on the biblical text in Deuteronomy.[21]

It appears that the author of the *Temple Scroll* identified these two passages with each other and therefore blended or homogenized them in his rewritten Bible. Seduction and rape are to be considered as identical offenses and carry the same penalty in the eyes of the author of the scroll. The one question we might pose is: Does the author of the scroll maintain the right of paternal refusal of the marriage (which appears in Exodus but not in Deuteronomy)? Yadin asserts that the *Temple Scroll* denies the father the right to refuse in either case, and notes that rabbinic halakhah harmonized the texts in the other direction, permitting refusal both in the case of seduction and in the case of rape on the basis of an *a minore ad maius (qal vaḥomer)* argument.[22] We believe it is dangerous to argue confidently from silence, as Yadin does here, that the *Temple Scroll* would compel such a marriage against the father's will, although it is certainly conceivable that it might.

The treatment of the law of the division of war spoils in the *Temple Scroll* is an example of "harmonization" which is particularly unusual. There appears to be a contradiction between the pentateuchal description of how

20. While harmonization is often employed to resolve contradictory biblical passages, Schiffman has pointed out that certain biblical contradictions are preserved in the *Temple Scroll,* such as what is done with the offerings of the firstborn animals. Cf. L. H. Schiffman, "Priestly and Levitical Gifts in the Temple Scroll," in *The Provo International Conference on the Dead Sea Scrolls: Technological Innovations, New Texts, and Reformulated Issues,* ed. D. Parry and E. Ulrich, STDJ 30 (Leiden: Brill, 1999), 480-96 (483).

21. The significant addition of והיא רויה לו מן החוק ("provided that she is permitted to him by the law") is not germane to our issues.

22. Yadin, 1:369.

the spoils captured in the war against Midian (Num. 31:27-28) were to be allocated and the recounting of David's division of his captured booty in 1 Samuel 30:24-25.[23] Numbers orders the booty to be divided equally between the
warriors, who then give ⅟₅₀₀th of their half of the booty to the priests, and the
rest of the nation, which is obliged to give ⅟₅₀th of their half of the spoils to
the Levites. However, 1 Samuel attests to David's initiating a policy of halving
the spoils equally between the warriors and those who remain with the baggage, without the mention of any tax whatsoever.

11QT 58:13-14 records a practice which differs, on the surface, from both
biblical accounts. From the total booty, ⅟₁₀th is to be given to the king, ⅟₁₀₀₀th
to the priests, ⅟₁₀₀th to the Levites, and the remaining spoils are to be divided
equally between the warriors and the people. How are we to explain the
amounts awarded to the priests and Levites? Yadin suggests that this aspect of
the law is composite, the result of harmonization of the passage in Numbers
with that in Samuel. He explains that the author of the *Temple Scroll* harmo-
nizes the biblical texts by viewing each of them as referring to a different stage
in the overall process. First, the shares of the king, the priests, and the Levites
were taken from the total booty, as described in Numbers, and only afterward
were the remaining spoils halved equally between the warriors and the non-
combatants as mandated by 1 Samuel.[24] The law in the *Temple Scroll* is then a
harmonization of the law in Numbers and the narrative in 1 Samuel 30.[25]

23. This example differs from the others involving legal exegesis of prophetic texts
that we shall discuss below, because it is only the implications of the narrative which stand
in contrast with the pentateuchal law. Nevertheless, it should be added to the others introduced later in the section on non-pentateuchal sources for law. Rabbinic literature treats
the Midianite narrative as not establishing precedent for the future (*b. Menaḥ.* 77b).

24. Note that the groups are termed תופשי המלחמה ("the warriors") and אחיהמה
אשר הניחו בעריהמה ("their brothers whom they left in their cities"). The former is the
term employed by Numbers, and the latter is more analogous to העדה ("the congregation") of Numbers than to הישב על הכלים ("the one who stays by the baggage") of 1 Sam.
30:24. Y. Yadin, *The Temple Scroll: The Hidden Law of the Dead Sea Sect* (New York: Ran-
dom House, 1985), 77, writes that the author of TS "used the text of the situation in Numbers, with its provisions for the priests and Levites, but altered the stages at which those
were to be allocated, so that their shares came 'off the top,' as fractions of the *total* booty.
Thus, the scroll gave one thousandth of the total to the priests, which is the equivalent of
one five-hundredth of the half as in Numbers, and one hundredth of the total to the Levites, equalling one fiftieth of the half. Thereafter, the balance was divided evenly between
the warriors and the others, as prescribed by David in the Book of Samuel."

25. There is one aspect of this law on the division of the spoils which cannot be explained on the basis of "organization as interpretation" — the assigning of one-tenth of
the spoils to the king. It is the result of some analogical form of midrash (see further below). It is likely, as Yadin has suggested, 1:360, that "Although there is no clear biblical basis

External Interpretation

When we turn to most other forms of Qumran legal interpretation, found in texts which do not take on the shape of "rewritten Bible," and in which the stance of the interpreter is outside the biblical text, a further significant distinction can be drawn from a formal standpoint between "explicit" and "implicit" interpretation. In the former, the biblical text which gives rise to the law is cited, and we can observe the connection between the biblical verse and its Qumranic reading. In the latter, which is perhaps more common in Qumran "codes," the biblical verse which underlies the law is not cited explicitly, and the relationship between the law and the verse must be inferred by the reader, often based on the imitation of the biblical language by the Qumran interpreter.

Legal Interpretation with Citation

At times, the law is conjoined with its interpretation through the use of a citation, almost always with a formula, such as כאשר כתוב, "as it is written," or כאשר אמר, "as it states."[26] This employment of a formula constitutes the clearest evidence that a given law relies on a specific biblical text. Such use is found in several passages in CD. The Sabbath code in CD (10:14–11:18) is framed by biblical citations; that is to say, the first and last laws in the list are "justified" by explicit scriptural texts: אל יעש איש ביום השישי מלאכה מן העת אשר יהיה גלגל השמש רחוק מן השער מלואו כי הוא אשר אמר שמור

---

for prescribing that the king is to be given one tenth of the booty, a likely source seems to be the section on the ways of the king which prescribes that the king is to be given one tenth of the grain, of the vineyards and of the flocks" (1 Sam. 8:15-17). The author of the law has extended the rights of the king from a tenth of the produce to a tenth of the war booty as well. Yadin also suggests that tithing in the context of war booty might be suggested by Abram giving a tithe to Melchizedek in Gen. 14:20.

26. Cf. M. J. Bernstein, "Introductory Formulas for Citation and Re-Citation of Biblical Verses in the Qumran Pesharim: Observations on a Pesher Technique," *DSD* 1 (1994): 30-70, for a discussion of the use of these formulas in nonlegal material. To the best of our knowledge, no thorough survey has been done of their employment in legal passages. 4QMMT presents a unique usage of formulas in legal contexts in that it employs כתוב ("written") even in situations where the Bible is paraphrased and not quoted. Elisha Qimron, in Qimron and John Strugnell, eds., in consultation with Y. Sussmann and with contributions by Y. Sussmann and A. Yardeni, *Qumran Cave 4. V: Miqṣat Maʿaśe Ha-Torah*, DJD 10 (Oxford: Clarendon, 1994), 140-41, insists that the term never introduces a citation in 4QMMT, but cf. M. J. Bernstein, "The Employment and Interpretation of Scripture in 4QMMT: Preliminary Observations," in *Reading 4QMMT: New Perspectives on Qumran Law and History,* ed. John Kampen and Moshe J. Bernstein, Symposium 2 (Atlanta: Scholars Press, 1996), 38-46.

את יום השבת לקדשו (10:15-17; "No one should do work on the sixth day, from the moment when the sun's disk is at a distance of its diameter from the gate, *for this is what it says, 'Observe the Sabbath day to sanctify it'*"), and אל יעל איש למזבח בשבת כי אם עולת השבת כי כן כתוב מלבד שבתותיכם (11:17-18; "No one should offer anything upon the altar on the Sabbath, except for the burnt offering of the Sabbath, *for thus it is written, 'Except your [offerings of] the Sabbath'*"). Both interpretations could be open to question; "keeping the Sabbath to sanctify it" (Deut. 5:12) need not refer to the cessation from prohibited activities some length of time before the actual onset of the Sabbath, nor need "apart from your Sabbaths" imply that only the Sabbath offerings were to be placed on the altar on that day. According to the exegesis of CD, however, those are indeed the intentions of those verses. More striking, however, is the fact that none of the intervening laws regulating behavior on the Sabbath is explicitly justified by citation. Isaiah 58:13, ממצוא חפצך דבר ודבר ("serving your own interests, or pursuing your own affairs"), seems to underlie 10:19-20, אל ידבר בדברי המלאכה ... לעשות את עבודת חפצו ("He is not to speak about matters of work . . . to do the work which he wishes"), and 11:2, לעשות את חפצו ביום השבת ("to do what he wishes on the Sabbath day"), but it could be argued that the usage is stylistic and not exegetical, since the verse is not explicitly cited in support of the law.[27] Thus the code reflects both explicit and implicit biblical interpretation, while also containing laws which have no discernible scriptural foundation whatsoever.[28]

Implicit Interpretation

The last-cited passage from Isaiah in CD leads us to two further issues on which we must touch, at least briefly. The first is the kind of implicit interpre-

27. Fraade, "Legal Midrash," 73 and n. 50, notes that *Mekhilta de-Rabbi Yishmael, Baḥodesh* 7, cites this verse in its remarks on Exod. 20:8, "Remember the Sabbath day to sanctify it." He stresses the ways in which CD's formulation diverges from that of the rabbinic text.

28. On occasion, biblical verses are employed explicitly, with citation formulas, to justify regulations which we would probably describe as sectarian rules. Thus we read in 1QS that non-members of the community are to be kept at a distance based on (כיא כן כתוב; "for thus it is written") Exod. 23:7, מ(כול) דבר שקר תרחק, perhaps interpreted as "from every speaker (דובר) of falsehood stay away" (where MT lacks כל, "every," but LXX has a word for "every"). Nor shall free gifts be taken from them based on (כאשר כתוב) Isa. 2:22, חדלו לכם מן האדם אשר נשמה באפו כיא במה נחשב הואה ("Turn away from mortals, who have only breath in their nostrils, for of what account are they?"), although it is not clear why the nonmember of the group should be defined as "the one whose breath is in his nostrils," or why this biblical verse should be employed in a legal interpretation.

tation which points to a particular reading of a biblical text, even though the text is not cited verbatim. Some of these, like the CD formulations based on Isaiah, indicate by the closeness of their formulation to the biblical original that they are "reading" the biblical text, while others do not manifest such overt connections. One example from 4QMMT is worth noting. Leviticus 22:16, והשיאו אותם עון אשמה באכלם את קדשיהם ("causing them to bear iniquity requiring a guilt payment, when they eat their sacred donations"), can be interpreted in more than one way, depending on the subject and meaning of והשיאו ("causing to bear") and the referent of אותם ("them"). 4QMMT B 11-13 asserts that certain offerings are to be eaten on the day they are brought, adding [כי לבני] הכוהנ[ים] ראו להזהר בדבר הזה בשל שלוא [היו] י, מסיא[י]ם את העם עוון, "[for] it is proper that the [sons of] the priest[s] be careful in this matter so that they [should] not cause the people to be[a]r guilt." Leviticus 22:16 is not cited with כאשר כתוב ("as it is written") or כאשר אמר ("as it says") as the basis of the law, but there is no doubt from MMT's formulation that it is the biblical source for this sentence, warning the priests not to cause laypersons to incur guilt. MMT has applied the passage to the law regarding the proper time for the consumption of offerings because of the words "when they eat of their holy things" in Leviticus, even though those words themselves are not cited in the formulation of MMT.

Non-Pentateuchal Legal Interpretation

The other aspect of Qumran legal exegesis which the Isaiah verse highlights is significant for the way it differs from later rabbinic interpretation. It is well-known that rabbinic literature was reluctant to rely on non-pentateuchal passages for legal exegesis, with the Babylonian Talmud indicating this tendency with expressions like דברי תורה מדברי קבלה לא ילפינן (*b. Ḥag.* 10b and *b. B. Qam.* 2b) and דנין דברי תורה מדברי תורה ואין דנין דברי תורה מדברי קבלה (*b. Nid.* 23a).[29] At Qumran, on the other hand, there appears to have been no such unwillingness to link legal practices to passages in the Prophets and Hagiographa, although there does not appear to be a substan-

29. Cf. *Encyclopedia Talmudit* [Heb.], s.v. דברי קבלה (Jerusalem: Talmudic Encyclopedia Publishing, 1956), 7:106-14, especially 112-14. Another formulation may be אין נביא רשאי לחדש דבר מעתה (*b. Meg.* 2b). Ginzberg, *An Unknown Jewish Sect*, 184-90, who is committed to the basic identification of the group in which CD arose as Pharisaic, struggles to show, on the one hand, that in rabbinic Judaism, too, laws are actually linked with non-pentateuchal passages, and on the other, that the passages we shall discuss belong to the rabbinic category אסמכתא, "supports" for the law, rather than its midrashic source. The latter portion of his position is probably untenable.

tial number of such instances. What is quite interesting, however, is the manner in which these texts are "cited" and employed. CD 11:19-20 prohibits the sending of offerings to the altar via an impure emissary and "cites" as the prooftext Proverbs 15:8, אל ישלח איש למזבח עולה ומנחה ולבונה ועץ ביד איש טמא באחת מן הטמאות להרשותו לטמא את המזבח *כי כתוב זבח רשעים תועבה ותפלי צדקם כמנחת רצון* ("No one should send to the altar a sacrifice, or an offering, or incense, or wood, by the hand of a man impure from any of the impurities, so allowing him to defile the altar, *for it is written, 'The sacrifice of the wicked is an abomination, but the prayers of the righteous are like an agreeable offering'*").[30] What appears in the original biblical context to be a contrast between the sacrifice of the wicked and the prayers of the righteous is turned by CD into logical support for a prohibition.

The section of CD dealing with oaths, ועל השבועה אשר אמר לא תושיעך ידך לך (9:9; "Concerning the oath, as for what it says, 'You shall not do justice with your own hand . . .'"), paraphrases 1 Samuel 25:26, מנעך ה' מבוא בדמים והושע ידך לך ("the Lord has restrained you from bloodguilt and from taking vengeance with your own hand"), which is a narrative statement implying divine disapproval of acting on one's own behalf without judicial process, and turns the verse into a prohibition, reformulating the citation as an apodictic statement. Finally, in a passage which remains somewhat obscure, a prooftext is brought for the prohibition against "declaring the food of [one's] mouth holy [to G]od," from Micah 7:2, כי הוא אשר אמר איש את רעיהו יצ[ו]דו חרם ("This is what it says, 'They hunt each other with nets'"). The exegesis of חרם, which means "net" in its biblical context, in the sense of "vow" is a good example of midrashic exploitation at Qumran of potential multiple meaning in the biblical text.[31]

---

30. MT reads זבח רשעים תועבת ה' ותפלת ישרים רצונו ("The sacrifice of the wicked is an abomination to the Lord, but the prayer of the upright is his delight"); nevertheless, it is clear that this verse is being referred to by CD. There is a need for further study of "inaccurate" or "variant" citations from biblical texts at Qumran preceded by words like אמר and כתוב to determine whether we should really expect verbatim quotations in such cases. It is known that MMT furnishes an exception to such expectations, as do this text from Proverbs and the verse from 1 Samuel cited below. For this phenomenon in the *pesharim*, cf. Bernstein, "Citation and Re-Citation," 53-54 nn. 67 and 70, and 57.

31. For other examples of legal exegesis of non-pentateuchal texts, cf. the interpretation of Isa. 2:22 in 1QS cited above (n. 28) and our earlier discussion of the integration of Numbers and 1 Samuel in the law of dividing the booty. Ezek. 45:11 is cited in three different passages as evidence for the equivalence of the *ephah* and the *bat* as a tenth of a *ḥomer*: 4Q159 (4QOrdinances[a]) 1 ii 13; 4Q271 2 2, and 4Q513 (4QOrdinances[b]) 1-2 i 4.

Methods of Interpretation

There are several fundamental distinctions that we can draw between and among different methods of legal exegesis through which we can better appreciate the broader framework of interpretation as well as its details.[32] Schiffman distinguishes between *perush* and *midrash* as the two most important terms for legal interpretation at Qumran, defining *perush* as "an exegesis based only on the analysis of the text in question, without recourse to other passages from Scripture," and *midrash* as "an exegesis in which a corroborative passage in Scripture plays a part" and "an exegetical form in which a passage is interpreted in light of a second passage."[33] In other words, while *midrash* deals with some intertextual hermeneutic technique, *perush* represents the way in which the authors of the scrolls *read* the biblical texts straightforwardly. Our first division, then, of the "methods" of interpretation will employ Schiffman's distinction.[34]

Perush

Definition and Limitation

There are passages in the Pentateuch which, despite the fact that the words they employ are not unusual, are open to more than one reading. Thus Numbers 5:13 describes the woman who is to be put to the *soṭah* ordeal with the words ועד אין בה והיא לא נתפשה, "there being no witness against her and she was not נתפשה." The final word can be translated either "caught (in the act)," or "seized," i.e., raped. A fragmentary copy of 4QD (4Q270 4 3) reads [אם] אמרה אנוסה היתי, "if] she says, 'I was forced,'" implying that the word נתפשה, "seized," was given the latter interpretation, and perhaps also that a woman who defended herself with such a claim was exempt from the ordeal.[35]

---

32. We have already discussed the category of "organization as interpretation," which relates to the way interpretation is expressed.

33. Schiffman, *The Halakhah at Qumran*, 3 and 76 respectively.

34. We did not set out our initial classification to employ Schiffman's terminology. After we had established categories and were searching for nomenclature, it became clear to us that this distinction supplied the very rubrics for which we were looking.

35. For text and commentary, cf. J. M. Baumgarten, *Qumran Cave 4, XIII: The Damascus Document (4Q266-73)*, DJD 18 (Oxford: Clarendon, 1996), 152-53. As Baumgarten notes, *Sifre Numbers* 7 contains the same exegesis, including the employment of the term אנוסה, "forced."

At times in legal passages the Bible employs terms which were no longer current in the Second Temple era, and one of the responsibilities of a biblical interpreter at that time was to make the Bible meaningful to his audience, by "translating" the term into language his audience understood. An interesting example of this feature of Qumran legal interpretation may be found in 4Q251 (4QHalakha A). Despite its fragmentary nature, it is quite clear that we have an interpretation of Exodus 22:28, מְלֵאָתְךָ וְדִמְעֲךָ לֹא
תְאַחֵר בְּכוֹר בָּנֶיךָ תִּתֶּן לִי ("You shall not delay the <u>fullness</u> [of your harvest] and the <u>outflow</u> [of your presses]. The firstborn of your sons you shall give me"), in which both of the underlined terms are obscure. The Qumran text reads אל יאכל איש דגן ותיר[וש ויצהר כי אם [הניף הכוהן] ראשיתם הבכורים והמלאה אל יאחר איש כי [התירוש] הואה ראשית המלאה [וה]דגן הוא הדמע (4Q251 9 1-2).[36] It appears that the Qumran legal text defines (note the use of הואה and הוא) מלאה as referring to the wine and דמע as referring to the grain, which are subject to being brought as firstfruits. We should translate "[No one is to consume grain, wi]ne or oil until [the priest has waved] their first part. *Let no one delay the firstfruits or the* מלאה, *for the first part of the* מלאה *is [the wine], [and] the* דמע *is the grain*." From a formal standpoint, this formulation of the exegesis is strikingly similar to that which is already familiar from nonlegal material at Qumran: e.g., כיא
הלבנון הוא עצת היחד (1QpHab 12:3; "For Lebanon is the council of the Community"), והמחוקק הוא דורש התורה (CD 6:7; "And the staff is the interpreter of the law"), and the series המלך הוא הקהל . . . . והכוכב הוא דורש
התורה . . . . השבט הוא נשיא כל העדה (CD 7:17-20; "The king is the assembly . . . and the star is the interpreter of the law . . . and the scepter is the prince of the whole congregation").[37]

Another sort of clarification of an obscure phrase is to be found in the Qumran interpretation of Leviticus 19:16, לא תלך רכיל בעמיך ("You shall not go around as a slanderer among your people"), which, in its biblical context, prohibits talebearing or gossiping about a fellow Israelite. In 11QT 64:6-7 this law is reformulated as כי יהיה איש רכיל בעמו ומשלים את עמו לגוי

---

36. Text according to E. Larson, M. R. Lehmann, and L. H. Schiffman, "4QHalakhah A," in *Qumran Cave 4. XXV: Halakhic Texts*, ed. J. Baumgarten et al., DJD 35 (Oxford: Clarendon, 1999), 34, with our addition of the definite article before תירוש and דגן in the restorations. The editors, p. 35, translate "for [wine] is the choice part of the flow [and] grain is the best part." Our suggested translation emphasizes the definition which we believe is the import of the language.

37. Admittedly in those passages the biblical word is followed by the identification, whereas here, if we are correct, the identification precedes the biblical term. Nevertheless, we see them to be functionally equivalent.

נכר ועושה רעה בעמו ("If a man passes on information against his people or betrays his people to a foreign nation, or does evil against his people"), where the biblical phrase is explicitly quoted (as is unsurprising in this "rewritten Bible") and then interpreted in the following two clauses. Whereas in the Bible the רכיל (slanderer) is one who defames another individual, in the *Temple Scroll* he is one who betrays his people and acts against their best interests. The law is followed by the condemnation of one who, already under sentence of death, יברח אל תוך הגואים ויקלל את עמו (9-10; "he flees among the nations and curses his people"). When 4Q270 (4QDᵉ) lists among its offenders אשר יגלה את רז עמו לגואים או יקלל א[ת עמו] (2 ii 12; "who reveals the secret of his people to the nations, or curses h[is people]"), the formulation is unbiblical, but clearly based on the kind of interpretation of the verse in Leviticus which we saw in the *Temple Scroll*. Note the juxtaposition of "revealing secrets" and "cursing" which is likely to be parallel to the two cases in the *Temple Scroll*.³⁸

Specificity of Detail

The laws regarding the number of witnesses required for testimony in court are found in two places in the Pentateuch, Deuteronomy 17:6 and 19:15.³⁹ The former passage demands "two or three witnesses" for a capital crime and explicitly excludes a single witness for the imposition of the death penalty. 19:15 denies a single witness any standing at all לכל עון ולכל חטאת ("regarding any crime or wrongdoing"), and asserts that facts can be established (יקום דבר) only on the basis of two or three witnesses.⁴⁰ The exegetical problem is

---

38. Lev. 19:16 is employed in a third passage as well, and we see how Qumran legal interpretation need not be completely consistent. 1QS 7:15-17 reads והאיש אשר ילך רכיל ברעהו . . . ואיש ברבים ילך רכיל ("And whoever goes round slandering his fellow . . . whoever goes round slandering the Many"). The biblical בעמיך ("among your people") appears to be read in two slightly differing ways: (1) "against [one within] your people," or "among your people," and (2) "against your people." The former, of course, is probably the intention of the biblical passage, while the latter reads the *bet* of בעמיך the same way 11QT does, but without restricting the "defamer" to the traitor described there. The rabbis referred to the multiple application of a single scriptural text as מקרא אחד יוצא לכמה טעמים, "a single verse goes forth to several meanings."

39. Num. 35:30 indicates that a murderer is to be executed לפי עדים, with no number specified, and denies to a single witness the right to have the death penalty imposed based on his testimony.

40. For discussion of the meaning of the biblical text, as opposed to the history of its interpretation, see B. S. Jackson, "'Two or Three Witnesses,'" in *Essays in Jewish and Comparative Legal History*, SJLA 10 (Leiden: Brill, 1975), 153-71.

quite clear: If two witnesses suffice, why does the Pentateuch demand three?[41] Some of the Qumran regulations for the acceptance of testimony are found in CD 9:16-23, and they include implicit interpretation of the verses in Deuteronomy.[42] In a capital crime, if a man is reported to have "sinned against the law" three separate times, with only one witness testifying to each event, the testimonies are accepted and "his judgment is complete." In monetary matters, however, two trustworthy witnesses are acceptable. Sandwiched in between these two laws is an ambiguous formulation within the capital punishment category. "And if they are two, and they testify on a different matter," the testimony is only sufficient to exclude the suspect from the pure food, but not to incriminate him fully.[43] The law is a result of the reading of the words "two or three witnesses" in the biblical text. Under normal circumstances two witnesses are effective even in capital cases; under unusual circumstances, namely, the repetition of an offense three times with a single witness each time, three witnesses are needed. There is thus no superfluity in the biblical text; the Qumran text does not need to go formally through the elaborate rabbinic presentation of the problem and its resolution, but resolves it implicitly by laying out the rules in the different cases.[44]

---

41. The question, of course, is predicated on the assumption that Scripture does not contain extraneous language, and that apparently superfluous terminology must be explained. For the mishnaic response to the question, cf. *m. Mak.* 1:7-9. Although Qumran does not manifest the rabbinic tendency to "omnisignificance," the attribution of meaning to every aspect of the text, a case such as this one clearly begged for interpretation far more than the "extra" *vav*s which sometimes generate rabbinic exegesis.

42. This passage engendered a series of studies by B. A. Levine, J. Neusner, L. H. Schiffman, N. L. Rabinovitch, and B. S. Jackson in the mid-1970s in *RevQ* (8 and 9). They focused on its legal significance, rather than the exegetical issue in which we are interested.

43. Reading אחר, "another," with the MS of CD, and not with the emendation to אחד (one) accepted by many scholars. According to the unemended text, two witnesses testifying to the same capital offense on two different occasions suffice to preclude the offender from the *tohorah* of the community. Among contemporary scholars, B. S. Jackson, "*Testes Singulares* in Early Jewish Law and in the New Testament," in *Essays in Jewish and Comparative Legal History*, 176-77, and Yadin, 1:380, also accept the MS reading.

44. Schiffman, *Sectarian Law*, 74-81, does not accept the dichotomy between two and three witnesses as referring to a single or repeated act(s), and claims that this Qumran text always demands three witnesses for capital offenses and two for others. In his reading, too, the apparently superfluous terminology carries exegetical significance. He notes correctly, 74, "that from the point of view of hermeneutics, the sect maintained that in groups of numbers, each had to have its own significance." The parallel he adduces is the assignment of significance to each of the numerical terms in the case of the dual limit of 1,000 and 2,000 *ammot* outside the levitical cities in CD 10:5-6 and 21.

Midrash

Varieties of Analogical Reasoning

When characterizing the forms of analogical reasoning that we believe are found in the scrolls, it is convenient to employ the terminology which is utilized later in rabbinic literature for similar techniques. We are fully aware that such usage runs the risk of anachronism as well as of giving the misleading impression that the authors of the Qumran texts themselves thought in just these terms. Even if they did, it is clear they did not formulate their interpretations in language which makes the methodology obvious, and, it must be admitted, our observations are therefore largely inferential. Nevertheless, by using "rabbinic" terminology we obviate the need to invent new terminology, and underline what in our opinion is the very significant phenomenon that Qumran and rabbinic legal interpretation are ultimately not unrelated to one another. Many of the classic rabbinic *middot* are forms of analogy, based on similarities of laws in location, circumstance, language, or logic.

Qal vaḥomer (a minori ad maius)

Rabbinic tradition claims that this mode of argumentation from the less significant to the more significant appears already in Scripture.[45] Fundamentally, it is an argument from analogy supported by logic.[46] Although *qal vaḥomer* is quite common in later rabbinic law, we know of only one (or perhaps two) possible example(s) of it in the scrolls. At CD 4:20–5:2 the sin of taking more than one wife is delineated and supported by three verses: Genesis 1:27 regarding the creation of humankind in the person of one male-female couple, Genesis 7:9 regarding the animals entering the ark two by two, and Deuteronomy 17:17 regarding the king who is not permitted to multiply wives for himself. Regardless of the relative function of the three cited texts as prohibitions, it appears clear to us that the citation of Deuteronomy 17:17, ולא ירבה לו נשים ("and he must not acquire many wives for himself"), argues that *even* the king, who might be thought to have special privileges, is not permitted to marry more than one wife, and therefore the passage is likely to be a good example of a *qal vaḥomer*.[47]

---

45. *Gen. Rab.* 92:7, including such pentateuchal examples as Gen. 44:8; Exod. 6:12; Num. 12:14; and Deut. 31:27.

46. We owe this characterization of *qal vaḥomer* to Rabbi Jeremy Wieder.

47. Ginzberg, *An Unknown Jewish Sect*, 182-83 and n. 125, is the only other treatment we are familiar with which refers to this passage as a *qal vaḥomer*, but he could not see the possibility of legal reasoning from the two verses cited from Genesis since they were not quoted with citation formulas and since in his view CD followed the rabbinic principle of

Binyan Av (Homogenization)

Milgrom has dubbed one of the exegetical techniques used in the scrolls "equalization or homogenization," defining it as an interpretive process in which "a law which applies to specific objects, animals or persons is extended to other members of the same species."[48] He points out that the "exegetical technique of homogenization most closely resembles the later rabbinic hermeneutical rule of *binyan 'āb*, lit. a structure (emerging out) of the father."[49]

When the *Temple Scroll* draws together from different portions of the Pentateuch legal material which is or appears to be contradictory, it needs to synthesize and harmonize the texts so that the laws are in agreement or, at

---

not deriving law from pre-Mosaic narratives! It is unsurprising that 11QT 57:17 interprets לא ירבה as "not take more than one," in full agreement with the exegesis in CD. If our analysis is accepted, the general implications of Milgrom's remarks in his appendix to Yadin, 1:161, "the Qumran sectarians did not resort to hermeneutical principles like this *argumentum a fortiori*, but based themselves solely on Scripture," need to be modified. In fact, Milgrom himself, "Laws of Purity," 94-95, furnishes another possible example of this hermeneutic technique, although he avoids use of the terminology: if minor impurities require ablutions and sunset for purification, certainly major impurities should require them as well. According to our view, this is probably a *qal vahomer*.

48. Milgrom, "Exegetical Principles," 171, noting that Yadin does not deal with this technique. Milgrom, 175, goes so far as to suggest that "the Temple Scroll's technique of homogenization is the forerunner of rabbinic *binyan 'āb*." He furnishes one example each of homogenization of objects, animals, and persons. In "Qumran's Biblical Hermeneutics: The Case of the Wood Offering," *RevQ* 16 (1993-95): 449, Milgrom asserts "that Qumran exegesis can be broken down into four types: conflation, harmonization, homogenization and application."

49. Milgrom, "Exegetical Principles," 175. He cites *Sifrei* on Num. 15:27, which comments on the command to bring a she-goat in her first year (עז בת שנתה) for a sin offering: "this is a *binyan 'āb*: any place that it says 'a she goat' it must be a yearling." Cf. בנין אב in *Encyclopedia Talmudit* [Heb.], 4:1-11 (ET with slightly less documentation, s.v. בנין אב/Binyan Ab, *Encyclopedia Talmudica* [Jerusalem: Talmudic Encyclopedia Institute, 1992], 4:410-20). There are a number of principles based on analogical reasoning in the rabbinic exegetical arsenal, and we should note here that despite significant similarities, this exegetical tool differs from the one called *heqesh*. The last mentioned article (p. 418) formulates the difference as follows: "If the comparison between the source and the derivative is derived from their proximity, then it is a *heqesh*, not a *Binyan Ab*." The narrowest sense of *heqesh* is "the comparison of two things which are mentioned in the same verse" (הקש, *Encyclopedia Talmudit* [Heb.], 10:558), equating the laws of two different legal topics based on their juxtaposition. The only example of *heqesh* in the narrow sense of which we know in the Qumran corpus was noted by Y. Elman, "Some Remarks on 4QMMT and the Rabbinic Tradition, Or, When Is a Parallel Not a Parallel?" in J. Kampen and M. J. Bernstein, eds., *Reading 4QMMT: New Perspectives on Qumran Law and History* (Symposium 2; Atlanta: Scholars Press, 1996), 101-2. The "human limb" of Num. 19:18 is taken by 11QT 50:5-6 to be a limb from a corpse, and not from a living person, because the rest of the verse deals with "one slain by the sword, or a corpse."

least, noncontradictory. In such instances, the *Temple Scroll* responds to exegetical/interpretive difficulties which are created by the Pentateuch itself. By omitting, rephrasing, limiting, and otherwise modifying the integrated passages, it offers resolutions for the difficulties. In Leviticus 17:13 the Bible charges a person who hunts and slaughters an animal or bird ושפך את דמו וכסהו בעפר, "to spill out its blood and cover it with dust." In Deuteronomy 12:23-24 and 15:23, however, we read regarding one who slaughters an animal: על הארץ תשפכנו כמים, "spill it [the blood] out on the ground, like water." The requirement of covering the blood is absent in the two verses in Deuteronomy. 11QT 52:11-12 and 53:5-6 "resolve" this discrepancy by introducing into the paraphrase of Deuteronomy's instruction to spill the blood the commandment from Leviticus to cover the blood with dirt (וכסיתו בעפר).[50]

Another sort of analogical reasoning is the basis for the consistent ruling in the scrolls which forbids marriage between uncle and niece. This prohibition is found in the *Damascus Document* (CD), the *Temple Scroll*, and 4QHalakha A.[51] While no explanation is given in *Temple Scroll*, CD, due to its polemical character, provides an extremely insightful elaboration: "And each one of them takes as a wife the daughter of his brother and the daughter of his sister. But Moses said: 'Do not approach your mother's sister, she is a blood relation of your mother.' The law of prohibited marriages is written for males, and like them [applies equally] to females; and if the brother's daughter uncovers the nakedness of her father's brother, and she is a blood relation."[52] Here, too, we see another clear illustration of extending the biblical regulation to an analogous circumstance, something like homogenization.[53] While the

50. Yadin, 1:75, overstating more than a little, calls this resolution "an extreme example of the author's method of harmonization by merging two variant commands." Vermes, "Bible Interpretation," *186, calls this technique "harmonizing expansion." The solution differs, of course, from that of the rabbis, who distinguish the verses in Leviticus and Deuteronomy from one another, reading the former narrowly to refer only to fowl and non-domesticated animals and the latter to domesticated animals.

51. CD 5:7-11; 11QT 66:15-17; 4Q251 17 2-5. Although the context in the last instance is fragmentary, it appears that the prohibition is expressed twice, once forbidding a man to marry his brother's or his sister's daughter, and once enjoining a woman from marrying her father's or mother's brother.

52. We have translated the last phrase awkwardly because its syntax is virtually intractable in the Hebrew. Is it possible that the text should read ואיך תגלה for ואם תגלה, "How can a brother's daughter uncover . . . seeing that she is . . . ?"

53. This example may be especially significant when considering Milgrom's claim that "though some of the rabbinic *middot* are attested in the Qumran documents, homogenization, the forerunner of *binyan 'āb*, is amply and exclusively represented in the Temple Scroll" ("Exegetical Principles," 175). The prohibition of uncle/niece relationships, which is found in CD as well, seems at least to mitigate his contention. Ginzberg, *An Unknown Jew-*

biblical text specifies only the illicit relationship of an aunt and a nephew, CD extends this law to the case of an uncle and niece. In this case, CD provides a sort of logical justification for its position, an explanation of its legal reasoning. In accounting for the problem of the absence of uncle-niece relationships within the biblical listing of illicit relationships, the author of CD appears to argue that the text was written for males but should be applied equally to females. How does he know this? It may be the simple observation that the degrees of kinship of the two cases are identical that forces the logical conclusion that the law must be applied to the one not mentioned in Scripture as well.

It is possible that analogical reasoning of this sort operates on a much larger scale as well in the scrolls. The Qumran calendar included several festivals which were not listed in the Pentateuch (cf. 11QT 19-21 and 43, as well as 4Q365 23 [above, n. 11]). The Bible associates only one festival explicitly with new grain. A fifty-day counting period beginning with the Day of Waving the Sheaf (עמר) culminates in the Feast of the Firstfruits of Wheat (= Festival of Weeks), on which a new cereal offering (מנחה חדשה) is to be brought (Lev. 23:9-22 and Num. 28:26-31). Yadin assumes quite reasonably that the author of the *Temple Scroll*, along with all other Jews in late antiquity, identified the sheaf as an offering from the new barley and the new cereal offering as coming from the new wheat.[54] Fifty days later was the Feast of the Firstfruits of Wine, and after another fifty days, the Feast of the Firstfruits of Oil. Milgrom suggests that the motivation for the calendrical innovation is homogenization based on the common obligation to bring new oil, wine, and grain as firstfruits (Num. 18:12).[55] To employ our formulation, analogical reasoning demands that if new grain has a festival, new oil and new wine should have one as well, since the three items are associated with each other several times in the Pentateuch. The author of the *Temple Scroll* posits via homogenization the existence of new wine and new oil festivals, and further "homogenizes" them by placing them at fifty-day intervals from each other.[56]

---

ish Sect, 183, calls the rule involved here a הקש. It is also possible that this is an even stronger exegetical technique than harmonization because the biblical law and the Qumran addendum are virtually mirror images of each other.

54. Yadin, 1:102.

55. Milgrom, "Exegetical Principles," 172-73.

56. The New Wood Festival is a complicated topic that we shall not deal with here. For the present, see Yadin, 1:122-31, and Milgrom, "Qumran's Biblical Hermeneutics," pp. 449-56. It is certainly worth noting that the wood offering festival does not seem to share the same properties as the New Wine and New Oil festivals. This is best reflected in the lack of a fifty-day interval between the New Oil and New Wood festivals, a detail we would expect to see if the New Wood Festival was also derived from the same "homogenization" as the other festivals.

Metaphorical Analogy

Another fascinating variation of the analogical approach to exegesis can be seen in laws recently published in some of the 4QD fragments and in 4QMMT. In the former, in a passage which survives sufficiently in four copies (4Q267 7 12; 269 9 1-2; 270 5 14-15; and 271 3 7-9) to be restored virtually to completeness, we read of the responsibility of a father to inform his prospective son-in-law regarding all his daughter's physical blemishes: "why should he bring upon himself the judgment of the curse which says 'whoever leads a blind man astray from the path'?" Deuteronomy 27:18 reads ארור משגה עור בדרך ("cursed be anyone who misleads a blind person on the road"), whose simple sense is indisputable as a prohibition against misdirecting the blind. But in the exegesis of 4QD the essence of the curse is divorced from its literal context and applied to a case in which a similar injustice is being perpetrated. On the surface, the situations are not, strictly speaking, the same; the literal commandment is being read metaphorically in 4QD. But, once again, analogical reasoning indicates that misleading a prospective son-in-law by not informing him of the potential bride's defects is of the same nature as leading a blind person astray.

The same text in 4QD (4Q267 7 13; 269 9 2-3; 270 5 15-17; 271 3 9-10) continues with a second example of this method of biblical interpretation. The father is warned not to give his daughter to one who is not fit for her, "for that is two kinds (כלאים), an ox and an ass, and woolen and linen clothing together," a reference to two biblical injunctions against mingling species (Deut. 22:10-11). 4QMMT B 75ff., in a section dealing with improper marriages, alludes to all three types of forbidden mixtures: animals, fibers, and sowing.[57] It is clear that, in the view of the Qumran legists, the biblical texts dealing with mixing diverse kinds (in addition to their literal interpretations) are to be taken metaphorically as the equivalent of the union of inappropriate couples. While this interpretive technique is significantly different from "homogenization," it is still fundamentally a form of analogical reasoning.[58]

---

57. Qimron and Baumgarten disagree as to whether it is a question of intermarriage between priests and laypersons or Israelites and foreigners. Cf. Qimron and Strugnell, *Qumran Cave 4. V: Miqsat Ma'aśe Ha-Torah*, 55.

58. Dr. Shani Berrin pointed out to us that Ben Sira 25:8 contains the antecedent of this correlation of incompatible marriages and plowing with mixed breeds. Rabbinic literature observes that the marriage of a Jew to a Gentile woman violates all the laws of mixed kinds and compares that of Hamor to Dinah (Gen. 34) to plowing with ox and donkey together (*Yalqut Shim'oni* 931 ad Deut. 22:10 and *Tanḥuma Vayishlaḥ* 7, respectively). For another example of metaphorical analogy employing the same biblical law, but in a wisdom, as opposed to a legal, context, cf. 4Q418 (4QInstruction^d) 103 ii 6-9.

Gezera Shava (Argument from Analogous Expressions)

We have seen analogical reasoning which appears similar to the rabbinic *binyan av,* where broad similarity in some details of the law is the only analogical feature. There are, in addition, other kinds of legal exegesis where the analogy is not to be found in the circumstances of the laws, but in some other factor such as linguistic similarities in their biblical formulation. This methodology appears most similar to the later rabbinic hermeneutic technique of *gezera shava.*[59] There are several likely illustrations of *gezera shava* in the *Temple Scroll.* In 11QT 51:11-18 the author collocates material from Deuteronomy that deals with honest judgments and the prohibition to accept bribes, conflating the verses from Deuteronomy 16:18-20 with those from Deuteronomy 1:16-17. The latter passage contains the phrase לא תגורו מפני איש ("you shall not fear anyone"). In employing this phrase at the conclusion of the homogenized text, the author writes והאיש אשר יקח שוחד ויטה משפט צדק יומת לא תגורו ממנו להמיתו (51:17-18; "the person who takes a bribe and perverts righteous judgment *shall be put to death; you shall not fear him to put him to death*"). Yadin notes quite correctly that the scroll imposes the death penalty because the phrase לא תגורו ("you shall not fear") has only one other pentateuchal occurrence, that in the law of the false prophet (Deut. 18:22, לא תגור ממנו; "You shall not fear him"), a case in which the death penalty is imposed. The author of the *Temple Scroll* apparently extrapolates, based on the common linguistic usage, that the law must be identical in the case of accepting bribes.[60] Although Yadin does not employ the term *gezera shava,* this is a very likely example of that hermeneutic, especially since the words appear exactly twice in the Pentateuch. It should also be noted that the author of the scroll draws his language from Deuteronomy 18 and not Deuteronomy 1 when he writes לא תגורו ממנו להמיתו, rather than לא תגורו מפניו להמיתו, thus making his exegetical process clearer to us.

Another likely occurrence of *gezera shava* involves the age of the participant in the consumption of the paschal sacrifice. It is not completely clear from the language of this passage which pentateuchal passage about the pas-

---

59. For rabbinic *gezera shava,* see s.v. גזרה שוה/G'zeyrah Shavah in *Encyclopedia Talmudica* [Eng.], 6:304-16, and M. Chernick, *Gezerah Shavah: Its Various Forms in Midrashic and Talmudic Sources* (in Hebrew) (Lod: Haberman Institute for Literary Research, 1994). What is significant for our first example is Chernick's remark that "the basic formal rule for 'plain' gezerah shavah [*sic*] is that its source is a word or phrase repeated only twice in the Pentateuch" (p. 1 of unpaginated English abstract; cf. "The Types of the 'Plain' *Gezera Shava,*" 12-37).

60. Yadin, 2:229.

chal offering forms the model for its composition. The author of the *Temple Scroll* (11QT 17:6-8) records an age restriction of twenty years (line 8, מבן עשרי[ם] שנה ומעלה) for those who may participate in the offering. Although the Pentateuch does not stipulate, either in Exodus 12 or in Deuteronomy 16, the age at which an individual may participate in the paschal meal, it is likely that the *Temple Scroll* finds an exegetical source for the number. Numbers 1:1-3 specifies that the census is to include כל עדת בני ישראל . . . מבן עשרים שנה ומעלה ("the whole assembly of the Israelites . . . from twenty years up-ward"); of the paschal sacrifice it is written ושחטו אתו כל קהל עדת ישראל ("the whole assembly of the congregation of Israel shall slaughter it"). Accord-ing to Yadin, "The analogy [היקש in the Hebrew version] is obvious."[61] But why should there be an analogy between the census and the paschal offering without any external connecting feature?[62] Therefore we are inclined to believe that, if this legal detail is dependent on exegesis and is not a free addition to the text, it is more likely to belong to some category of what rabbinic exegesis calls *gezera shava,* rather than analogy of a less specific sort. It is interesting that the book of *Jubilees* (49:17) records a similar age restriction for performing the paschal sacrifice.

As we noted earlier, one of the needs of legal exegesis is the specification of terms. The expression דרך רחוקה, "far away (lit., 'a distant way')," is a clas-sic example of such a case. One is permitted to avail himself of the opportu-nity to bring the "Second Passover" (cf. Num. 9:9-14) if he is בדרך רחקה; the right to redeem second tithe crops for money and spend that money in "the place which the Lord has chosen" is permitted כי ירחק ממך המקום (Deut. 14:24; "should the place be too distant for you"); the latter phrase also fur-nishes the criterion for the availability of non-sacral slaughter of animals in Deuteronomy 12:21. In the two surviving parallels to these three instances, the *Temple Scroll* replaces this biblical רחק with the precise distance of three days.[63] Living a distance of three or more days' journey from the temple al-lows the landowner to bring the monetary value of the second tithe produce to Jerusalem (11QT 43:12) and permits the slaughtering and eating of meat without having to bring it to the temple as an offering (52:14).

The obvious question, of course, is what prompts the equation of "dis-tance" with "a three days' journey"? Yadin has suggested that the source is verses like Exodus 3:18, ועתה נלכה נא דרך שלשת ימים במדבר ונזבחה לה'

61. Yadin, 1:97.
62. Whether Yadin's description of this technique as *heqesh* was meant to connote the term in the narrow sense or not, his language still seems imprecise.
63. Unfortunately, that portion of the *Temple Scroll* which deals with the Second Passover has not survived.

אלהינו ("let us travel *three days* in the desert and sacrifice to the Lord our God").[64] This is a very loose sort of "analogical reasoning," since there is no particular reason to compare the two passages. Schiffman, on the other hand, has suggested quite convincingly that the author of the *Temple Scroll* used *gezera shava* to identify the precise meaning of the biblical term.[65] He points to Exodus 8:23-24 where Moses asserts that the people will travel דרך שלשת ימים ("a three days' journey") into the desert to sacrifice, and Pharaoh replies, רק הרחק לא תרחיקו ללכת ("only do not go too far away").[66] The use of רחק (go away) in conjunction with "three days" furnishes a *gezera shava* for other places where רחק is employed to mean "a three days' journey."

"Nontechnical" Midrash

While there exist in the legal material in the scrolls many examples of "technical" midrash, deriving from various types of analogical reasoning and often paralleling hermeneutical tools of the later rabbis, not all Qumran midrash fits this characterization. Some midrash satisfies our initial requirement, borrowed from Schiffman, of "an exegesis in which a corroborative passage in Scripture plays a part," but does not exhibit any definable hermeneutic technique. A good example is CD's treatment of the "Sabbath limits." CD 10:21 forbids a man from walking outside his city על אלף באמה ("more than a thousand cubits"). Schiffman writes, "This law is clearly the result of *midrash halakhah*. Ex. 16:29 was understood by means of *perush* to apply not only in the desert period but to all time. However, the verse does not define the limits of *taḥtaw* or *meqomo*. The process of *midrash* was used to define these terms."[67] Like their tannaitic counterparts, the sectarians used the description of the boundaries of the levitical cities recorded in Numbers 35:2-5 to clarify the ambiguous terms in Exodus. They applied both of the measurements of 1,000 and 2,000 cubits found in Numbers in defining the Sabbath limits (rabbinic תחום שבת). No man was allowed to walk 1,000 cubits outside of the camp, unless he did so while pastur-

---

64. Yadin, 1:317. Vermes, "Biblical Interpretation," *186, does not seem to envision any exegetical reason for the specification, categorizing it under "Clarifying Additions."

65. L. H. Schiffman, "Sacral and Non-Sacral Slaughter according to the *Temple Scroll*," in *Time to Prepare the Way in the Wilderness*, ed. D. Dimant and L. H. Schiffman, STDJ 16 (Leiden: Brill, 1995), 77.

66. Schiffman's suggestion seems much more plausible than that of Yadin mentioned above and that of A. Shemesh, "'Three Days' Journey from the Temple': The Use of This Expression in the Temple Scroll," *DSD* 6 (1999): 126-38, who believes the term is meant to denote the halakhic boundaries of the Land of Israel.

67. Schiffman, *The Halakhah at Qumran*, 91.

ing his animals, in which case the limit was extended to 2,000 cubits (CD 11:5-6).[68] Several centuries later, R. Akiva (*m. Soṭah* 5:3), asserting, against the majority view among the tannaim, that the Sabbath limit is a biblical rather than rabbinic injunction, understood the 1,000-cubit limit as describing the levitical pastureland (מגרש), and applied only the 2,000-cubit limit to defining the *teḥum shabbat*. This Qumran ruling is a clear illustration of the use by the sectarians of midrash which does not conform to any familiar hermeneutic technique. On the one hand, the interpretation is not based on the verse in Exodus alone, but on the other, there is no device to which we can point which links to it the verse in Numbers. This represents one of many instances of midrash that cannot be classified among the other types of midrash we have detailed.

Conclusion

As we noted earlier, to date there has been no systematic study of legal biblical exegesis at Qumran, and the work which has been dedicated to this topic has often been non-systematic and frequently treated legal exegesis as a marginal subject under the larger rubric of biblical interpretation at Qumran. In this initial foray into the subject, we have attempted to bring together, categorize, and examine some of the fundamental ways in which the sectarians, and/or their predecessors, approached the legal portions of Scripture. We hope this paper will encourage further investigation into the hows and whys of legal interpretation per se, as well as some of the crucial issues that unfortunately remained beyond the scope of the present study. The further study of topics such as interpretive authority, "biblical" and "extrabiblical" legislation, and the relative roles which inspiration and exegesis played in the interpretation of legal texts will not only deepen our understanding of the group of Jews whom we refer to as the Dead Sea sect, but will also undoubtedly provide insight into the relationship between them and other groups of Jews in late antiquity. As we hope to demonstrate in future studies, we believe that the conclusions derived from such investigation will prove to be indispensable to an analysis of what different groups of Jews in late antiquity held in common and what set them apart. The overall result is likely to shed light both on the Jews who produced the Qumran writings in the late Second Temple period and on those who produced the mishnaic, talmudic, and midrashic corpora during the rabbinic period.

68. אל ילך איש אחר הבהמה לרעותה חוץ מעירו כי אם אלפים באמה ("No one should go after an animal to pasture it outside his city more than two thousand cubits"). As Schiffman points out, the parallels between the formulations of both of the laws in CD and the limits detailed in Numbers are indisputable.

Biblical Interpretation in the "Pseudo-Ezekiel" Fragments (4Q383-391) from Cave Four

MONICA BRADY

Since the time they were first grouped together, one thing has been clear about the fragments assigned to manuscripts 4Q383-4Q391 — they are closely connected to biblical passages.[1] The particulars of that connection, however, are not so obvious or easy to ascertain. Although initial study led John Strugnell to characterize the fragments as "un écrit *pseudo-jérémien,* contenu dans cinq ou peut-être six mss . . . ," it was not long before he amended his description by adding that the work contained a "notable pseudo-Ezekiel sec-

---

1. The fragments were first mentioned as a group by John Strugnell in 1956. See the *Communication de J. Strugnell* in J. T. Milik, "Le Travail d'Édition des Fragments Manuscrits de Qumrân," *RB* 63 (1956): 49-67, esp. p. 65. Milik mentioned them in 1959 (*Ten Years of Discovery in the Wilderness of Judaea,* trans. J. Strugnell, Studies in Biblical Theology 26 [London: SCM Press, 1959], 36). The first treatment of a few fragments of the collection appeared in 1988 with a joint publication by J. Strugnell and D. Dimant ("4QSecond Ezekiel," *RevQ* 13 [1988]: 45-58). Others followed, and now 4Q383 and 4Q385-4Q390 have been published by Dimant in the Discoveries in the Judaean Desert series (*Qumran Cave 4.XXI: Parabiblical Texts, Part 4: Pseudo-Prophetic Texts,* DJD 30 [Oxford: Clarendon, 2000]). 4Q384 and 4Q391 were published separately by Mark Smith, *Qumran Cave 4.XIV: Parabiblical Texts, Part 2,* J. C. VanderKam, consulting ed., DJD 19 (Oxford: Clarendon, 1995), 137-93.

This article is drawn in part from my dissertation, "Prophetic Traditions at Qumran: A Study of 4Q383-391" (Diss., University of Notre Dame, 2000).

tion."[2] Further attempts to define the relationship between these texts and biblical materials led Devorah Dimant to divide the work into three, describing parts that seemed distinct from both the Jeremiah and Ezekiel components as pseudo-Moses in character.[3]

Most likely the desire quickly to come up with an apt title for a previously unknown work or works contributed to the different labels assigned to the work early on, such as "pseudo" Jeremiah, "pseudo" Ezekiel, "second" Ezekiel, "pseudo" Moses, etc. That the work has already borne so many titles is testimony to the fact that although in general terms we are quite sure of a connection between these fragments and biblical books such as Jeremiah and Ezekiel, we are not so sure when it comes to specifics exactly what the connection(s) is (are). For example: Was the text in its entirety meant to be a reworking of the biblical Ezekiel, of Jeremiah, or of some combination of both? Did the biblical books simply serve as source materials for a work of similar themes? What authority did the words of these prophets have? What role might a pseudo-Ezekiel or pseudo-Jeremiah character have played for the scrolls community? Are the connections limited to these prophets, or are the biblical ties more complex? How exactly do we explain the similarities and differences between biblical materials and what is found in 4Q383-4Q391? Do we have enough clearly preserved material to determine whether it is appropriate to see one of these prophets as the overarching figure or organizing principle of these fragments?

In other words, the larger questions of biblical interpretation posed by this volume are key in the very task of characterizing or labeling these fragments. When we can come to some understanding as to the precise use of biblical materials in these fragments — the choices of passages, the modes of interpretation, the apparent concerns — then we will have made some progress toward the elusive goals of categorization and naming of the texts. It seems to me, however, that this process is only at a beginning. Naming the

2. Compare his 1956 description ("Le Travail d'Édition des Fragments Manuscrits de Qumrân," 65) with his assessment of the collection in 1960 ("The Angelic Liturgy at Qumrân — 4QSerek Šîrôt 'Ôlat Haššabbāt," *Congress Volume, Oxford, 1959*, VTSup 7 [Leiden: Brill, 1960], 344).

3. Dimant's view was set forth in "New Light from Qumran on the Jewish Pseudepigrapha — 4Q390," in *The Madrid Qumran Congress: Proceedings of the International Congress on the Dead Sea Scrolls, Madrid, 18-21 March 1991*, ed. J. Trebolle Barrera and L. Vegas Montaner, STDJ 11:2 (Leiden: Brill, 1992), 2:405-48. She has since abandoned at least a portion of this position, arguing in her DJD edition that the fragments represent two distinct works — "Pseudo-Ezekiel" and "Apocryphon of Jeremiah C" — but not a third related to Moses, as she had argued previously (see the summary of her view on p. 3 of DJD 30).

text is something which probably should happen much later.[4] This is in part because the collection is somewhat large and in ways diverse. It is also because it is extremely fragmentary. While there are some fragments which might be called large by Qumran standards, they break off at the most inopportune moments, giving the reader little context or framework for interpretation. It may be the case that because of the incomplete state of preservation the most precise title would be "text related to Jeremiah and Ezekiel." At least for now, such a title is fitting, if not ultimately satisfying.

Not only do the early changes in titles point to uncertainties regarding the relationship between these fragments and biblical books, they also highlight a methodological problem that has plagued the approach to this collection. It is an understandable problem — one that might surface for anyone faced with categorizing or analyzing a collection of diverse and previously unknown fragments and finding that some bear more fruit from analysis than others. However, it is also one which has contributed much confusion to the task. This is the problem of examining individual fragments in isolation while attempting to characterize the whole.

It has been Dimant's approach to use formal or literary elements — contents, themes, elements of style, etc. — as the criteria for sorting fragments.[5] In many ways this approach lends itself to separation of fragments into isolated pieces — this one mentions Jeremiah, this other Ezekiel, still another the Law; or, this passage is poetry, another historical narrative, another dialogue between a prophet and the Lord. This approach and its findings are

---

4. Although understandable, the rush to name texts such as these can be premature or unhelpful when we are still far from a complete understanding of the work. Inevitably, as we have seen with other Qumran documents, more information comes to light, some titles are found to be inaccurate or imprecise, and texts must be renamed. Multiple name changes often then become burdensome, complicating the discussion of fragments.

5. See her studies of individual fragments, including "New Light from Qumran on the Jewish Pseudepigrapha — 4Q390"; "An Apocryphon of Jeremiah from Cave 4 (4Q385B = 4Q385 16)," in *New Qumran Texts and Studies: Proceedings of the First Meeting of the International Organization for Qumran Studies, Paris 1992*, ed. G. J. Brooke, STDJ 15 (Leiden: Brill, 1994), 11-30; "4Q386 ii-iii: A Prophecy on Hellenistic Kingdoms?" *RevQ* 18 (1998): 511-29; "A Saying about the Past from the Composition Pseudo-Moses: 4Q389 2" [Hebrew: 4Q389 2 — 'נאום על העבר מתוך החיבור'פסוידו משה], in *A Light for Jacob: Studies in the Bible and the Dead Sea Scrolls in Memory of Jacob Shalom Licht*, ed. Y. Hoffman and F. Polak (Jerusalem: Bialik Institute/Tel Aviv University, 1997), 220-26; and "A Quotation from Nahum 3:8-10 in 4Q385-6 from Qumran," in *The Bible in the Light of Its Interpreters: Memorial Volume for Sarah Kamin*, ed. S. Japhet (Jerusalem: Magnes Press, 1994), 31-37 [Hebrew: ציטטה מנחום ג, ח-'ו בקטע מקומראן 4Q385 6].

what led Dimant to break from Strugnell's initial assessment of the fragments and posit three distinct works.

Dimant began by noticing that, in terms of form and content, a few fragments stood out as distinct from each other. Eventually, each of three exemplars was set forth by Dimant as the primary representative of a distinct work. They were Ezekiel's vision of the dry bones (4Q385 2; 4Q388 8 3-7; 4Q386 1 i 1-9), Jeremiah's activities surrounding the exile (4Q385 16), and the pair of fragments which Dimant associated with Moses (4Q390 1-2).[6] For Dimant, the Ezekiel fragment suggested a larger "Pseudo-Ezekiel" text, the fragment related to Jeremiah seemed to represent an "Apocryphon of Jeremiah," and the fragments which appeared to contain divine speech addressed to Moses suggested a larger work entitled "Pseudo-Moses."[7]

In other words, Dimant analyzed three individual fragments, came to certain conclusions about their form, style, content, and connections to biblical passages, and then postulated larger works of uniform style, of which these are representatives. The problems arose when Dimant set about sorting the remaining fragments into the three categories. These can be summarized by a few examples: If "Apocryphon of Jeremiah" is a historical narrative, characterized by reports of Jeremiah's activity, with Jeremiah mentioned in the third-person singular (as in 4Q385 16), what does one do with 4Q383 1, which, although it mentions Jeremiah, contains first-person speech ("And I, Jeremiah . . .")? How should a fragment such as 4Q385 6 + 9 + 22 + 24 + 34, which is based on Nahum 3:8-10, be categorized, since it reworks a passage from yet another prophet, but also mentions Egypt, like fragments assigned to the Jeremiah and Ezekiel subdivisions? And probably most problematic, on what basis are smaller and smaller fragments containing isolated phrases such as "A]braham your father" (4Q385 18), "]number of priests[" (4Q385 43), "]statutes[" (4Q388 2), etc., assigned to separate categories?

Dimant's approach certainly has merit in some venues, such as the examination of a novel or letter or other complete work, or even as a later stage

---

6. These manuscript and fragment numbers reflect those of the *Preliminary Concordance* (R. Brown, J. Fitzmyer, W. Oxtoby, and J. Teixidor, *A Preliminary Concordance to the Hebrew and Aramaic Fragments from Qumran Caves II-X, Including Especially the Unpublished Material from Cave 4* [printed from the card index; arranged for printing by Hans-Peter Richter; privately printed in Göttingen, 1988]), and B. Z. Wacholder and M. Abegg (*A Preliminary Edition of the Unpublished Dead Sea Scrolls: The Hebrew and Aramaic Texts from Cave Four*, Fascicle III [Washington, D.C.: Biblical Archaeology Society, 1995]). In DJD 30, some of these are represented by different numbers. See the chart at the end of this article for corresponding numbers.

7. See Dimant, "New Light," 405-48, esp. 405-13.

in this task. But when the material under study is fragments, with many of the beginnings, middles, and endings unknown, it is extremely problematic to speak definitively about their formal elements, and to categorize them on such basis. What has happened is that fragments have been examined one by one, in isolation. Their salient features have been noted, and used to separate the fragments. Jeremiah is separated from Ezekiel, dialogue from narrative, Deuteronomic language from poetic, and so on. Certainly information gleaned from analysis of the fragments is helpful, but it is pushed beyond its limits when it is used as the basis for assigning the fragments to distinct works. When fragments are that small and without a clear context, commonalities are overlooked while differences are highlighted.

Separating fragments because of differing formal elements assumes a world with rather strict literary conventions, which we know not to be the case in biblical literature. It would rule out the possibility that the organizing principle of the work is broad, perhaps combining smaller themes or units within a larger category (such as the prophets are in the Hebrew Bible). It would also rule out the possibility that diverse forms could exist in one work. A simple example illustrates this. Imagine that one found the following phrases on separate fragments: (1) "What wrong did your fathers find in me that they went far from me . . . ?"; (2) "Search her squares to see if you can find a man, one who does justice and seeks truth . . ."; (3) "Egypt rises like the Nile, like rivers whose waters surge . . ."; (4) "Zedekiah was twenty-one years old when he became king; and he reigned eleven years in Jerusalem . . ."; (5) "The Levitical priests shall never lack a man in my presence to offer burnt offerings, to burn cereal offerings, and to make sacrifices forever. . . ."

All five of these verses, drawn from the book of Jeremiah, should suffice to make the point that one may find within a single work such forms as first-person speech, third-person narrative, poetry, and dialogue, and themes as diverse as adherence to the law, the condemnation of Egypt, and the recounting of the reign of a king. Now imagine that the five verses above were torn into smaller pieces. It would be quite difficult then to determine their dominant features, and quite problematic to use this limited information to separate them into categories.

Why consider the fragments together when there are differences in content and form? If we look back at what originally led to the placement of these fragments in the same general category, we find different types of physical evidence. There are the similarities of hand, of leather, and of damage patterns, as well as the presence of overlaps, at times between three or four fragments from different manuscripts. Although the physical evidence (particularly relating to hand and leather) cannot provide definitive conclusions about ordering of fragments or the overall shape of the work, it also cannot be ignored or passed over in favor of formal elements. Instead, it seems that in the absence of a complete copy of the work, physical evidence must be considered first, before matters of form and style. Since there is some compelling physical evidence (hand, damage patterns, the overlaps, and the presence on 4Q386 1 i-iii of very different types of material) to consider fragments together, then this should be done first, and the possibility of a work of diverse forms and content should not be excluded.

Dimant herself wrote in her 1992 article:

> A strong case for such an hypothesis [her proposal to subdivide the manuscripts] could, of course, be made on the basis of material evidence, if the fragments showed different scribal hands. But there is no unambiguous evidence of this kind. The fragments display very similar scribal hands, and more or less the same material aspect. Of the few minute material and scribal differences detectable in the fragments most are either insufficiently distinctive, or are distinctive only in a handful of fragments. This is undoubtedly what led Strugnell to join these fragments in the first place.[8]

As she prepared the fragments for publication in DJD 30, Dimant appears to have wrestled with her approach, particularly the issue of examining fragments in isolation.[9] She began to recognize the need to look at all of the fragments together. However, formal and stylistic elements were still used as the criteria for sorting.[10]

Unfortunately, the result is that a considerable amount of confusion regarding proper categorization of fragments, naming of manuscripts, numbering of fragments, and criteria for all of those efforts remains. As noted, with the publication of DJD 30, Dimant abandoned the category "Pseudo-Moses." A category which once was viewed as possessing its own distinctive themes, style, and vocabulary is now subsumed under "Apocryphon of Jeremiah C," which itself was once described as distinct from the pseudo-Moses material. Perhaps the most helpful step at this point would be to set aside the categories, numbers, and names, and to consider the fragments as a group, al-

---

8. Dimant, "New Light," 407-8.

9. Dimant writes, "At that point I realized that only an exhaustive inventory of all the fragments of 4Q385-390 could provide a reliable key for comprehensive classification." See the general introduction to DJD 30 (3).

10. "The Ezekiel-like phraseology and themes of 4Q386 have nothing in common with the Deuteronomistic idioms and the review of history of 4Q390. Once this was recognized, each manuscript served as criterion for sifting the entire collection, a method which proved to be correct." See p. 2 of the general introduction to DJD 30.

beit a heterogeneous one, assembled first because of their common physical traits. In doing so, commonalities which were overlooked when fragments were separated are now revealed.

While a final or complete picture of what is going on in these very fragmentary texts may continue to elude us, we *can* make a good start toward describing their dominant features with respect to biblical interpretation. This can be done through a survey of biblical materials across the collection. This will include a look at the biblical books which figure most prominently in the fragments, and the ways in which they do so.

Survey of Biblical Interpretation in 4Q383-391

First, some basic descriptive points might be helpful. The nine manuscripts which originally constituted the group called "Pseudo-Ezekiel" contain roughly 225 fragments, with a little more than half of these leather and the rest papyrus.[11] The fragments range in size from quite small, preserving only a letter or two, to fairly sizable, preserving the width of a column for eleven to twelve lines, and in some cases even two or three columns (e.g., 4Q386 1 i-iii and 4Q390 2 i-ii). Between five of the nine manuscripts, four instances of overlapping text have been identified. Two of these overlaps connect four manuscripts (4Q385, 4Q387, 4Q388, and 4Q389), one connects three (4Q385, 4Q386, and 4Q388), and the last illustrates contact between two manuscripts (4Q385 and 4Q387). There are no overlaps with the papyrus manuscripts, nor with 4Q383 (which is quite small) and 4Q390.

As a collection, the manuscripts exhibit the following general qualities. (1) Most contain first-person speech, second-person address, and third-person narrative. In several cases, these are parts of a dialogue framework; the Lord speaks with a pseudepigraphic figure, issuing commands and surveying future events in response to the addressee's questions. (2) Some contain language which is somewhat poetic. (3) Vocabulary and forms from Biblical and later Hebrew are present. (4) All exhibit biblical connections, but in different ways and to varying degrees. (5) Many share language and themes from other known ancient works, both from Qumran and elsewhere.

As already stated, the biblical books with which the group shows the most points of contact are the prophets, especially Jeremiah and Ezekiel. The

---

11. The papyrus fragments are confined to 4Q384 and 4Q391 and, although almost equal in number to the leather fragments, actually represent a much smaller amount of preserved material, since most of them are quite tiny.

foregoing discussions have hinted at some of the connections, but a more focused look is in order. We begin with the most obvious or straightforward ties.

Although in many passages the identities of characters are not clear, in others the names of the prophets are mentioned. Jeremiah's name appears ten times,[12] while Ezekiel is referred to by name three times.[13] In addition, the epithet "son of man" occurs three times.[14]

Beyond precise mention of prophets' names or titles, there are numerous other connections between this collection of manuscripts and the biblical prophetic books. These include: (1) paraphrasing or reworking of specific relatively large biblical passages related to Jeremiah and Ezekiel; (2) reworking of smaller units of texts (verses or phrases) drawn from Jeremiah and Ezekiel; (3) the use of language and themes common to Jeremiah, Ezekiel, and other prophets; (4) the use of terms or language associated only with Jeremiah and/or Ezekiel; (5) the presentation of material in the form of dialogues between the Lord and another figure, in ways similar to the prophets in the biblical books; (6) reworking of smaller units of text from other prophets; and (7) the incorporation of paraphrased Pentateuchal passages and themes, especially those which are taken up by the biblical prophets. The remainder of this section will entail discussion of these seven biblical connections one by one.

(1) There are four larger biblical passages reworked in the collection. All occur in 4Q385, although one is also preserved in both 4Q386 and 4Q388.

(a) The first is 4Q385 1, which paraphrases Ezekiel 30:1-5. That passage falls in the middle of Ezekiel's prophecies against foreign nations (Ezek. 25–32), and speaks of the day of the Lord coming upon Egypt (a theme found elsewhere in the collection; see below). As in the biblical text, Ezekiel reports the reception of a word of the Lord, in which he is commanded to prophesy. The word of the prophet is presented in more summary fashion in fragment 1 than in the biblical account.[15] In addition, the order of destruction of various

---

12. The name occurs once in 4Q383 (1 2; in first-person speech), eight times in 4Q385 (16 i 2, 6, 8; 16 ii 3, 4, 6; 25 1; and 39 2; all in third-person narrative), and once in 4Q389 (3 5; also in third-person narrative). In all but one case (4Q385 25 1) the shortened form of the name is used.

13. All three instances occur in 4Q385 (1 1 [third person, introducing Ezekiel's words]; 3 4 [second person, addressed by the Lord]; 4 5 [third person, introducing Ezekiel's vision]).

14. See 4Q385 2 5; 12 4; and 4Q386 1 ii 2. Other phrases clearly connected to prophets also appear ("the words of" [4Q385 1 1]; "the vision which he saw" [4Q385 4 5]; "prophesy" [4Q385 1 2; 2 5, 6, 7 and the overlaps in 4Q386 1 i]).

15. For example, the phrase "thus says the Lord" in Ezek. 30:2 is omitted in frg. 1 2. 4Q385 2 and 16 exhibit similar condensing of biblical details.

locations is inverted. Also, some words and phrases not found in Ezekiel 30 appear.[16] Although it is not clear whether the fragment contained dialogue between Ezekiel and the Lord, it is at least clear that the passage contained third-person narration, a bit of first-person speech by the prophet, and the Lord's word to the people, as reported by Ezekiel.

(b) A second larger biblical passage treated in the collection is a portion of the vision of the dry bones in Ezekiel 37. The text is reworked in 4Q385 2 (and perhaps 12?), with overlaps in 4Q386 1 i and 4Q388 8. The ten lines of 4Q385 2 have been treated extensively, by Dimant and Strugnell, and others.[17] The dialogue between Ezekiel and the Lord preserved in fragment 2 incorporates major elements of the biblical account of the vision, but within a different framework, creating a new interpretation intended for a different time and context. The result is that a vision originally intended to describe the return of the people to the land of Israel is reinterpreted to deal with the question of reward for the faithful at the end time.

Fragment 2 mirrors Ezekiel 37 in the following ways: (1) the perspective provided is that of Ezekiel, who recounts his interaction with the Lord; (2) questions are asked, and these frame the account; (3) three times the Lord commands the prophet to prophesy, concerning roughly the same matters; and (4) the fact that the Lord's actions will cause the people to know that he is the Lord is emphasized.

In other ways, however, fragment 2 departs from the account in Ezekiel 37: (1) the actual vision of the dry bones is not preserved in fragment 2 (although some form of it probably appeared before line 1); (2) the role of Ezekiel is somewhat elevated in fragment 2, in the sense that his questions frame the dialogue and move things forward (as opposed to the Lord asking Ezekiel a single question in the biblical account, and when the prophet declines to answer, it is the Lord's speeches and commands which propel the account forward); (3) fragment 2 focuses on the timing of events, while Ezekiel 37 is more concerned with the nature of events; (4) the contents of the prophecies, as well as their presentation, differ somewhat; (5) the commands to prophesy are more compact in fragment 2, and the biblical reports that Ezekiel did so are absent in fragment 2; (6) fragment 2 contains some nonbiblical elements (the questions about when events will occur, and the cryptic phrase about a tree which will bend and straighten) which may have

16. Line 4 contains a form of the verb קלל, and line 5 contains nonbiblical phrasing (בשער]י [מצרים ואבד]ן).

17. 4Q385 2 was presented in Strugnell and Dimant's first article on the collection, "4QSecond Ezekiel," *RevQ* 13 (1988): 45-58.

parallels in other writings; and (7) elements treated in Ezekiel 37 (such as re-vivification and the opening of the graves) are not taken up in fragment 2. This summary of similarities and differences is necessarily brief and cursory, but it gives the reader some sense of the treatment of the biblical vision of the dry bones in this collection.

(c) A third larger passage from Ezekiel which appears in the collection is the chariot vision of Ezekiel 1 (and perhaps 10) preserved in 4Q385 4. The first four of the fifteen lines preserved may contain some dialogue, although it is difficult to determine this since the fragment is quite broken. The vision itself is then introduced clearly in line 5 ("the vision which Ezek[iel] saw[. . .").

In 1990 Dimant and Strugnell published a detailed edition of fragment 4.[18] Their study examined the relationship between the fragment and Ezekiel 1, 10, and other *merkabah* traditions. They concluded that fragment 4 is perhaps the oldest witness to postbiblical explicit exegesis of the biblical *merkabah* vision. They also summarized the interpretive methods of the author of fragment 4 as follows:

(1) *omission* of repetitious or redundant details;
(2) *substitution* of biblical terms by nonbiblical ones;
(3) slight *rewriting* of the biblical version, such as by a shorter and simplified sequence of the description;
(4) small interpretive *additions* are introduced;
(5) use of *other* parallel or related *biblical* texts (Ezek. 10; Isa. 6; 2 Chron. 3).[19]

As we have seen already in fragments 1 and 2, these same sorts of techniques are apparent in other fragments of the collection.

(d) The final fragment which paraphrases a larger stretch of text is 4Q385 16. Unlike the others, it reworks a larger amount of biblical material (from several chapters, namely, Jer. 40–44 and 52) less closely, focusing on events surrounding the deportation, and employing biblical details as needed. It is the largest fragment that is unquestionably concerned with the prophet Jeremiah. The two columns (of about ten lines each) appear to con-

18. Dimant and Strugnell, "The Merkabah Vision in Second Ezekiel," *RevQ* 14 (1990): 331-48.
19. Dimant and Strugnell, "The Merkabah Vision," 346. Also, see their helpful table on p. 344, which illustrates how, in general language and sequence of events, frg. 4 follows Ezek. 1. The table also shows those parts of frg. 4 (particularly lines 9-12) which seem to derive more from the account of the vision in Ezek. 10. The discussion which follows the chart shows ways in which frg. 4 departs from the biblical sources (see pp. 345-46).

tain accounts of two separate events involving Jeremiah, drawing upon both biblical and extrabiblical sources. Each account seems to preserve a reception of a word of the Lord by Jeremiah, delivery of the word to the people, and some summary contents of the word, which in both cases involve divine commands about keeping the covenant and/or laws and commandments.

Column i contains third-person narrative which describes events surrounding the deportation of Israelites to Babylon. The events recounted are as follows: (1) Jeremiah goes forth from the presence of the Lord (presumably after receiving a word) (line i 2). (2) Jeremiah joins the captives who, we are told, were taken previously from Jerusalem to Babylon, an activity which involved the king of Babylon (Nebuchadnezzar) and his chief bodyguard, Nebuzaradan. The vessels of the house of God, as well as the priests and the children of Israel, were taken (lines i 3-6a). (3) At a river, Jeremiah commands the people what they ought to do in the land of their captivity. They are to listen to the voice of Jeremiah, to the words God commanded him, and to keep the covenant of the God of their fathers in the land of their captivity, something the people, their kings, and their priests failed to do previously (lines i 6b-11).

Column ii appears to contain first-person speech by both the Lord and the people, set within a framework of third-person narrative which describes events which occurred in Tahpan(h)es. The contents are as follows: (1) The setting is Tahpan(h)es (line ii 1), and (presumably) the people ask Jeremiah to pray for them or to inquire of God on their behalf (lines ii 2-3). (2) It appears that Jeremiah does as asked and prays for them, or perhaps gives forth "lamentation and prayer" on their behalf, lamenting over the people of Jerusalem (lines ii 3-5). (3) The location of activity, Tahpan(h)es, in Egypt, is then reiterated (line ii 6), probably in the context of introducing a word of the Lord which has come to Jeremiah, intended for the people of Israel, Judah, and Benjamin (line ii 7). (4) The word then follows (lines ii 8-10), containing directives to seek God's law and keep his commandments, possibly including those to avoid foreign idols.

(2) Passages that rework smaller units of text from Jeremiah and Ezekiel include the following:

(a) 4Q386 1 iii 1 (Jer. 51:7 [and also 25:15-29]): 4Q386 1 iii 1 reads ". . . and He came to Babylon. And Babylon is like a cup in the hand of the Lord. . . ." For the closest language, compare Jeremiah 51:7: "Babylon was a golden cup in the Lord's hand, making all the earth drunken; the nations drank of her wine, therefore the nations went mad." Also, see Jeremiah 25:15-29 for the fuller biblical description of the cup of judgment.[20]

---

20. The theme of drinking from the cup of the Lord's judgment can be found else-

(b) 4Q387 3 iii, and overlaps in 4Q389 1 ii 10 and 4Q388 1 ii 4-7 (Ezek. 29–30): The words of the fragment echo the language of the oracle against Egypt in Ezekiel 29–30. See especially 29:6-16, which describes the fate of Egypt. 4Q387 3 iii picks up the themes of deliverance to the sword and desolation of the land prominent in that passage.

(c) 4Q387 4 i 4 (Ezek. 38:22): Although 4Q387 4 i is quite fragmentary, with much of the surface worn away, a few legible words connect it to Ezekiel 38:22. The scant contents of the line before line i 4 differ from what comes before Ezekiel 38:22, suggesting that the fragment is not reworking this section of Ezekiel but rather drawing upon a single verse. Line i 4 reads וגשם שוטף וא[בנ]י א[ל]גב[יש אש וגפרית [אמטיר עליו ("and flooding rain and h]a[i]l [s]ton[es], fire and sulfur [I will rain upon him"), while Ezekiel 38:22 reads:

ונשפטתי אתו בדבר ובדם וגשם שוטף ואבני אלגביש אש וגפרית
אמטיר עליו ועל אגפיו ועל עמים רבים אשר אתו

With pestilence and bloodshed I will enter into judgment with him; and I will rain upon him and his hordes and the many peoples that are with him, torrential rains and hailstones, fire and brimstone.[21]

(d) 4Q391 65 (Ezek. 40–42): Fragment 65 is also quite broken, but has clear connections to Ezekiel. A vision at the river Chebar is mentioned (line 4), followed by various measurements which comport with those in the descriptions of the construction of the new temple in Ezekiel 40–42.[22] In addition, the word גבוה, or "height," is also used in the biblical description (see Ezek. 40:42; 41:8, 22). Finally, the word חמשפש ("postern," line 8), although not used in the biblical account, appears elsewhere at Qumran in Aramaic in 5Q15, a text about the New Jerusalem based upon Ezekiel 40–48.

(3) Beyond specific passages, language and themes pervasive in Jeremiah, Ezekiel, and other prophets are employed in the collection. These include the following:

---

where in Ps. 75:9; Lam. 4:21; Isa. 51:17, 22; Ezek. 23:31-33; and Hab. 2:16 (also see the interpretation of this line in 1QpHab XI 10, 14-15). In the book of Jeremiah, the "cup" of judgment is equated with "the sword" (see Jer. 25:28-29 and 50:35-37, in which the sword is turned upon Babylon). The sword of judgment appears in Ezekiel as well (see Ezek. 30, esp. vv. 4, 11, 24-25; and recall 4Q385 1, which reworks Ezek. 30:1-5).

21. Compare Ezek. 13:11-13 as well, although that passage does not contain the reference to sulfur or brimstone.

22. For line 6 (thi]rteen[), see Ezek. 40:11; for line 7 (]cubit and height of five[), see 40:42 and 41:8, 22.

(a) the Lord's hiding of his face (4Q385 44; 4Q387 3 ii, 3 iii; 4Q388 6; 4Q389 1 ii; 4Q390 1);

(b) the covenant of Abraham, Isaac, and Jacob (4Q385 2, 16, 41, 45; 4Q387 1, 2; 4Q388 1 ii 4, 8; 4Q389 1 ii; 4Q390 1, 2 i);

(c) the committing of evil in the presence of the Lord (4Q388 1 ii; 4Q389 1 ii; 4Q390 1, 2 i, 3);

(d) the desolation of the land following the destruction of Jerusalem (4Q383 1; 4Q386 1 ii-iii; 4Q387 1; 4Q390 1);

(e) Egypt, and her destruction (4Q385 1, 8, 16, 31, 6 + 9 + 22 + 24 + 34; 4Q386 1 ii; 4Q387 3 iii; 4Q388 1 ii, 12 ii; 4Q391 1, 5, 70);

(f) sword of judgment (4Q385 1; 4Q387 3 iii; 4Q388 1 ii, 9; 4Q390 1, 2 i);

(g) lands of captivity/enemies (4Q385 16 i, 44; 4Q387 1, 3 ii; 4Q389 1 ii; 4Q390 1);

(h) statutes and commandments (4Q385 16; 4Q387 2, 3 ii; 4Q388 2; 4Q389 1 ii; 4Q390 1, 2 i).

(4) There are also specific terms which in the Hebrew Bible are associated only with Jeremiah and/or Ezekiel. A few of these are found in the collection, including:

(a) the river Sor (4Q389 3 7; compare *Bar.* 1:4);

(b) the river Chebar (4Q391 65 4; compare Ezek. 1:1; 3:15; etc.);

(c) Tahpanhes (4Q384 7 2 and 4Q385 16 ii 1; compare Jer. 2:16; 43:7-9; 44:1; 46:14; and Ezek. 30:18).

(5) In addition, in ways similar to the prophets in the biblical books, named or unnamed pseudepigraphic figures engage in dialogue with the Lord concerning the people, the covenant, law, recompense for the righteous, punishment of the unfaithful, and other matters in several fragments of the collection. These include the following.

(a) 4Q385 2: The vision of the dry bones is set in the framework of a dialogue between the Lord and Ezekiel.

(b) 4Q385 3: Ezekiel questions the Lord about timing of events to come.

(c) 4Q386 1 ii: Ezekiel (?) questions the Lord about future events.

(d) 4Q390 1 and 2: The Lord speaks to an unnamed addressee, surveying future events, especially times of sinfulness and punishment.

(6) As was suggested earlier, the ties to biblical prophets are not limited to the books of Jeremiah and Ezekiel. With regard to themes and language, there are many resonances with other prophetic books (as in the list of themes above). In addition, there are a couple of passages from the minor prophets which are reworked in the same ways as passages from Ezekiel and Jeremiah. These are Nahum 3:8-10 and Amos 8:11.

(a) 4Q385 6 + 9 + 22 + 24 + 34: As suggested by the numbers, this fragment consists of multiple fragments placed together. Their placement was possible because of the close connection to Nahum 3:8-10 (the portion of the oracle against Nineveh which is concerned with Egypt). Lines ii 4-9 of the composite fragment follow Nahum 3:8-10 closely, although they do not present the MT verbatim. Some substitutions, additions, and omissions of words occur.[23] There is also a change in the party to whom the passage is addressed. In Nahum 3:8-10, Nineveh (represented by second-person forms ["Are you better than Thebes . . . ?"]) is addressed, with Thebes (No-Amon) described using third-person suffixes. In the composite fragment, it appears that Amon, rather than Nineveh, is addressed, with both second- and third-person forms referring back to Amon. The result is a prophecy directed against Amon, announcing her imminent destruction in the words of Nahum.

(b) 4Q387 2 8-9: Although the ends of lines 8-9 are broken and twisted, enough letters are visible to piece together the sense of the lines. They can be reconstructed as follows:]ם[א]וצמא ולל[א]/ללח[א]/ללל[א]/ל[מ] לן[מ]ים ושלח[תי רעב[ ]ול[א] ("[And] I [will send] a famine,[ ] but no[t] of br[ead,] and thirst, but no[t] of [wa]ter[ ]if [ ]"). They appear to be a close approximation of Amos 8:11: והשלחתי רעב בארץ/לא רעב ללחם ולא צמא למים/כי אם לשמע את דברי יהוה ("I will send a famine on the land; not a famine of bread, or a thirst for water, but of hearing the words of the Lord"). The verse occurs in Amos in the middle of the vision of the basket of fruit (chap. 8), which symbolizes the immediacy of Israel's destruction.[24] The words for hunger and thirst are paired elsewhere in the Hebrew Bible (see Deut. 28:48; 2 Chron. 32:11; Isa. 5:13; Neh. 9:15), likewise in stretches of text dealing with Israel's punishment for breaking the covenant.

(7) Beyond the prophets, fragments from the collection also rework and/or draw language from Pentateuchal passages. Often they are Pentateuchal passages which are of concern in the prophetic books.

(a) 4Q387 1: This fragment draws upon Leviticus 26:15-44 (see also Ezek. 38–39; 43–44). The vocabulary of fragment 1 fits very closely the language of Leviticus 26:15-44, the warning of the punishment that will result from dis-

---

23. The composite fragment uses הוכן (ii 4) rather than התיטבי (Nah. 3:8),]שכ[נה (ii 4) instead of הישבה (Nah. 3:8), בסעדך (ii 7) for בעזרתך (Nah. 3:9), and]דרכ[ים (ii 8) for חוצות (Nah. 3:10). לבריח]יך (ii 6) is an addition to what appears in Nah. 3:9. פוט (Nah. 3:9) and רתקו (Nah. 3:10) are omitted in the composite fragment. Also, some changes in forms occur (קץ [ii 6]/קצה [Nah. 3:9]; לוב [ii 7]/ולובים [Nah. 3:9]; לגלה/ה [ii 7]/בגולה [Nah. 3:10]; תלך [ii 7]/הלכה [Nah. 3:10]).

24. Note that the word גאון (line 6 of the fragment) also occurs in Amos, just above in 8:7.

obeying the covenant and its commands, particularly those just enunciated regarding proper observance of festivals and Sabbaths.[25] This punishment consists primarily of defeat by enemies and removal from the land.

Interestingly, some of this vocabulary, as well as other words in the fragment, can be found in Ezekiel.[26] Ezekiel 38 introduces the oracle of Gog and the land of Magog whom the Lord would bring against his people (38:1-16), only to turn on them and defeat them (38:17–39:10), making known the Lord's glory before all nations (39:13, 21). All nations would then know the Lord, and that he delivered Israel into captivity because of their unfaithfulness and brought them back because of his mercy (39:21-24). The Lord promises to restore the house of Israel, bringing them out of the lands of their enemies and back to Israel, where they will cease their treacherous ways (39:25-29). Ezekiel's vision of the new temple then follows (40–48), containing detailed specifications for the temple, as well as commands for proper observance of festivals and Sabbaths (as first set out in the law of Moses, in Lev. 23–26), something the people failed to carry out in the past.

It seems, then, that fragment 1 draws upon the interplay of language and themes between Leviticus (especially chap. 26) and Ezekiel.[27] The laws regarding proper Sabbath and festival observance are spelled out in Leviticus, along with the threat of removal from the land which would come from breaking the covenantal laws. Using language common to Leviticus, the later chapters of Ezekiel remind the people of their removal from the land due to their unfaithfulness and breaking of the covenant. Once they have paid for their iniquity, the Lord bestows his mercy upon them and returns them to their land. A new temple, with proper observance of festivals and sacrifices, is then envisioned.

(b) 4Q387 5: Although broken, fragment 5 2 (בערותם לקרוב איש[[אל שאר בשרו]) appears to contain a clear reference to the biblical law regarding incest (see Lev. 18:6: איש איש אל כל שאר בשרו לא תקרבו לגלות ערוה; "None of you shall approach anyone near of kin to uncover naked-

---

25. Examples of common vocabulary include the following: עזב (Lev. 26:43/4Q387 1 2); שעיר (Lev. 4:23-24; 9:15/1 4); פרר (Lev. 26:15, 44/1 5); ביד איביכם (Lev. 26:25/1 7); שבת and שמם (Lev. 26:32-35, 43/1 8); and ארצות איביכם (Lev. 26:34-44 [6X]/1 9).

26. Ezekiel uses מועדי (Ezek. 44:24/4Q387 1 3 [reconstructed from overlap]); חלל (Ezek. 44:7/1 3); זבח (Ezek. 39; 43–44/1 4 [reconstructed from overlap]); שעיר (Ezek. 43:22, 25; 45:23/1 4); פרר (Ezek. 44:7/1 5); ארצות איביכם (Ezek. 39:27/1 9); and אדמתכם (Ezek. 39:26, 28/1 10).

27. Parallels between Ezekiel and the Holiness Code (particularly Lev. 26) have long been noted, including phrases and expressions found only in those two places. Frg. 1 provides additional evidence of this relationship.

ness").[28] שאר occurs at Qumran in reference to one's kin or relative in CD 5:11; 7:1; 8:6; etc. Also, see 4Q477 2 ii 8, which refers to the blood relative with the same phrase as line 2 (וגם אוהב את שיר בשרו), although with different orthography.[29] Although the context is not clear, the lines preceding and following the reference refer to unfaithfulness and profaning the Lord's name, and apparent punishment for doing so.

(c) 4Q389 2: Fragment 2 draws upon events from the time of Moses (Num. 13–14; also compare Deut. 1–2) to fashion a retrospective speech set in the mouth of God and addressed to some later group in a state of exile. The speech seems to be designed to highlight past divine deeds and perhaps compare and contrast past human and divine actions with those from the later time of the audience. The biblical passage serves as the source for an example from the past presented in the Lord's speech. The order of elements is essentially the same in the fragment as in the biblical sources: (1) Kadesh Barnea is mentioned (4Q389 2 4; Num. 13:26; Deut. 1:19). (2) A divine oath is made there (4Q389 2 5 describes it as a past event; Num. 14:21, 28-30 describe the actual event; Deut. 1:34-36 contains Moses' recollection of it). (3) The concession that the children of the wanderers would be permitted to enter the land is noted (4Q389 2 6 [past event]; Num. 14:31-33 [the Lord's actual speech concerning this]; Deut. 1:39 [Moses' recollection of the Lord's speech]). (4) God walks with the people in the desert (4Q389 2 7 [past event]; Num. 14:34ff. [not specifically stated as "walking with the people," but assumed]; Deut. 2:7; 29:4-5 [recollection of the Lord's words]). (5) The length of the sojourn is set at forty years (4Q389 2 8 [past event]; Num. 14:33-35 [the Lord's speech]; Deut. 2:7; 29:4-5 [Moses' recollection of the Lord's speech]).

It should be noted that Numbers 13–14 is another Pentateuchal passage picked up by Ezekiel. See especially Ezekiel 4:6, which makes reference to the forty years of wandering (Num. 14:33), Ezekiel 20:32-39, which compares apostasy in Canaan to the apostasy in the wilderness after being led out of Egypt (Num. 14:13-25), and Ezekiel 20:9, 44, which picks up the theme that delivery from exile is evidence of the power and faithfulness of the Lord, not of Israel's deserving it (Num. 14:13-19).

---

28. The phrase שאר בשרו also occurs in Lev. 25:49 to refer to a blood relative.

29. 4Q386 1 ii 4 appears to contain yet another orthography (ומשרו; "and from his kin").

Conclusions

As the foregoing survey indicates, in general, the greatest number of connections to the biblical prophets occurs with the book of *Ezekiel*. Language, themes, and specific passages from throughout the book appear in this collection. On a somewhat smaller level, there are ties to the book of *Jeremiah*, especially chapter 25 and the later chapters of the book. There are also resonances (of vocabulary and themes) with *multiple prophetic books*, particularly those parts concerned with exile from the land as punishment for unfaithfulness to the covenant. Likewise, there are clear connections with various *Pentateuchal passages*, often ones which are of concern in the prophetic books. Finally, there are similarities of *vocabulary with many other biblical books* (including Esther, Daniel, Isaiah, and the Psalms) which are too numerous to describe here.[30]

How might we characterize the use of these biblical books in 4Q383-391? There are certainly several types of biblically based writings which these manuscripts are not. They are not simply copies of biblical books.[31] Nor do

---

30. While the focus here is on biblical interpretation in these fragments, it should at least be noted that there are extensive connections with a variety of other known works, including *2 Baruch*, *2 Esdras* (= *4 Ezra*), the *Animal Apocalypse*, the book of *Jubilees*, and the *Damascus Document*. The following list provides a sampling of the types of ideas, themes, and other qualities shared with such works:

(1) framework of dialogue between a prophet and the divine, characterized by questions, often introduced by עד מתי (4Q385 2 [// 4Q386 1 i; 4Q388 8]): Dan. 8:13; 12:6; 4 Ezra 4:33; 6:59; 2 Bar. 41:1, 5-6.
(2) chronological notices marked by years, weeks of years, jubilees (4Q387 3 ii; 4Q390 1 and 2 i): *Jubilees* (esp. 1 and 23); 11QMelch 2; *T. Levi* 16-17.
(3) Belial, sons of Belial (4Q386 1 ii; 4Q390 2 i): *Jub.* 1:20; 15:33; CD 4:13, 15; 5:18; 8:2.
(4) angels of the Mastemoth (4Q387 3 iii; 4Q390 1, 2 i): CD 16:5 (angel of the mastemah); 1QM XIII 11 (angel of mastemah); 4QPseudo-Jubilees[a] 2 i 9; 2 ii 13-14 (prince of the mastemah); *Jub.* 10:8 (spirits of Mastemah); 19:28 (Prince Mastemah); 11:5, 11; 17:16; etc. (prince of the Mastemah).
(5) internal dispute over the law and commandments (4Q385 41; 4Q387 2): *Jub.* 23:19; 1 Macc. 2:27, 50.
(6) hastening of the time of judgment (4Q385 3): 4 Ezra 4:26-46; 2 Bar. 20:1-2; 54:1; 83:1; *Barn.* 4:3.
(7) Jeremiah in Babylon and/or Egypt (4Q385 16; 4Q389 6): *Paraleipomena Jeremiou, Lives of the Prophets, Epistle of Jeremiah.*
(8) keeping the covenant in the lands of captivity (4Q385 16): 2 Macc. 2:2-3; *Epistle of Jeremiah.*

31. Six copies each of the biblical books of Ezekiel and Jeremiah have been found at Qumran (with varying amounts preserved). These make up 12 of 49 biblical prophetic books preserved (21 MSS of Isaiah, 8 of Daniel, and 8 of the Twelve Prophets).

they exhibit the qualities of related literature such as commentaries or *pesharim*.[32] In addition, the evidence does not suggest that the larger composition included a complete reworking of either Jeremiah or Ezekiel. Fragments do not suggest a systematic reworking or interpretation of the books in their entireties.

Did the biblical books serve simply as sources for the larger work? In some ways, since they are the place from which various units of biblical text were borrowed, the answer is yes. However, the picture is more complex than that.

How, then, are biblical materials used in these fragments? Our survey indicates that the usage takes several different forms. In the examples in which larger passages of biblical text (ten or more verses) are employed, we have seen that the biblical material is not quoted. Nor is it subjected to extensive exegesis or commentary. Instead, it appears to be paraphrased or reworked to achieve a shorter, summary version of the biblical text. Details are summarized, phrases omitted, and other words added.[33]

Often these units of reworked biblical material are placed within a framework which is nonbiblical. Indeed, the work moves freely between biblical and nonbiblical elements (as in 4Q385 2 [// 4Q386 1 i and 4Q388 8], in which Ezekiel's vision of the dry bones was summarized and placed in the framework of a dialogue between the prophet and the Lord). But at other times, such as in 4Q385 1, a summary version of a biblical passage is presented, but without the dialogue framework. Smaller reworking is done with the smaller units of biblical text (verses and phrases).

Many of the other uses of biblical material are more on the order of strong allusions to specific biblical texts. Biblical words and phrases are placed into larger frameworks of narrative or speech not as direct quotes but as summarized references to a biblical theme or idea (e.g., "the covenant of Abraham, Isaac and Jacob"; "I walked with them forty years . . ."; "they will do evil in my sight"; "I shall hide my face from them . . ."; etc.). Often these are phrases which have also found their ways into the wider body of literature (see n. 30; e.g., *Jubilees* and other works have picked up such phrases from biblical books). And at times in 4Q383-391 (as in the wider body of literature), these biblically rooted units of material appear alongside phrases and themes more common to the nonbiblical works (see, e.g., 4Q390 1 and 2 i, which

32. There are 17 *pesharim* on prophetic books, with 6 devoted to Isaiah, 2 each to Hosea, Micah, and Zephaniah, and 1 each to Nahum and Habakkuk, and 3 to Psalms. There are no *pesharim* on Jeremiah or Ezekiel.

33. The best examples of this are 4Q385 1, 2, 4, 16; and 4Q386 1 i.

combine biblical language and themes with elements common to the *Damascus Document* and *Jubilees* [angels of the Mastemoth, Belial, chronology of jubilees, etc.]).

In many fragments the combination of biblical with nonbiblical elements, and the placing of these in a larger framework, particularly those of question and answer dialogue between the Lord and a prophet (4Q385 2, 3; 4Q386 1 i-iii; etc.), seem to suggest that the writer was concerned not so much with explicating passages of biblical text, but more so with employing biblical passages, ideas, and themes to advance his message. In essence, the biblical passages function as B. Z. Wacholder has suggested, as "vehicles to depict contemporary issues and presage the future."[34] The writer appears to draw upon biblical language, themes, and specific passages, as well as relevant material from other works, to fashion a new text framed by dialogue between the Lord and a pseudepigraphic figure, or simply divine speech to a pseudepigraphic figure. The biblical elements often function to fill out the details of a later time — e.g., exilic and postexilic sinfulness is characterized through biblical descriptions (such as unfaithfulness in the wilderness), questions of when the faithful will be rewarded are answered through a reworking of the vision of the dry bones, descriptions of the land as desolate are filled out from descriptions of Babylon and Egypt in desolation in Jeremiah and Ezekiel.

When our survey of biblical usage in the collection is considered, seemingly disparate elements (which led Dimant to subdivide the collection) can in fact be reconciled. Although, on the one hand, close study reveals differences in content and form between various fragments, on the other hand, it also highlights certain commonalities. This is particularly clear if one considers the fragments against the backdrop of apparent sources, biblical and nonbiblical, from which the work is derived.

While at first the presence in one work of two different major prophets — Jeremiah and Ezekiel — may seem incongruous, a look at their biblical books turns up similarities. Between the two there are countless examples of shared language and religious concerns, as well as the fact that they both allude to and/or specifically treat the same events in the history of Israel — the time in Egypt, wandering in the desert, destruction of the temple, exile and captivity.[35] Both prophets are directly associated with destruction and exile,

---

34. See B. Z. Wacholder, "Deutero-Ezekiel and Jeremiah (4Q384-4Q391)," in *The Dead Sea Scrolls Fifty Years after Their Discovery: Proceedings of the Jerusalem Congress, July 20-25, 1997,* ed. L. H. Schiffman, E. Tov, and J. C. VanderKam; G. Marquis, executive ed., Israel Exploration Society in Cooperation with the Shrine of the Book (Jerusalem: Israel Museum, 2000), 445-61.

35. W. Zimmerli, *Ezekiel 1: A Commentary on the Book of the Prophet Ezekiel, Chap-*

not only predictions but also personal experience of them. And, as the *Lives of the Prophets* indicates, both die in the lands of their exile.[36] It is also the case that, when looked at in small portions, each book exhibits seemingly disparate elements, both of form and content. However, these are incorporated into the larger, overarching organizational principles of the books, around certain themes and concerns.

It is against this backdrop that certain "Mosaic" elements which Dimant once found distinctive can be understood. At first glance, fragments such as 4Q387 1 and 4Q389 2 may seem more clearly connected to Pentateuchal passages involving Moses. 4Q387 1 is concerned with Sabbath and other regulations set forth in Leviticus, while 4Q389 2 refers to "forty years," "Kadesh Barnea," and "the land." However, a closer look at the language reveals that rather than being distinct from Ezekiel, these sorts of matters are taken up in that book. Similarly, traits associated with Moses in the biblical text are elsewhere associated with Jeremiah (see *Lives of the Prophets* 2:19, where Jeremiah is portrayed as a partner of Moses [also, see 2:14, 17]).

Probably one of the best examples of physical evidence which illustrates the union of seemingly disparate elements is 4Q386 1 i-iii. Preserved in this three-columned fragment are many of the different types of biblical interpretation described above as found in different fragments of different manuscripts. Column 1 i (which overlaps with 4Q385 2 and 4Q388 8) contains the passage reworking Ezekiel's vision of the dry bones. In contrast, column 1 ii contains part of a dialogue between the Lord and the prophet (concerned with when the people of Israel would be gathered to the land) which has no close connection to any biblical passage, and introduces language quite similar to 4Q390 and elsewhere (describing events of future times, referring to figures such as Belial, etc.), as well as some unusual poetic lines. Finally, column 1 iii contains the reference to Babylon as a cup in the hand of the Lord (from Jer. 51:7), along with other language reminiscent of Jeremiah. Had these columns been found physically separate from one another and been classified

---

ters 1–24, Hermeneia (Philadelphia: Fortress, 1979), esp. 44-46, discusses Ezekiel's close relation to Jeremiah, including common themes such as submission to Babylon, an anti-Egyptian attitude, reference to the time of Moses, the expectation of a new future for Israel among the exiles, and inner transformation of the people in the promised age of salvation.

36. According to 2:1, Jeremiah died in Tahpanhes, Egypt (a city which, as noted, is mentioned in both Jeremiah and Ezekiel and in this group of manuscripts). Ezekiel's death is described in 3:1, as follows: "And he died in the land of Chaldea, in the time of the captivity, after uttering many prophecies to those who were in Judaea. . . ." See the edition of C. Torrey, *The Lives of the Prophets*, JBL Monograph Series 1 (Philadelphia: Society of Biblical Literature and Exegesis, 1946), 21-22, 35, 37.

according to Dimant's criteria for subdivisions, most likely they would have been placed in distinct categories. However, their physical connection supports attempts to determine their thematic connection (likewise in the rest of the collection).[37]

In general, the composition appears to be concerned with the exilic and postexilic time periods. Details surrounding the destruction of Jerusalem by Nebuchadnezzar, the deportation of the people, Jeremiah's activity in Babylon and Tahpanhes, the destruction of Egypt, the unfaithfulness which led to the destruction, and several other related themes are drawn from Jeremiah and Ezekiel, likely sources for priestly/prophetic condemnation of unfaithfulness characterized by failure to adhere to the Lord's statutes and commandments. These, combined with language, themes, and formal elements from other works, serve to create a composition which likely attempts to address matters of sin, exile, and the hope of return from exile. Unfortunately the fragmentary nature of the collection prevents a clear and comprehensive understanding of its organizing principle.

It is at least clear, however, that the work represented by 4Q383-391 would be at home in the writings of Qumran, as something which was copied and studied there. Its use of biblical materials fits in the wide range of biblical interpretation found among the scrolls. Likewise, many of its themes and ideas are shared with other Qumran works. The theme of exile, in particular, resonates with the situation of those living in the desert, away from other Jews. 4Q383-391 draw heavily upon the historical situations of exile in Egypt (4Q385 1; 4Q389 2) and in Babylon (4Q385 16; 4Q390 1-2), fitting them into the larger message of an ongoing condition of exile which it seems will end only after God's judgment, preceded by periods of great wickedness and disobedience to the covenant (see especially 4Q387 1, 2, 3 ii-iii; and 4Q390 1-2).[38] Such a work might be of great importance to a group which saw itself as living under a (re)newed covenant in the latter days predicted by the prophets.

37. In fact, Dimant acknowledged the linkage of disparate elements in this manuscript and looked to biblical examples for an explanation. See "4Q386 1 ii-iii," 522: "The Vision of the Dry Bones develops a biblical vision and links it to the individual recompense of the righteous, whereas the vision in col. ii-iii is non-biblical, and concerns the destiny of the People of Israel. Nevertheless, both visions share common traits in that they belong to the sphere of eschatological final processes. Perhaps the juxtaposition of the two is influenced by the similar thematic sequence in Ezekiel 37-39."

38. This view of exile not only fits well with writings from Qumran, but also with many of the apocalyptic texts discussed above. See the surveys of this theme by J. VanderKam, "Exile in Jewish Apocalyptic Literature," and M. Abegg, "Exile and the Dead Sea Scrolls," in *Exile: Old Testament, Jewish, and Christian Conceptions*, ed. J. Scott (Leiden: Brill, 1997), 89-109 and 111-25.

Table of Corresponding Manuscript and Fragment Numbers			
Manuscript and Fragment Numbers according to the PC	DJD XXX	Manuscript and Fragment Numbers according to the PC	DJD XXX
4Q383 1	4Q383 1	4Q387 2	4Q387 3
4Q385 1	4Q385b	4Q387 3 ii	4Q387 2 ii
4Q385 2	4Q385 2	4Q387 3 iii	4Q387 2 iii
4Q385 3	4Q385 4	4Q387 4 i	4Q387 4 i-ii
4Q385 4	4Q385 6	4Q387 5	4Q387 A
4Q385 6 + 9 + 22 +24 + 34	4Q385a 17a-e	4Q388 1 ii	4Q388a 7
4Q385 8	4Q385a 13b	4Q388 2	4Q388a 3 1-4
4Q385 12	4Q385 3	4Q388 4	4Q388a 3 5-7
4Q385 16	4Q385a 18	4Q388 6	4Q388a 6
4Q385 18	4Q385a 9	4Q388 8	4Q388 7
4Q385 25	4Q385a B	4Q388 9	4Q388 6
4Q385 31	4Q385c C	4Q388 12 ii	4Q388 3
4Q385 39	4Q383 2	4Q389 1 ii	4Q389 8
4Q385 41	4Q385a 5b	4Q389 2	4Q389 2
4Q385 43	4Q385a 5a	4Q389 3	4Q389 1
4Q385 44	4Q385a 4	4Q389 6	4Q389 A
4Q385 45	4Q385a 3a-b	4Q390 1	4Q390 1
4Q386 1 i-iii	4Q386 1 i-iii	4Q390 2	4Q390 2
4Q387 1	4Q387 1	4Q390 3	4Q390 3

Qumran Pesharim

SHANI BERRIN

The purpose of this study is to answer the question, "What is *pesher?*" There are undoubtedly those who would maintain that this question could be adequately addressed in a phrase or so: perhaps "contemporizing exegesis," or "Qumranic midrash," or "eschatological commentary." These descriptions all have some validity, and each is effective, to some extent. However, each employs technical terminology in a very loose fashion; the resultant blurring of attributes necessitates elucidation. To this end, the analysis in this chapter will be based upon the following, more comprehensive, definition of *pesher:* "a form of biblical interpretation peculiar to Qumran, in which biblical poetic/prophetic texts are applied to postbiblical historical/eschatological settings through various literary techniques in order to substantiate a theological conviction pertaining to divine reward and punishment." This definition can be seen to encompass characteristics of form, content, method, and motive.[1] There has been much scholarly debate regarding each of these aspects of

1. Here, I follow upon the approach of George Brooke, who categorized the various positions of scholars on the definition of *"pesher"* in his "Qumran Pesher: Toward the Redefinition of a Genre," *RevQ* 10 (1981): 483-503. Brooke endeavored to determine what constitutes a "genre" as a prerequisite to determining what the nature of a particular genre is (cf. W. H. Brownlee's comments regarding "the question as to which is the more basic distinction, literary form or mode of exegesis," in "Biblical Interpretation among the Sectaries of the Dead Sea Scrolls," *Biblical Archaeologist* 14 [1951]: 54-76, p. 76). In his study, Brooke suggested a hierarchical model for the formulation of a generic definition of *pesher:* (1) form and content are both inseparable "primary factors," (2) "secondary factors" revolve around method, and (3) literary tradition provides a context for classification (491-94; see also his *Exegesis at Qumran: 4QFlorilegium in Its Jewish Context,* JSOTSup 29 [Sheffield: JSOT Press, 1985], 149-56). Our own approach in this chapter is more descrip-

our definition. Each of the four elements will serve as a heading in this chapter, providing the structure for the discussion of the nature of *pesher.*

Form

Qumran *pesher* is most easily identified by the use of the word itself. *Pesher* consists of: a citation of a biblical text (the "lemma"); an introductory formula using the word *pesher* (such as "its *pesher* concerns . . ."); and an application of the text to a historical, eschatologically significant reality, outside of its original context. The term *pesher* is used to refer both to a particular instance of such *pesher* interpretation and to a composition that consists of the systematic application of *pesher* interpretation to a particular work (termed "continuous" or "running" *pesher,* following J. Carmignac).[2] The fifteen works published as a group in Horgan's *Pesharim* are generally accepted as representing the existing corpus of such continuous *pesher* compositions.[3] These continuous *pesharim* are the focus of the discussion in this chapter, though some of my remarks are relevant to related phenomena, including "thematic" *pesher* compositions[4] and isolated occur-

---

tive than prescriptive, and is more integrative than hierarchical; I also add "motive" as a separate element. Paul Mandel employs similar categories of form, content/intent, and exegetical stance/hermeneutical methods in his comparison of Qumranic and rabbinic exegesis in "Midrashic Exegesis and Its Precedents," *DSD* 8, no. 2 (2001): 149-68; see esp. 158.

2. Carmignac, "Le Document de Qumrân sur Melkisédek," *RevQ* 7 (1969-71): 361.

3. M. P. Horgan, *Pesharim: Qumran Interpretations of Biblical Books,* CBQMS 8 (Washington, D.C.: Catholic Biblical Association of America, 1979). On the additional works 3Q4, 4Q168, and 5Q10, listed as, respectively, "3QpIsa," "4QpMic?" and "5QpMal?" by F. García Martínez and E. J. C. Tigchelaar, *The Dead Sea Scrolls Study Edition* (Leiden: Brill, 1998), see Horgan, 260-66, and G. L. Doudna, *4Q Pesher Nahum: A Critical Edition* (London: Sheffield Academic Press, 2001), 25.

4. See George Brooke's contribution to this volume. This term was also coined by Carmignac, "Le Document de Qumrân sur Melkisédek," in application to 4QCatena[a] (177), 4QFlorilegium (174), and 11QMelchizedek (13), which are systematic applications of *pesher*-like methodology to verses of distinct works. Like the continuous *pesharim,* these compositions contain eschatological applications of cited biblical texts, and they feature introductory formulae, some of which include the word *pesher.* However, the texts are selected from a number of biblical sources, rather than sequentially following a particular biblical work.

A. Steudel has identified 4QFlor and 4QCat[a] as two copies of a single composition, and renamed them "4QMidrash Eschatologie[a,b]." She classifies this work with 11QMelch as "thematic midrash" rather than thematic *pesher. (Der Midrasch zur Eschatologie aus der Qumrangemeinde [4QMidrEschat.[a,b]]* [Leiden: Brill, 1994]. See Brooke's earlier inclination in this direction, "Qumran Pesher," 501-3). Although Steudel's important work on these

rences of *"pesher"* interpretation in non-*pesher* compositions.[5]

The skeletal *pesher* form may be expressed as: Biblical *lemma* + *interpretation* with *formula*.[6] Continuous *pesharim* are comprised of a series of these "units" of citation/interpretation. These *pesharim* are the earliest extant compositions to feature such systematic citation and interpretation of biblical text. The direct citation of the biblical *lemma* characterizes *pesher* as an example of

---

texts is very useful, it must be noted that some new problems are posed by the nomenclature and some of the criteria for classification. The term "midrash," perhaps even more than the term *pesher,* is in need of more precise definition rather than ever wider application. Moreover, Steudel's classification of 4Q252 and 4Q176Tanḥumim as thematic midrash (185-87) overlooks the significant distinction between the multiplicity of biblical base texts in 4Q177, 4Q182, 4Q183, and 11QMelch, as opposed to the specific selection of Genesis in 4Q252 and the primacy of Deutero-Isaiah in 4Q176. In 4Q252, the author's "thematic control" is limited by the selected base text. 4Q176 does exhibit thematic selection, but the best-preserved portion of the work primarily consists of excerpts from, rather than interpretation of, sequential passages in Deutero-Isaiah. Cf. C. D. Stanley, "The Importance of 4QTanhumim (4Q176)," *RevQ* 15, no. 60 (1992): 569-82.

5. Cf. G. Vermes, "Interpretation, History of," in *Interpreter's Dictionary of the Bible,* ed. Keith R. Crim et al., supplementary volume (Nashville: Abingdon, 1976), 439; J. A. Fitzmyer, "The Use of Explicit Old Testament Quotations in Qumran Literature and in the New Testament," in Fitzmyer, *Essays on the Semitic Background of the New Testament,* Society of Biblical Literature (Missoula: Scholars Press, 1974), 3-58, revised from *NTS* 7 (1960-61): 297-333; and D. Dimant, "Pesharim," in *ABD,* 248. Particularly challenging to attempts at classification are isolated instances of *pesher*-like exegesis that do not use the word *pesher* at all, such as CD 7:15-20; 1QS 5:15-17; 8:14-16; 1QM 11:11-12. (On the converse, isolated cases of the use of the *pesher* formula which do not seem *pesher*-like in content, technique, or motive, see below, n. 47.)

6. For comprehensive discussions of standard *pesher* structures and citation formulas and their variations, see Horgan, *Pesharim,* 239-44; Brooke, "Qumran Pesher," 497-501; B. Nitzan, מגילת פשר חבקוק (*1QpHab*) (Jerusalem: Mosad Bialik, 1986), 81-89; and M. J. Bernstein, "Introductory Formulas for Citation and Re-citation of Biblical Verses in the Qumran Pesharim: Observations on a Pesher Technique," *DSD* 1 (1994): 30-70. See also, F. L. Horton Jr., "Formulas of Introduction in the Qumran Literature," *RevQ* 7 (1971): 505-14, and I. Rabinowitz, "*Pêsher/Pittârôn:* Its Biblical Meaning and Its Significance in the Qumran Literature," *RevQ* 8 (1973): 226-30. For other forms of explicit biblical citations at Qumran, see Fitzmyer, "The Use of Explicit Old Testament Quotations in Qumran Literature and in the New Testament." L. H. Silberman, observing that the introductory "formula" may be so simple as a demonstrative pronoun, determined that the use of the word *pesher* should not be viewed as an essential generic feature ("Unriddling the Riddle: A Study in the Structure and Language of the Habakkuk Pesher [1 QpHab]," *RevQ* 3 [1961-62]: 327-30). Although *pesher* compositions will contain a number of "short" introductory formulas, I would maintain that the use of at least some formulas including the word *pesher* must be seen as a necessary formal characteristic of a *pesher* composition. The extent of the use of the technical term as a generic feature is one of the foci for the disagreement concerning the categorization of "thematic midrash"/"thematic *pesher,*" noted above.

explicit biblical interpretation.[7] Another distinctive quality of the *pesher* interpretation, evidenced in the introductory formula, is that *pesher identifies* elements of its base text. This observation is congruent with the etymological relationship between the roots פשר and פתר.[8] Rabbinic usage of פתר has often been understood in a broad sense as "explaining" or "interpreting" difficult verses or halakic traditions. Actually, פתר is used primarily in the more technical and specific sense of "apply" or "refer." In the Palestinian Talmud, rabbis limit the scope of a problematic halakic statement by applying it to a specific instance: "פתרא בy."[9] In aggadic midrash, the same term is used to apply a *scriptural* citation to a particular matter, ". . . פתר קריא ב." P. Bloch described this *"petira"* form, such that the formula introduces a "homiletic interpretation . . . individualizing, graphically defining, or illustrating." It attributes a "concrete instance" to the "abstract idea of the text." Bloch rendered the formula as, "he specifically referred the verse to. . . ."[10] Qumran *pesher*, like the similarly named rabbinic *petira*, provides an identification.

The characteristic form of *pesher* may thus be said to comprise the following basic structure: "biblical citation + *identifying* interpretation with *identifying* formula, typically including (or assuming) a form of the word *pesher*."

---

7. This characterization has its roots in the early tendency to contrast *pesher* to works of "rewritten Bible," specifically the *Genesis Apocryphon*. See, for example, Vermes, "Bible Interpretation at Qumran," *ErIsr* 20 (1989): 184*-91*. Studies by M. J. Bernstein and G. Brooke on 4Q252 (previously called 4QPesher Genesis[a]) have refined the distinction between *pesher* and rewritten Bible and further honed generic criteria. Cf. G. J. Brooke, "The Genre of 4Q252: From Poetry to Pesher," *DSD* 1 (1994): 160-79, and "The Thematic Content of 4Q252," *JQR* 85 (1994): 33-59; M. J. Bernstein, "4Q452: From Re-written Bible to Biblical Commentary," *JJS* 45 (1994): 1-27, and "4Q252: Method and Context, Genre and Sources: A Response to George J. Brooke," *JQR* 85 (1994): 61-79. The Brooke-Bernstein debate has largely revolved around issues concerning the function and aim of 4Q252, assessing the work's "theme(s)" (or lack thereof) and "structure." (See below, under the heading "Motive.") In his initial assessment of 4Q252, however, Brooke stressed a differentiation between implicit and explicit interpretation. *Pesher*, which cites its lemma, exemplifies "explicit" biblical interpretation.

8. See below, under "Method," on the meaning(s) of these and related roots, especially in reference to dream interpretation.

9. Cf., e.g., *y. Ter.* 3:6 (42b) in reference to Exod. 22:28, פתר ליה בביעור; and *y. Qidd.* 1:2 (59c) in reference to Deut. 15:17, פתר ליה בהענק.

10. Translation of Silberman, "Unriddling the Riddle," 328. Bloch renders "ר' פ' פתר . . . קרא ב" as "R. . . . legt den Vers mit Bezug auf . . . aus" ("Studien zur Aggadah," *MGWJ* 34 [1884]: 8-9, 266; cf. 264-69; 385-92). Silberman emphasized that the structure of *pesher* is like that of the *petira*, in that the *pesher* citation is followed by an introductory formula, and an identifying interpretation. See Mandel, "Midrashic Exegesis," 159 n. 22; I. Fröhlich, "Le Genre Littéraire des *Pesharim* du Qumran," *RevQ* 12 (1986): 385.

Content

Uniformity in the *content* of *pesharim* may be sought in either the (prophetic) biblical *base text* or in the (historical/eschatological) *pesher application*. We will begin with the subject matter of the application, as it is more easily discernible. We will then proceed to examine qualities that are shared by the biblical texts used in extant *pesharim*.

The Historical/Eschatological Application

An essential feature of *pesher* is the application of the base text to historical reality.[11] There is a logical relationship between an "identifying" form and historical content. We may look once again at the rabbinic *petira*. A formal attribute of the *petira* is its identification of an allusive biblical text. At Qumran, *pesher* contemporizes biblical verses, identifying their referents in history. In an *aggadic petira*, the proposed referent may be a tangible religious object, or even a concept or *halakic* category, but it is often a *historical individual or event*.[12]

---

11. Cf., e.g., N. Wieder, "The Dead Sea Scrolls Type of Biblical Exegesis among the Karaites," in *Between East and West: Essays Dedicated to the Memory of Bela Horovitz*, ed. A. Altmann (London: East and West Library, 1958), 75; Nitzan, מגילת פשר חבקוק, 27; C. Roth, "The Subject Matter of Qumran Exegesis," *VT* 10 (1960): 52. Wieder maintained that this attribute distinguished *pesher* from midrash, but Silberman, "Unriddling the Riddle," 326, presented the views of I. L. Seeligman regarding a similar historicizing quality in midrash. Seeligman had stated that the purpose of "earliest Jewish exegesis, i.e. Midrash," was to contemporize in the broadest sense: to make the ancient text relevant to current concerns (*Septuagint Version of Isaiah: A Discussion of Its Problems* [Leiden: Brill, 1948], 82). Seeligman also presented particular examples from Daniel and the Passover Haggadah that he showed to be "contemporizing" in the more restricted sense of applying the text to a specific later historical reality, and not merely to one's own situation generally (82-86). Cf. D. Patte, *Early Jewish Hermeneutic in Palestine*, SBLDS 22 (Missoula: Scholars Press, 1975), esp. 75-81, 99-100, 123-25.

12. A detailed analysis of every *petira* in the rabbinic corpus is beyond the scope of this investigation. However, the following preliminary observation may be observed. The use of פתר in aggadic midrash includes applications of verses to the following: the first ten generations of mankind (*Gen. Rab.* 2:3); the generation of "Separation" (*Gen. Rab.* 38:1); Noah (*Gen. Rab.* 33:1 on Ps. 36:7); Abraham (*Gen. Rab.* 39:3 on Ps. 45:8, and two more times); Rebecca; Moses (two times); Aaron (*Lev. Rab.* 10:3); Miriam; Pharaoh; the Sinai experience (three times); the tribe of Reuben; the tribes of Reuben, Gad, and half of Manasseh; the participants in the Exodus; Joshua; Doeg and Ahitofel (*Gen. Rab.* 38:1 on Ps. 59:12); Solomon (three times); Isaiah; Ezekiel; "the True Prophets"; successive foreign kingdoms (*Gen. Rab.* 2:4; *Gen. Rab.* 38:1 on Ps. 59:12); successive exiles

P. Mandel does not discern a historical focus in the *petira* itself, but does point to this sort of specificity in the case of the related phrase עליו מפרש בקבלה, an expression he demonstrates to be the *Tannaitic* forerunner to the *amoraic* פתר עליו קרא.[13] We view all three of the above exegetical forms as exhibiting a "historical" focus, with the understanding that "history" refers to the course of human events, past, present, and future.[14] However, an important distinction between the historical content of Qumran *pesher* and the rabbinic *petira* or עליו מפרש is the specific eschatological focus of the former.[15]

_____

(*Gen. Rab.* 99:1 on Ps. 68:17); future redemption (גאולה של מחר, *Lev. Rab.* 23 on Ps. 25:15).

This list was compiled from a word search of "*aggadic* midrash" in the CD-Rom Concordance of the Bar Ilan Responsa Project, which yielded sixty-eight occurrences. Even among the applications to tangible objects, a prominent referent for *petira* applications is the temple (also the tabernacle, the altar, the high priest), a locus with a historical dimension. The evidence of the midrashic examples does not support Dimant's contrast of the *petira* and *pesher*, in which she stated that "the *petira* always deals with moral lessons, while the subject of the *pesher* is historical eschatological" ("Qumran Sectarian Literature," in *Jewish Writings of the Second Temple Period: Apocrypha, Pseudepigrapha, Qumran Sectarian Writings, Philo, Josephus*, ed. M. E. Stone, CRINT II.2 [Philadelphia: Fortress, 1984], 506).

13. See "Midrashic Exegesis," 160. This point is further developed in some of Mandel's other works. I would like to express my gratitude to Paul Mandel for generously providing me with a copy of a forthcoming article on the rabbinic "*petiḥta*," "על 'פתח' ועל הפתיחה-עיון חדש," and a work-in-progress related to the "*petira*," "להוראת הביטוי עליו מפרש בקבלה: עיון במדרש הכתובים של התנאים, as well as for various insights he shared with me in private conversation during the early stages of my research.

14. Thus, Dimant states that the Community saw the "mysteries of God" to be "the secrets of the divine fore-ordained plan of history according to which all human events take place (cf., *e.g.*, 1QS 3:23)." These mysteries, which were communicated by the prophets, "include the significance of the entire sequence of history from the remote past to the *eschaton*," with the final age being of greatest interest to the sect ("Qumran Sectarian Literature," 508). Cf. A. Lange, "The Essene Position on Magic and Divination," in *Legal Texts and Legal Issues*, ed. M. J. Bernstein, F. García Martínez and J. Kampen (Leiden: Brill, 1997), 426-27. Contrast Doudna's position, especially his argument that *ex eventu* prophecy is not found in *pesher* (*4Q Pesher Nahum*, 59). I would agree with Doudna that references to past events in *pesher* are not of general antiquarian interest, but aim to place the historical event in an eschatological context. Still, I maintain that these past events are presented as fulfillments of biblical prophetic predictions, and not merely as "background" to predictions of the future.

15. Mandel describes the expression עליו מפרש בקבלה as referring to an activity in which "verses in the later [biblical] books . . . are interpreted as referring, in an oblique way, to earlier biblical events" ("Midrashic Exegesis," 158-59). He associates this with the term "back-referencing" used by J. Kugel (*In Potiphar's House* [Cambridge: Harvard University Press, 1994], 261). Mandel indicates that the Tannaitic rabbis related the messages of the prophets to the past, while the Qumran community placed them in the eschatological

K. Elliger in particular stressed the eschatological import that *pesher* attributes to the biblical text, emphasizing the *pesher*'s understanding of the eschatological age as having already begun. This eschatological meaning is taken as *the* meaning of the base text, which cannot be understood without a new revelation. Elliger delineated the prime "hermeneutical principles" of *pesher* as the beliefs that (1) biblical prophecies refer to the end time and (2) the end time is now.[16] He offered internal support for these principles from 1QpHab 7:1-8. The first principle is clearly stated in the *pesher* interpretation to Habakkuk 2:2, "God told Habakkuk to write down the things that are going to come upon the last generation, but the fulfillment of the end-time He did not make known to him . . . God made known to [the Teacher of Righteousness] all the mysteries of the words of the prophets."[17] The second principle is im-

---

present. The later rabbis placed them in both periods, and even expanded the range of applications to the conceptual plane.

16. "Prophetische Verkündigung hat zum Inhalt das Ende, und Die Gegenwart ist die Endzeit" (Elliger, *Studien zum Habakuk-Kommentar vom Toten Meer*, BHT 15 [Tübingen: J. C. B. Mohr, 1953], 150). This quote has become the standard epigrammatic representation of Elliger's contribution to our topic. Brownlee's first "hermeneutical principle" of *pesher* was that "everything the ancient prophet wrote has a *veiled, eschatological meaning*" ("Biblical Interpretation," 60).

The second half of Elliger's principle emphasizes the concept of the "eschatological present" mentioned above. A number of scholars have contrasted the Qumran community's anticipation of future salvation with the early Christian sense that "the new has come" (2 Cor. 5:17). So, O. Betz, "Past Events and Last Events in the Qumran Interpretation of History," *WCJS* 6 (1977): 27-34. Cf. F. F. Bruce, *Biblical Exegesis in the Qumran Texts* (Grand Rapids: Eerdmans, 1959), 68; Fitzmyer, "The Use," 13. Whereas early Christianity saw the past as having been supplanted by the present, Qumran's "typological exegesis" viewed the biblical past as paradigmatic for the future (Betz, "Past Events," 33; Betz adopted the term from D. Flusser, פרושים צדוקים, ואסיים בפשר נחום, *Essays in Jewish History and Philology, in Memory of Gedaliahu Alon* [Tel Aviv: Hakibbutz Hameuchad, 1970], 133-68 [= "Pharisäer, Sadduzäer und Essener im Pescher Nahum," in *Qumran*, ed. K. E. Grözinger et al. (Darmstadt: Wissenschaftliche Buchgesellschaft, 1981)]).

This contrast is important, but following Elliger it must be equally stressed that the Community saw this future as having already begun; there is a partial sense of "realized eschatology" at Qumran. Thus, even Betz states, "the present has eschatological significance" (34) and "past events permeate the present, thereby revealing its significance, and they reach out for the future" (33). Cf. MMT C 20-22: "And we know that some of the blessings and the curses have (already) been fulfilled as it is written in the bo[ok of Mo]ses. And this is at the end of days . . ." (in E. Qimron and J. Strugnell, *Qumran Cave 4. Miqsat Ma'ase Ha-Torah*, DJD 10 [Oxford: Clarendon, 1994], 61).

17. So, too, 1QpHab 2:7-10 on Hab. 1:5, "all which is to come upon the last generation" is told by "the priest, into whose heart God placed knowledge to interpret (לפשור) all the words of the prophets by whose hand God recounted all which is to come upon his nation and[. . .]"

plied by the subsequent *pesher* (1QpHab 7:8 on Hab. 2:3), which states that the "last end-time" will be prolonged, i.e., spanning a period of time that extends at least to the life of the author of the *pesher*, who is witnessing the fulfillment of some of these prophecies, and thus living in the end time.

The "eschatological" nature of the application must be clarified. Not all of the applications in the extant *pesharim* are explicitly located in "the End of Days" (אחרית הימים).[18] Nonetheless, Steudel has convincingly demonstrated an extended use of the term "end of days" at Qumran.[19] With the sense of the "end of days" as encompassing past, present, and future, the "eschatological" valence may be seen as more theological than strictly chronological. Past events, even long-past events, may still be understood as relevant to, and part of, the approach of the end time.[20] The eschatological significance of *pesher* applications must be viewed as a salient feature of *pesher*.

Another aspect of the theological content of *pesher*, and one that has received insufficient attention, is dualism. In Nitzan's discussion of the content of *Pesher Habakkuk*, she describes the sectarian conception of a dualistic struggle on three interrelated planes: the internal political, the international political, and the cosmic.[21] The *pesharim* document this tripartite struggle in each of its aspects, aiming to trace the fulfillment of the prophetic word to its ultimate resolution on all three planes, with the triumph of the Community. The eschatological content of *pesher* should thus be described more specifically as reflecting basic sectarian tenets: dualism, historical determinism, and the election of the Community.[22]

18. For example, in 4Q169 *Pesher Nahum*, frgs. 3-4, the last three columns feature eschatological terminology: קץ אחרון, אחרית הקץ, אחרית הימים, but col. i does not. Moreover, the dominant understanding of this composition associates col. i with Alexander Jannaeus, while positing a later context for the other columns. Thus, col. i would appear to predate the "End of Days" of the later columns.

19. In "אחרית הימים in the Texts from Qumran," *RevQ* 16 (1993-94): 225-46. Cf. Doudna, *4Q Pesher Nahum*, 63-66.

20. In n. 14 above, it was claimed that "history" encompasses eschatological, and even future, events; here the claim is that the "eschatological age" encompasses past events. These complementary observations can be viewed as corollaries to Elliger's principles.

21. Nitzan, מגילת פשר חבקוק, 12-19.

22. Nitzan, מגילת פשר חבקוק, 19-28. Nitzan contextualizes these concepts within apocalyptic tradition. Similarly, J. J. Collins views determinism as a key feature of Qumran *pesher* ("Jewish Apocalyptic against Its Hellenistic Near Eastern Environment," *BASOR* 220 [1975]: 31-34). He compares the *pesharim* to the Egyptian Demotic Oracle, and associates the "prophecy by interpretation" in these works with Hellenistic political oracles and with the phenomenon of pseudepigraphy. In describing a broad Hellenistic Near Eastern apocalyptic "zeitgeist," Collins further maintains that "like the esteem for antiquity, [determinism] attests to a sense of alienation from the present" (34).

The Prophetic Base Text

C. Roth argued further for the eschatological valence of the biblical base texts themselves, in addition to that of the *pesher* applications.[23] An evaluation of the extant continuous *pesharim* does not support the view that all of the base texts are intrinsically "eschatological," i.e., dealing explicitly with אחרית הימים. However, it may be stated that the base texts all *lend themselves* to dualistic eschatological application.[24] The "eschatological" quality of each text may be evaluated on the basis of terminology (קץ האחרון, אחרית הקץ, אחרית הימים) and thematic content.[25] *Pesharim* that comment upon strongly eschatological base texts include 1QpHab,[26] 1QpZeph (1Q15),[27] 4QpIsaᵃ (4Q161),[28] 4QpIsaᶜ

23. Roth, "Subject Matter," 53. Cf. the objections of Brooke, "Qumran Pesher," 486-87, though in a different context Brooke does emphasize the association of the term "latter days" with *pesharim* ("The Genre of 4Q252," 174).

24. There is of course some degree of circularity inherent in this observation, since our starting point is that the *pesharim* use the base texts for just such applications. To minimize the impact of this circularity, I have intentionally characterized the biblical base text *without* reference to its use by the *pesher* (as a corrective to Roth's approach in "The Subject Matter of Qumran Exegesis").

25. It must be noted that determining "eschatological" content is not an entirely objective task, and that perhaps even the term אחרית הימים is neither a necessary nor sufficient indicator. Thus, in *ABD*, G. W. E. Nickelsburg identifies "eschatological" material in every chapter of Ezek. 34–48, except 38–39, the Gog prophecies, in which the phrase אחרית הימים actually appears (s.v. "Eschatology," subheading "Ezekiel," 581; he refers only to chaps. 34–37, 40–48).

26. The base text of *Pesher Habakkuk* is concerned with divine retribution against the wicked, and divine salvation of the righteous. Chap. 2, God's response to Habakkuk, has been described as the eschatological section of the book by Y. Kaufman, תולדות האומה הישראלית, vol. 3, bk. 2 (Tel Aviv: Mosad Bialik, 1966), 360-65 (cited in Nitzan, in reference to אחרית הימים, in מגילת פשר חבקוק, 74 n. 131). In Hab. 2:3, כי עוד חזון למועד ויפיח לקץ ("For there is still a vision for the appointed time; it speaks of the end"), we may take קץ as a technical, eschatological term. Although the author of the book of Habakkuk does not himself claim to describe the "end time," the *pesher* assumes that Habakkuk perceived himself as doing so. The passage in 1QpHab 7:1-8, cited above, not only describes the prophecy as eschatological, but also implies that the prophet himself shared the perception: God told Habakkuk to record that which would befall the last generation.

27. The extant fragment of this work is a citation of Zeph. 1:18–2:2 with a beginning of a *pesher*. Chap. 1 of Zephaniah does not use the term "last" or "end," but it is the classic description of the eschatological "Day of the Lord," the apocalypticists' doomsday. The cited passage describes the "day of God's wrath."

28. Chaps. 10–11 of Isaiah are traditionally understood eschatologically, though explicit eschatological terminology is not as pervasive as might be expected from this paradigmatic messianic text. "On that day" (10:27) points in such a direction.

(4Q163),²⁹ 4QpIsaᵈ (4Q164),³⁰ and 4QpZeph (4Q170).³¹ The base texts of the following *pesharim* focus upon divine retribution of sinners, thereby accommodating interpretations that reflect the dualistic perspective typical of the Qumran community: 1QpMic (1Q14),³² 1QpPs (1Q16),³³ 4QpIsaᵇ (4Q162),³⁴ 4QpIsaᵉ (4Q165),³⁵ 4QpHosᵃ (4Q166),³⁶ 4QpHosᵇ (4Q167),³⁷ 4QpNah

29. The scope of the passages covered by this poorly preserved papyrus is not clear. Isa. 9–10 and 29–30 constitute the bulk of the extant citations. These chapters, as was noted in reference to 4QpIsaᵃ, do not explicitly use the terminology of "end of days" or "last days," but are thematically "eschatological" in that they describe divine retribution and salvation on a cosmically significant scale.

30. Isa. 54 does not use the terminology of "last" or "final" days, but is thematically, and certainly traditionally, "eschatological." Terminologically, "eternal loving-kindness" contrasted with momentary wrath (v. 8) seems to be close to explicit eschatology.

31. This is a small fragment with 1:12, 13 and some *pesher.* See our comment on 1QpZeph, above.

32. The extant fragments of this *pesher* treat chaps. 1 and 6 of Micah, which deal with the divine punishment of sinners. Chaps. 4, 5, and 7 of this book include more "eschatologically oriented" prophecies, describing the ultimate and eternal salvation of the righteous, but we cannot be certain that these prophecies were subjected to *pesher* interpretation.

33. Ps. 68 refers to the punishment of sinners. The Sinai experience is seen as a paradigm for divine immanence, and for divine presence in the Jerusalem sanctuary. V. 17, in reference to the Mountain of God, assures that "God will dwell *for eternity.*"

34. Chap. 5 of Isaiah describes divine wrath against sinners; the *pesher* cuts off with a possible citation of 6:9, but in 6:11-13 God vows to make Israel desolate for its sins. If 6:9 is indeed to be restored, then the *pesher* would have, significantly, skipped over the narrative of Isaiah's selection and heavenly vision recorded in 6:1-8, and limited its scope to the surrounding prophetic rebukes.

35. The fragmentary state of this *pesher,* and its uncertain reconstruction, make it difficult to characterize its citations. Some key words and phrases lend themselves to *pesher* treatment, such as "poor ones" and "on that day."

36. The citation and *pesher* of only part of Hos. 2 is preserved, in which the husband refuses to take back his wayward wife, a metaphor for divine punishment of the wicked. Presumably, the *pesher* continued with a treatment of the rest of the chapter, which describes how "on that day" God will renew and seal his eternal covenant with his people, an eschatological image.

37. Chaps. 5 and 8 of Hosea are cited in the extant portions of this *pesher.* These chapters feature Judah and Ephraim in a manner that prefigures the dualistic opposition between Judah and Ephraim found in a number of Qumran texts. (For the identification of these terms with, respectively, the Qumran community and the Pharisees, see, inter alia, J. D. Amusin, "The Reflection of Historical Events of the First Century B.C. in Qumran Commentaries [4Q 161; 4Q 169; 4Q 166]," *HUCA* 48 [1977]: 123-52; Flusser, ". . . פרושים," 133-68). The biblical text focuses upon divine retribution for faithlessness and transgression. The extant base text thus accommodates an eschatological statement, though it does not explicitly comprise one. Compare the view of Roth, who maintains that the *pesher's*

(4Q169),[38] 4QpPs[a] (4Q171),[39] 4QpPs[b] (4Q172).[40]

The foregoing list demonstrates that the base texts of *pesher* are texts that are amenable to dualistic and eschatological readings, and further, that these texts are concerned with the fate of the wicked. This concern with theodicy is frequently expressed via references to divine wrath and retribution.[41] Explicit "eschatological" terms, i.e., אחרית and even קץ, do not appear regularly in these texts, but a number of the cited biblical passages feature implicit apocalyptic terms, such as "the Day of the Lord" or "that day." Eschatological *concepts* are discernible in many but not all cases.[42] However, other passages that are treated by *pesher*, e.g., Nahum, or Psalm 60, are more naturally considered noneschatological in their original, historically specific contexts. Here, particular phrases or relevant themes would have recommended the texts for eschatological/historical *pesher* interpretation.[43]

---

treatment of Hosea was prompted by the use of the term "End of Days" in Hos. 3:5 ("Subject Matter," 57).

38. The original context is explicitly and specifically directed against Assyria. Its suitability for *pesher* interpretation derives from its themes: divine wrath, and ultimate divine retribution against the wicked, especially the apparently flourishing and triumphant wicked.

39. Ps. 37 addresses salvation on the personal, rather than the national, level. The term אחרית in v. 37 is the "posterity" of the righteous individual (Horgan's translation, *Pesharim*, 199. NJPSV renders "future"). Thus, the psalm is "eschatological" in a sense but is more low-key than typical cataclysmic prophecies, and its terminology is subdued as well. (Terms of "finality" also include לעולם [18], לעד [27], and perhaps "inheritance" [9] for the dwelling of the righteous.) Ps. 45 is both national and eschatological, describing the Messiah who will be acknowledged by all nations and generations forever and ever. Ps. 60:8-9 appears in a specific historical context in which David implores God to return divine favor upon His people. The passage itself is not eschatological, though its themes would support such an application: messianic victory, and belief in ultimate divine favor despite current setbacks.

40. A citation of Ps. 129:7-8 is extant. It is a general attestation of Israel's belief in divine justice and favor despite persecution by its enemies.

41. The interconnection between fate, reward and punishment, and eschatological beliefs in ancient Jewish sectarian theology is brought out most explicitly in Josephus's description of Pharisaic, Sadducean, and Essene views on these issues. Cf. *War* 2.162-66; *Ant.* 13.171-73; 18.12-15.

42. This assessment is somewhat subjective. Chaps. 11 and 54 of Isaiah could be "poster passages" for biblical eschatology, but only if we assume they were read in a particular way that is not absolutely mandated by the texts themselves. Still, it is likely that the eschatological valence of base texts such as these was widely established before the composition of the *pesharim*. Cf. 4QFlor 1:14-16, which quotes Isa. 8:11 with the following characterization: ". . . about whom it is written in the book of Isaiah the prophet *for the end of days*." Cf. Fitzmyer, "The Use," 29.

43. Comparison with Fitzmyer's three categories of (non-*pesher*) biblical citations at

A more general characteristic of the base text is that all the texts subjected to *pesher* commentary are prophetic. The Targum to the single biblical occurrence of the Hebrew root פשר (at Eccles. 8:1, לדעת פשר דבר; "Who knows the interpretation of a thing?") associates the term with prophets or prophecies. H. Yalon pointed to this Targum in conjunction with 1QpHab 2:8-9, which states that God endowed the priest (the Teacher of Righteousness) with the ability to interpret (לפשור) all the words (דברי) of the prophets.[44] The comparison between Qumran *pesher* and the rabbinic *petira* is relevant here again. Extant examples of *"petira"* tend to address verses from the Prophets and poetic Hagiographa. In this context, recall Mandel's characterization of the *petira* as an amoraic descendant of "עליו מפרש בקבלה," for the term קבלה signifies the Prophets and Hagiographa.[45] The extant continuous *pesharim* interpret books of the Minor Prophets, Isaiah, and Psalms.[46]

Qumran may be useful here *(op. cit.)*. Some of the base texts of the *pesharim* require *"modernization"* or *"accommodation"* to achieve the desired eschatological meaning, while others are already "eschatological" and are just stretched beyond their original contexts in being *applied* to a later time. (However, Fitzmyer's term "the new eschaton" does not seem well suited as a description of this later time. The Community would have awaited not a "new eschaton," but the culmination of the current eschaton.)

44. Yalon, מגילות מדבר יהודה: דברי לשון (Jerusalem: Kiryat Sefer, 1967), 65. Cf. the citation of 1QpHab 2:8-9 above, and recall also 1QpHab 7:7, "God made known to him all the mysteries of the words of the prophets." (Yalon cites the Targum as ולמדע פשר מליא בנביאיא; in some MSS the text appears as ולמדע פשר מליא כנביאיא, "to know the interpretation of the words like the prophets.") Cf. P. S. Knobel, "The Targum of Qohelet," in *The Aramaic Bible: The Targums,* vol. 15 (Collegeville, Minn.: Liturgical Press, 1991), 42; E. Levine, *The Aramaic Version of Qohelet* (New York: Sepher-Hermon Press, 1978), 40.

45. For this sense of קבלה, see, e.g., *b. Roš Haš.* 7a, in which the use of Zech. 1:7 as a proof text is preceded by the following statement: דבר זה מתורת משה רבינו לא למדנו מדברי קבלה למדנו, "we do not learn this from the Torah of Moses our teacher, but we learn it from the words of 'Qabbalah.'" Cf. J. Levy, *Wörterbuch über die Talmudim und Midraschim* (Berlin and Vienna: B. Harz, 1924), s.v. קבלה, def. 2; W. Bacher, *Die Exegetische Terminologie der jüdischen Traditionsliteratur: Tannaiten* (Hildesheim: G. Olms, 1965), s.v. קבלה, 165; Mandel, "Midrashic Exegesis," 159.

46. See the list of specific texts above. Cf. Vermes, "Interpretation, History of," 439; "Bible Interpretation," 188*. Carmignac also noted that the base texts of the *pesharim* were from the Prophets and Psalms, though he did not apparently view the latter as prophecy (*Les textes de Qumran traduits et annotés,* 2 vols. [Paris, 1961-63], 2:46). For the prophetic status of the Psalms at Qumran, see Dimant, "Apocrypha and Pseudepigrapha at Qumran," *DSD* 1, no. 2 (1994): 156-57; "Qumran Sectarian Literature," 507. Note the catalogue of Davidic compositions in 11QPsᵃ, in which David is described as a prophet (27:11). Along similar lines, Silberman observes that in a *"petirah"* midrash in *Ecc. Rab.* 12:1, the author of Ecclesiastes is referred to as "the prophet," and that *Ecc. Rab.* 1:1 claims

In sum, the use of an eschatologically significant prophetic/poetic *base text* must be viewed as a typical, and perhaps even an essential, feature of *pesharim*.[47] A theologically distinctive, historical, and specifically eschatological *application of the base text* is certainly essential.[48]

---

that Solomon wrote Proverbs, Ecclesiastes, and Song of Songs under the influence of the Divine Spirit (ברוח הקודש), and that they are therefore prophetic (cited in "Unriddling the Riddle," 328). In any case, biblical poetry tends to be perceived as prophetic, and specifically as eschatologically significant, both in its original contexts and, specifically, in its apprehension among Jews of the Second Temple period.

47. In light of 4Q252, it might best be stated that the determinative aspect of the base text is that it is "prophetic" with a lowercase, but not an uppercase, *p*. Nitzan had observed that the word *pesher* does not seem to be used at Qumran for the interpretation of Pentateuchal verses (מגילת פשר חבקוק, 31). She notes only the following two possible cases: 1Q22DM ("Dires de Moise," line 3, in DJD 1, 91-97, D. Barthélemy and J. T. Milik, ed.): [ור]פש; and 1Q30 (i:6, in DJD 1, 132-33; truncated context). The word is associated with Pentateuchal verses in 4Q159 (4QOrdinances) frag. 5, lines 1, 5 (DJD 5, 8-9), and 4Q180 frag. 1, lines 1, 6 ("4QAges of Creation" in DJD 5, 77-78), but exegesis is not evident in these contexts. Cf. W. H. Brownlee, "The Background of Biblical Interpretation at Qumran," in *Qumrân: sa piété, sa théologie et son milieu*, ed. M. Delcor (Paris: Leuven University Press, 1978), 185. The usual restoration of פשרו at 11Q13 (11QMelch) 2:4 following a citation of Deut. 15:2 has been contested by Milik on other grounds, and should be reassessed ("Milkî-ṣedeq et Milkî-rešaʿ dans les anciens écrits juifs et chrétiens," *JJS* 23 [1972]: 102. Cf. P. J. Kobelski, *Melchizedek and Melchirešaʾ* [Washington, D.C.: Catholic Biblical Association of America, 1981], 11-12).

However, it is now widely known that 4Q252 contains a more significant Pentateuchal *pesher*, consisting of a citation, a formula with *"pesher,"* and a historical identifying interpretation. In this case, since chap. 49 of Genesis described *"aharyt haymym,"* Gen. 49:3 was surely understood as prophetic. Bernstein comments on the use of the term פשר in 4Q252: "perhaps the interpretation of a poetic or prophetic text is automatically 'pesher' regardless of the type of interpretation involved. Such texts are deemed always to be opaque and in need of the *pesher* process in order to be understood properly" ("4Q252: From Re-written Bible," 18). Dimant says of "isolated *pesharim*" in CD: "the texts commented upon in this way are mostly prophetic but a few are taken from ancient songs found in the Torah (Num. 21:18; Deut. 32:33). This means that these songs were considered prophetic and were interpreted as such" (*ABD*, s.v. "Pesharim," 248; note, nonetheless, that these "isolated *pesharim*" do not actually use the word *pesher*).

48. Dimant sees the contemporizing eschatological content of *pesher* as the *only* basis for a generic definition of *pesher*, stating, "A definition of the *Pesharim* ought to be based on a feature truly distinctive to it. Such is their subject matter, namely the special historical-eschatological exegesis of prophecy relating to the sect's own position in history and rooted in its peculiar attitude to the base-text. The traditional exegetical devices and literary forms are employed in the service of these particular ideas, and only in this respect can the *Pesharim* be defined as a special genre" ("Qumran Sectarian Literature," 507). Brooke's approach to genre as deriving from a number of essential features seems more appropriate than determining genre by only a single peculiar feature. Thus, for example, a

Method[49]

The source of *pesher,* or method of arriving at *pesher* interpretation, has been alternately claimed to be "revelation" or "exegesis."[50] The characterization of *pesher* as "inspired exegesis" indicates a synthesis of "revelation" and "exegesis," both of which must be seen as central to *pesher.*

Revelation

One avenue of insight into this issue is the etymology of the term *pesher.* The late Hebrew root פשר is related to the Aramaic פשר, which is cognate to the Akkadian *pašāru.*[51] The root meaning of the Akkadian, "to unbind or release,"

---

ballad is defined as "a song that tells a story" (see *OED,* s.v. "ballad," def. 5; C. Baldick, *Concise Oxford Dictionary of Literary Terms* [Oxford: Oxford University Press, 1990]). Neither "being a song" nor "telling a story" is a characteristic that is exclusive to ballads, yet it is the combination of these essential components that will classify a ballad as such. In fact, by embedding the term "exegesis" in her description of the "subject matter" of *pesher,* Dimant has inadvertently demonstrated the need to acknowledge a number of components in determining genre.

49. Brooke categorizes "method" as a secondary factor in determining the genre *pesher.* He describes midrashic techniques and devices as an "important clue" to understanding *pesher,* but judges them as not "constitutive" of the genre, observing that the particular method of a given identification cannot even always be determined ("Qumran Pesher," 496-97). Despite this fuzziness in our apprehension of particular techniques, the very use of exegetical technique at all is indicative of a particular approach to the biblical text that characterizes *pesher.* The basis of *pesher* in "revelation" and "exegesis" is central to our definition of *pesher.* If a text is going to be linked to a later reality, the link will be as essential as both the text and its historical analogue. In an expression of equivalence or approximation, e.g., "a = b," "a ≈ b," or "a | b," the =, ≈, or | sign is just as requisite as the elements "a" and "b," though it is more complex, and subject to greater interpretation. The existence of a conceptual, methodological link is a premise that must be seen as "inseparable," to adopt Brooke's term, from the historical content and identifying form of *pesher.*

50. However, see Silberman's argument that the two are not mutually exclusive ("Unriddling the Riddle," 326). Note also Collins's phrase, "prophecy by interpretation" ("Jewish Apocalyptic," 32-34. Cf. Doudna, *4Q Pesher Nahum,* 58-61).

51. The nature of these relationships is complex and variously understood in the academic literature. A thorough lexicographic treatment of *pesher* and related terms is provided by S. D. Sperling, "Studies in Late Hebrew Lexicography in the Light of Akkadian" (Ph.D. diss., Columbia University, 1973), 53-92, esp. 65-72. Cf. Nitzan, מגילת פשר חבקוק, 29-33; Horgan, *Pesharim,* 230-37, and the works cited by her, p. 230 n. 3, esp. L. Oppenheim, *The Interpretation of Dreams in the Ancient Near East,* Transactions of the American Philosophical Society 46, part 3 (Philadelphia: American Philosophical Society, 1956), 217-25; Cf.

was extended to denote specifically the "unbinding of dreams."[52] As is well known, Aramaic פשר appears frequently in the book of Daniel in the sense of dream interpretation (e.g., 4:3; 5:12).[53] The Hebrew פשר as used at Qumran is a Hebraization of this Aramaic פשר.[54] Thus, the term *pesher* has an ancient basis in the sense of "loosening" as applied to dream interpretation.[55]

In the Bible, dreams are viewed as prophetic, but their hidden significance, their *"pesher"* or *"pitaron,"* can be brought to light only by specially endowed individuals. Ostensibly, biblical prophecies are themselves revealed mysteries, already made accessible to humanity by means of a divinely inspired agent. Herein, however, lies the unique view of the Qumran community. The community understood the figure of the prophet as analogous to that of a dreamer, reporting a dream. The agency of an additional select individual was required for the unraveling of the coded predictions. The word *pesher* indicates this deciphering of coded prophetic messages. In Daniel 5:8,

---

Akkadisches Handwörterbuch, vol. 2, s.v. *pašāru(m),* with the primary definition of "lockern, (auf)lösen."

52. For the "unbinding" or "unsealing" of "closed revelation," cp. תפתחו החזון, in 4Q299Mysteries[a], frg. 3c, line 3, and 4Q300Mysteries[b], frg. 1b, line 3 (L. H. Schiffman, DJD 20, 43, 101). The antithetical idiom, ח.ת.מ.חזון, is found in Dan. 9:24 and 4QMyst[a], frg. 3c, line 2. (See Mandel's discussion of פתח, in "הפתיחה ועל פתח על".)

53. יפשור is also used for dream interpretation at 4QEnochGiants[b] I ii 14-15 (and restored at I ii 23; cf. J. T. Milik, *The Books of Enoch: Aramaic Fragments of Qumrân Cave 4* [Oxford: Clarendon, 1976], 305).

54. Nitzan cited סרך as a similar Qumranic Hebraizing of an Aramaic word (מגילת חבקוק פשר, 33). See the discussion of סרך as two separate roots in Schiffman, *The Halakhah at Qumran* (Leiden: Brill, 1975), 60-68, and the literature cited there. The use of the root פתר to denote dream interpretation in Biblical Hebrew (only in chaps. 40–41 of Genesis, passim) has been viewed by some as cognate with the Aramaic. Horgan (*Pesharim,* 236) has even raised the possibility of a hypothetical proto-Semitic root *ptr* that could account for Akkadian *pšr,* Hebrew *pšr,* and Aramaic *ptr,* with Hebrew *ptr* borrowed from the Aramaic, and Aramaic *pšr* borrowed at a later stage from Akkadian or Hebrew. However, Sperling argues against an etymological relationship between פשר and פתר ("Studies," 92). Rabinowitz has been faulted for overly simplifying the lexical equation between Qumran *"pesher"* and the biblical Aramaic and Hebrew words designating dream interpretation, in *"Pêsher/Pittârôn,"* 220. Cf. the critiques of Brooke, "Qumran Pesher," 488; Nitzan, 31-32.

55. H. Basser pointed to an additional rabbinic Hebrew sense of פשר as "coming together." He saw this secondary etymology as relevant to the closeness with which *pesher* interpretations are "bound" to their biblical base texts (*"Pesher Hadavar:* The Truth of the Matter," *RevQ* 13 [1988]: 389-405, 391). Sperling discussed a shared sense of "to settle" or "mediate" for Akkadian *pašāru* and Aramaic and late Hebrew *pšr,* but he viewed this usage as limited to the legal sphere; he took only the root meaning "unloose" to be of relevance to Qumran *pesher* ("Studies," 77-86).

15, 26 the Aramaic פשר refers to the deciphering of mysterious prophetic/predictive writing, the "writing on the wall." At Qumran, *pesher* is intended to reveal the "true meaning" of a divinely revealed text.

Sperling observed that the Akkadian cognate term may refer not only to the releasing of the mysteries hidden in dreams (i.e., revelation), but also to the releasing and exorcising of the negative outcomes portended by dreams.[56] In contrast, the wording of Genesis 40–41 implies that the *pitaron* only revealed the events portended by the dreams, but does not effect or affect their fulfillment. The biblical dreamers "dreamed according to the *pitaron* of their dreams" (Gen. 40:5; 41:11); thus, the *pitaron* is the actuality represented by the dream, whether or not any human agent discerns that reality and its relationship to the dream. Similarly, at Qumran, *pesher* is revelatory, not magical. It supplies information about, but does not effect, reality.[57]

For Elliger[58] and Rabinowitz,[59] the revelatory nature of *pesher* was particularly associated with its eschatological content. Rabinowitz describes an affinity between *pesher* and apocalyptic literature, citing 1QpHab 2:2-3, "and God recounted to him all that was to come. . . ." The *pesher* states that the Teacher's words come "from the mouth of God."[60] We would agree with Rabinowitz that *pesher* functioned as the "revelation of revelation," specifi-

---

56. Sperling, "Studies," 58-62.

57. Horgan suggests that the use of the root פתר rather than פשר in Genesis may have been a deliberate choice to avoid association with magic (*Pesharim*, 235). Schiffman takes the opposite view on both biblical dream interpretation and Qumran *pesher*, stating that "the efficacy of prophecy depends on its correct interpretation" (*Reclaiming the Dead Sea Scrolls* [New York: Doubleday, 1994], 223). This position is apparently predicated on a presumed parallel to other ancient Near Eastern views of dream interpretation. However, it does not seem to be explicit in the Jewish sources themselves.

58. Elliger, *Habakuk-Kommentar*, 163.

59. Rabinowitz, *"Pêsher/Pittârôn,"* 220. Rabinowitz went to great lengths to define *pitaron* and *pesher* as "presage," which he explained has two meanings: "the presage of reality" (or the "as yet unfulfilled prognostic") and the "realized" or "fully actualized presage" (223).

60. Cf. Schiffman, *Reclaiming*, 225-27. Schiffman also cites 1QpHab 2:6-10 and 7:1-5 as evidence of the divine source of the Teacher's knowledge regarding the meaning of Habakkuk's prophecies. Rabinowitz states further that *pesher* sees realities as having been "incorporated in the divine word, . . . the word wherein one endowed with the necessary skill might detect the reality that would emerge . . . and which could thus be disclosed to others in 'ordinary language.'" The verb פתר/פשר refers to "the practice of this art." Although acknowledging that the act of creating the *pesher* involved a skill or art, Rabinowitz describes that art only in a negative sense — it is not exegetical. Oddly, whereas Rabinowitz saw *"pesher* as revelation" as a reason to dissociate *pesher* from midrash, Brownlee saw this feature as common to both ("Biblical Interpretation," 76).

cally the revelation of historical/eschatological reality, a "decoding" and "deciphering." Unlike Rabinowitz, though, we see this characteristic as only part of the distinctive nature of *pesher*. In the following section, we address the equally essential ingredient of exegesis.[61]

Exegesis

The lexical tie between citations and interpretations in *pesher* is undeniable. Nonetheless, one might ask whether this correlation points to an exegetical process as the means to the derivation of the *pesher*, or whether the *pesher* should be seen as simply a literary expression of revealed content. In reality, this distinction cannot hold up, whether in our evaluation of ancient perceptions or in our own critical analysis. The modern scholar can hardly define, much less accept, the premise that the author received a "revelation" of the true eschatological meaning of the biblical verse. (This is not just because of the "unscientific" nature of this approach, but also because of the fact that these meanings have clearly turned out to be false.) The author of *pesher* is likely to have perceived himself as engaging in a "seamless, undifferentiated" activity, but there is no doubt that this activity involved exegetical methods.[62]

61. Rabinowitz refers to Oppenheim in supporting his thesis that text-based explication is irrelevant to achieving revealed *pesher* application (*"Pêsher/Pittârôn,"* 225). In light of the etymological parallel to Akkadian *pašāru*, Rabinowitz argues that we may extrapolate a similar parallel in the method (or nonmethod) of *pesher* and Akkadian dream interpretation. He cites Oppenheim to the effect that "no exegetic or hermeneutic approach is involved when one speaks of the interpreting of dreams in the ancient Near East" (*Interpretation,* 220). However, I would interpret the ancient parallels as offering evidence of the presence of exegesis elsewhere in the Near East, rather than its absence. G. Manetti argues in favor of discerning exegetical devices in Mesopotamian sign interpretation, and shows associative links between "signifieds" and "signifiers" (*Theories of the Sign in Classical Antiquity,* trans. from Italian by C. Richardson [Bloomington: Indiana University Press: 1993], 1-13). Cf. Stephen Lieberman, "A Mesopotamian Background for the So-Called *Aggadic* 'Measures' of Biblical Hermeneutics: Especially Gematria and Notariqon," *Hebrew Union College Annual* 58 (1987) 157-225. Even Oppenheim concedes some use of "exegetic methods" in dream interpretation (*Interpretation,* 221). M. Fishbane elaborates specifically upon shared exegetical techniques in Qumran *pesher* and ancient Near Eastern divination ("The Qumran Pesher and Traits of Ancient Hermeneutics," *WCJS* 6, no. 1 [1977]: 97-114). See also, A. Finkel, "The Pesher of Dreams and Scriptures," *RevQ* 4 (1963-64): 364-70.

62. The adjectives are borrowed from Stephen Lieberman's description of rabbinic hermeneutic and exegetical self-consciousness, "Mesopotamian Background," 223. Earlier, he noted that the employment of numerous and varied exegetical techniques will precede the formation of an "abstract classification" of a repertoire. "Exegetes usually wend their

Silberman has brought the book of Daniel into the context of this discussion. It is true that God reveals hidden meanings to Daniel, but it must also be recognized that these meanings are already present, though encoded, in the book's dreams and in the handwriting on the wall. Symbolism and wordplay are clearly in evidence.[63] Like Daniel, 1QpHab claims revelation as the source of its interpretations; exegetical ties are operative in both instances.

Brownlee was the first and most staunch proponent of taking exegesis as the generic determinant of *pesher*.[64] He compiled thirteen "Hermeneutical

way through their duties without bothering to consider whether they are using the Australian crawl, the backstroke, or the butterfly stroke" (221).

Although the author of *pesher* is likely to have proceeded without sensitivity to discrete methodological steps, it is nonetheless likely that he and his audience would have appreciated the general "exegetical" nature of his activity. This is a plausible inference from the understanding of the Qumran community's attitude to halakic exegesis, as described below, in the section entitled "Motive." The self-awareness of the Qumran community as biblical interpreters is evident in its terminology and in its explicit citation of biblical text. Vermes raised the latter point in response to J. Neusner's suggestion that *pesher* not be considered exegesis since it reacts to events rather than Scripture (*Ancient Judaism and Modern Category Formation* [Lanham, Md.: University Press of America, 1986], 50). Vermes rejected the idea that *pesher* is "historiography disguised as Bible Interpretation," pointing to the systematic nature of continuous *pesher* ("Bible Interpretation," 190*). Patte raised the question of the relationship between history and scripture in apocalyptic literature, where the situation is less straightforward, as is the related issue of the attitude to "unwritten" Torah presumed in such works (*Early Jewish Hermeneutic*, 142). For an insightful examination of the community's self-perception in regard to revelation through Torah study, see A. Baumgarten, "The Zadokite Priests at Qumran," *DSD* 4 (1997): 137-56, esp. 142-43 and the literature cited there.

63. "Unriddling the Riddle," 331. The *"mene-tekel . . ."* of the writing may have appeared to be gibberish at first, but once the meaning is revealed, we discern an intrinsic relationship between the interpretation and the sense of the words. Silberman cites R. H. Charles on the intrinsic relationship between "Mina, mina, a shekel, and two half-minas" (or half a mina) and the allusion to political breakup. Cf. ICC, *Daniel*, 115, 133-37. Although the connection is indeed strong, it is not universally appreciated, and the conventional view of the book of Daniel perceives only its revelatory aspect. This mistaken approach is found even in the work of E. Slomovic, who sought to appreciate a synthesis in *pesher*, which he recognized as both employing literary devices and relying upon "charismatic revelation." Nevertheless, he stated that *pesher* resembles midrash in its use of hermeneutical rules, but also exhibits a revelatory aspect that is closer to exegesis found in the Bible itself, particularly the book of Daniel. In his view, this latter perspective "minimizes the function of hermeneutics, [and] rejects in the main a methodological connection between the text and the commentary" ("Toward an Understanding of the Exegesis in the Dead Sea Scrolls," *RevQ* 7 [1969]: 5). On the use of exegetical techniques in dream and oracle interpretation, see the previous note.

64. Hence, his definition of *pesher* as a sort of midrash. Cf. Brownlee, *Midrash Pesher of Habakkuk*, SBLMS 24 (Missoula: Scholars Press, 1979); "The Historical Allusions

Principles or Presuppositions" for 1QpHab. Some of these were overarching concepts, such as the eschatological significance of the prophetic base text (principle #1), while others were very specific techniques: e.g., interpreting words in the lemma as abbreviations, in the manner of rabbinic *notariqon* (#12), or as anagrams (#9).[65] Subsequent scholars have compiled additional lists of *pesher* techniques, identified and organized according to their own respective hermeneutics.[66]

The most developed and useful classification is that of Nitzan.[67] Her categories are: (1) paraphrase,[68] (2) allegory,[69] (3) polyvalence,[70] and (4) "re-

---

of the Dead Sea Habakkuk Midrash," *BASOR* 126 (1950): 10-20; "The Habakkuk Midrash and the Targum of Jonathan," *JJS* 7 (1956): 169-86; and "Biblical Interpretation," 75-76. Brownlee did not see *pesher* as equivalent to midrash in literary form, or in content, but he saw an equivalence in the "mode of exegesis." Brownlee drew a parallel between the use of hermeneutic principles for rabbinic halakic exegesis and for the eschatological interpretations of *pesher*. As the rabbis sought scriptural support for laws they believed to be of divine origin, maintaining that these laws were really in the Pentateuch, and could be derived from it, so did *pesher* seek support for historical predictions. His limitation of the comparison to *halakic midrash* presumably lies in the authoritative nature of the exegeses which would not be applicable in the case of rabbinic *aggada*.

65. "Biblical Interpretation," listed on pp. 60-61. Cf. Silberman, "A Note on 4QFlorilegium," *JBL* 88 (1959): 158-59.

66. Thus, for example, Fishbane listed techniques that are found in both *pesher* and ancient Near Eastern interpretations of oracles, dreams, and omens ("Qumran Pesher," 98-100). He names (1) citation and atomization; (2) multiple interpretations; (3) paranomasia; (4) symbols; (5) *notarikon*, including acrostic, acronym, and anagram; (6) gematria (albeit with the caveat that the last technique is "not certain at Qumran"). Bruce lists the following: (1) atomization; (2) variant readings; (3) allegorization; (4) "reinterpretation" (*Biblical Exegesis*, 16). Horgan apparently uses the criterion of the level of adherence to the base text. Her categories are (1) the adoption and adaptation of the actions, ideas, and words of the lemma to a different historical context; (2) the removal of isolated elements ("key words, roots, or ideas") from the lemma to use as the basis for describing a new historical reality; (3) metaphoric identification of lemma elements; (4) loose connection to the lemma (*Pesharim*, 244).

67. Nitzan, מגילת פשר חבקוק, 40-54.

68. She distinguishes between *"stylistic paraphrase"* (which restates an idea of the lemma) and *"exegetical paraphrase"* (which applies the lemma in a new way); Nitzan, מגילת פשר חבקוק, 40-42. Cf. Brownlee, #5; Bruce's "re-interpretation"; Horgan's "adoption and adaptation. . . ."

69. She differentiates between the use of *traditional* Jewish *allegory* and the development of original *sectarian allegory*, in which new symbolic traditions were established (Nitzan, מגילת פשר חבקוק, 43-46). Cf. Brownlee, #6; Bruce's "allegorization"; Horgan's "metaphoric identification." Nitzan focuses specifically on "building imagery."

70. Nitzan, מגילת פשר חבקוק, 46-51. Cf. Bruce's "variant readings." Nitzan speaks of the multiplicity of both readings and meanings. The term *"multiple meanings"* refers to

contextualization."[71] These exegetical methods constitute the first step in a bilevel process, aiming toward the "correlation" of the prophecy to (contemporary/eschatological) reality.[72] First, an application is derived from words, phrases, or ideas in the lemma. Then, literary considerations determine the description of the composite event. The literary techniques of expression include structural balance, especially parallelism, and the use of secondary biblical texts.[73] Nitzan's most significant contribution is her clarification of this second stage of *pesher* — the literary development of a unified work.[74] The prevailing conception of the "literary approach" of *pesher* is its negation, following Elliger's determination that "atomization" is the key "exegetical" technique of *pesher*.[75] Elliger thereby denies the lemma any significance beyond

---

the use of various denotations and connotations of a particular word or sound ("polysemy"; Carmignac's "amphibologie," *Les Textes,* 47), as well as the use of wordplays deriving from paronomosia or isolexism. *"Multiple readings"* describes the formation of *pesher* through deviations from a given root. This category could be further divided, though only theoretically, between actual textual variants, and exegetical wordplays upon the letters or sounds of a word, such as anagram, or paragram. On a practical level, since we do not know what the biblical *Vorlage* of the *pesher*'s author looked like, we cannot know where variants from it appear in his lemma, let alone whether a particular variant would be deliberate or inadvertent. Even when *lemma* and *pesher* clearly reflect more than one reading, we cannot be certain whether the variation is textual or exegetical within the *pesher*. In this context, Nitzan addresses the relevant rabbinic technique of "*'al tiqre*" (p. 51). Cf. M. J. Bernstein, "4Q252 i 2 לא ידור רוחי לעולם, Biblical Text or Biblical Interpretation?" *RevQ* 16, 3 (1994): 421-27. Doudna argues against the supposition that the authors of the *pesharim* were aware of and used textual variants (*4Q Pesher Nahum,* 67-70). It is our contention that textual variants were utilized, but that the way this was done is presently irretrievable. Cf. G. J. Brooke, "The Biblical Texts in the Qumran Commentaries: Scribal Errors or Exegetical Variants?" in *Early Jewish and Christian Exegesis: Studies in Memory of William Hugh Brownlee,* ed. C. A. Evans and W. F. Stinespring (Atlanta: Scholars Press, 1987), 85-100.

71. This is our rather free rendering of Nitzan's "נתוק ההקשר," 51-54. This term is preferable to the "atomization" of Elliger and Bruce, or even Horgan's intermediate description of the "removal of isolated elements."

72. Nitzan's התאמה, 33; the word "correlation" was used in this context by Finkel ("The Pesher of Dreams," 364). Cf. S. Berrin, "Lemma/*Pesher* Correspondence in Pesher Nahum," in *The Dead Sea Scrolls Fifty Years after Their Discovery,* ed. L. H. Schiffman, E. Tov, and J. C. VanderKam (Jerusalem: Israel Exploration Society, 2000), 341-50.

73. Cf. Nitzan, מגילת פשר חבקוק, 81-103, on "style." Brownlee listed the use of other scriptural passages as his thirteenth "hermeneutical principle," but it is more appropriate to describe this technique in terms of style and expression.

74. Cf. esp. pp. 51-54.

75. Elliger himself had acknowledged literary practices in *pesher*. He saw lemma/*pesher* correlation as functioning to strengthen the perception of the *pesher* as the true revelation of the prophetic words (*Habakuk-Kommentar,* 127-30). This was effected by

its individual elements. Nitzan, however, demonstrates the sensitivity of the *pesher* to the literary structure of the lemma in 1QpHab.[76] To illustrate atomization, Elliger introduces the analogy of one who takes apart a mosaic and then uses the separate tiles to produce a totally new, independent mosaic of his own. Elliger's own depiction of *pesher,* however, less resembles a new mosaic than a collection of independent mosaics formed from the pieces of the fragmented original whole.[77] Nitzan demonstrates that the *pesher* is a new organic structure in its own right, derived from the structure of its base text.[78] This composition is the final product of the "inspired exegesis" of its author.

Motive

The emergence of an appreciation of motive as a generic factor may largely be traced to the competing analyses of 4Q252 in the 1990s.[79] Bernstein formulated an evaluative criterion from an exegetical perspective, separating "simple-sense exegesis" *(peshat)* from more tendentious interpretation. He thus stressed the aim of the exegete in the classifying of exegetical texts.[80] In response, Brooke's subsequent analysis of 4Q252 attempted to establish a "thematic purpose."[81] This contrasted with Bernstein's view that the goal of

---

the use of words, or synonyms of words, from the lemma. Still, he saw the relationship of the *pesher* to the lemma as primarily that of "atomization." That is, the particulars of the biblical text are used by the *pesher,* but the overall context is not significant (139-42).

76. Nitzan's stated goal was to fill in gaps left by previous scholars who had attended to techniques in the formation of specific *pesher* interpretations in 1QpHab, rather than to the *pesher* composition as a whole (מגילת פשר חבקוק, 39).

77. In fact, it is this disjointed nature of *pesher* which distinguishes it from midrash in his opinion, and reflects the literary inferiority of the former to the latter (*Habakuk-Kommentar,* 163-64).

78. She further argues that the exegetical technique of "atomization" of the biblical text is only a last resort, and that an attempt is made to adhere to biblical structure (מגילת פשר חבקוק, 54).

79. See above. L. H. Silberman's treatment of 1QpHab stands out in earlier scholarship as having addressed the issue of motive as well as those of form, content, and method ("Unriddling the Riddle," 323-64; esp. 325, where he refers to "intentions").

80. Cp. Brooke's initial stylistic distinction between "explicit" and "implicit" interpretation, noted on page 113 above. The seeds of both Bernstein's and Brooke's criteria can be found in Vermes, "Interpretation, History of," 438-41.

81. Brooke, "Thematic Content," 33-59. Bernstein argues against the supposition of a unifying theme. In his opinion, the "content" of 4Q252 consists of resolutions to exegetical problems in Genesis, and the "structure" is a sequential stringing of these exegeses. Bernstein insists that "the overt must take precedence over the implicit" ("4Q252:

the composition was the resolution of textual difficulties. The debate over the motivation of 4Q252 has served to emphasize by contrast the clear aims of the continuous *pesharim:* to identify biblical texts as referring to eschatologically significant historical events, thereby demonstrating and predicting fulfillments of biblical prophecy.

Mandel's distinction between the eschatological content of Qumran *pesher* and the historical content of the rabbinic עליו מפרש led him to a radical conclusion regarding the motive of the Tannaitic authors of the latter. He argues that the absence of eschatological figures and events in those Tannaitic passages reflects a conscious rabbinic opposition to the eschatological fulfillment interpretations of Qumran and early Christianity.[82] Mandel's observations about these rabbinic forms and formulas dovetail well with an earlier proposal put forth by Silberman to the effect that Qumran *pesher* was one stage in a developmental line running from Daniel to the rabbinic *petira*.[83]

The analyses of Silberman and Mandel may be combined as follows. The book of Daniel, Qumran *pesher,* the Tannaitic עליו מפרש, and the amoraic *petira* represent successive chronological developments of a basic exegetical approach. All supply an "identification" or "specific reference" for a "text" of divine origin, using an explicit formula; and all evince a concern with historical content (apparently a necessary feature in the first three cases, and a frequent one in the last). The "texts" in the later examples are biblical texts. The identification in עליו מפרש is never eschatological — by design, according to Mandel. The content is restricted to the past. The term פרש indicates "specificity," but avoids the connotation of "revelation" implied in the roots פתר/פשר employed in the other three modes of exegesis.[84] Of these three other types, Qumran

---

Method," 71). See also, I. Fröhlich, "Themes, Structure, and Genre of Pesher Genesis: A Response to George Brooke," *JQR* 85 (1994): 83-90. It is now generally agreed that 4Q252 is a sort of "commentary" comprised of sections of biblical interpretation in various genres, including one in the *pesher* genre (col. iv: 3-6, a comment on Jacob's blessing of Reuben, which includes the formula פשר. Note also the "*pesher*-like" comment upon the blessing of Judah in col. v).

82. Mandel, "Midrashic Exegesis," 163-68.

83. Silberman, "Unriddling the Riddle," 327-30.

84. On the relationship between פתר/פשר and פרש, see too I. Heinemann, "להתפתחות המונחים המקצועיים לפירוש המקרא," in לשוננו 16 (1948), 22, and Schiffman, *The Halakha at Qumran*, 32-41, esp. 41. Schiffman summarizes Qumran usage as follows: "*Pesher* is a term used to denote 'aggadic' interpretation while *perush* denotes interpretation for the purpose of discovering the details of the *halakha*." Cp. Mandel, "Midrashic Exegesis," 159 n. 22. He views the Tannaitic terminology as a rejection of sectarian revelation, and cites further, rabbinic opposition to those who attempted to reveal aspects of the Torah (מגלה פנים בתורה. Cf. p. 166, and the literature cited).

pesher, like Daniel, is characterized by eschatological content, while the rabbinic *petira* exhibits variable content, including eschatology.[85]

We would further propose that in addition to the noted similarities in terminology, form, content, and purpose, Qumran *pesher* and the amoraic *petira* share another significant feature: a sense of the multivalence of biblical text.[86] Whereas the Tannaitic עליו מפרש sought to provide the literal meaning of a univalent biblical text,[87] and early Christian contemporizing exegesis provided allegorical interpretations of a biblical text that was viewed as devoid of literal meaning, Qumran *pesher* and the amoraic *petira* would have operated on the assumption of a multivalent biblical text possessing both literal and nonliteral meanings.[88]

This understanding of *pesher* would be consistent with what is known about the Qumran community's approach to halakic exegesis. At Qumran, halakah is seen as twofold, with the *nigleh* and the *nistar* both firmly rooted in the Hebrew Bible, each in its own way.[89] We maintain that the working hypothesis for Qumran historical exegesis should suppose a similar duality.[90] Thus, the exoteric sense of the prophetic base text (analogous to the halakic *"nigleh"*) pertained to the original context of the monarchic period, while the more significant esoteric meaning (analogous to the *"nistar"*) referred to the contemporary eschatological situation. The text itself could be appreciated as a sort of *"nigleh,"*[91] though the aim of *pesher* was to uncover the mystery, or

85. On the expanded frame of reference of the *petira*, including applications to the future, see Mandel, "Midrashic Exegesis," 161 n. 29, and Silberman, "Unriddling the Riddle."

86. On multivalence and the *petira*, see Heinemann, "להתפתחות," 21 (Silberman also cites Heinemann's "Altjüdische Allegoristik," in *Bericht des Jüdisch-Theologischen Seminars* [Breslau, 1935], 19-21, 45).

87. This description derives from Mandel's unpublished study on the term עליו מפרש.

88. Finkel comments upon the "allegorical" nature of both *pesher* and the *petira* in "The Pesher of Dreams," 364-70.

89. Cf. Schiffman, *The Halakha at Qumran*, 22-32; *Reclaiming* 247-49. Schiffman contrasts the rabbinic concept of "dual Torah" which involves the transmission of revealed oral traditions, with Qumran *perush*, which presupposed progressive revelation through textual interpretation (*The Halakha at Qumran*, 32, 41, 56, 76, and sources cited). The community perceived that "revealed things" were accessible to all Jews, while the "hidden things" were hidden from the larger population but were revealed exclusively to the community.

90. See, however, the cautious remarks of S. T. Fraade, "Interpretive Authority in the Studying Community at Qumran," *JJS* 44 (1993): 50-51.

91. This supposition of an appreciation of the base text and its original context has significant ramifications for the analysis of the Qumran *pesharim*, and is essential to the approach to *pesher* that I have put forth in "Lemma/*Pesher* Correspondence," and followed

"*raz*" — the truth that was concealed in the prophetic text (1QpHab 7:4-5).[92]

Although "motive" is rarely viewed as a "generic factor," it may be the key to the most informative description of *pesher*. After all, the *identifying form* of *pesher*, its sectarian contemporizing *eschatological content*, and the conception of *inspired exegesis* inherent in its production are all means to a particular end. Each of these factors is essential for the maximal achievement of authorial motive: the communication of the theologically significant truth latent in the selected biblical base text.

---

throughout my dissertation, and now in *The Pesher Nahum Scroll from Qumran: An Exegetical Study of 4Q169* (Leiden: Brill, 2004).

92. The term רז has been employed for this sense of "hidden mysteries"; cf. 1QpHab 7:5, 8, 14. This eschatologically significant term is frequent in Daniel and apocalyptic literature (cf., inter alia, Horgan, *Pesharim*, 237; Bruce, *Biblical Exegesis*, 7-11).

Thematic Commentaries on Prophetic Scriptures

GEORGE J. BROOKE

There are many ways of categorizing the early Jewish exegetical works found in the Qumran caves.[1] A basic list based on content and method would include the following. First, there are interpretations of legal texts, of which the hallmark is either the implicit or explicit juxtaposition of scriptural texts to expound and develop a legal point. Second, there are interpretations of scripture in poetic, liturgical, and wisdom texts; these are characterized by their use of scripture implicitly in a rephrased and reformulated way often alongside other scriptures, so that the allusions to scripture form a kind of scriptural anthology. Third, there are exhortations, in which scriptural passages are used by way of providing examples, either positively or negatively, to encourage a particular kind of behavior in the reader or hearer. Fourth, there are interpretations of scriptural narratives in which the stories are retold and in the retelling various explicatory phrases are used to clarify points of detail or to explain more overtly the actions of the participants in the story. Fifth, there are the interpretations of prophetic texts, in many of which the circumstances of the community are read back into the unfulfilled prophecy. Such unfulfilled prophecies can be recognized in blessings and curses, in psalms and in prophetic oracles of all kinds, and their exegesis adopts a method very close to that of ancient

---

1. Many studies of the exegetical works found at Qumran have been devoted misleadingly almost exclusively to the so-called *pesharim*. Various attempts have been made to open up the understanding of the enormous breadth of scriptural exegesis evident in the sectarian and nonsectarian compositions found at Qumran. Amongst the most successful is J. Maier, "Early Jewish Biblical Interpretation in the Qumran Literature," in *Hebrew Bible/Old Testament: The History of Its Interpretation*, vol. I, *From the Beginnings to the Middle Ages (until 1300)*, ed. M. Sæbø (Göttingen: Vandenhoeck & Ruprecht, 1996), 108-29.

dream interpretation. Commentary on such prophecies can also take several different forms, but two have commonly been identified.

Since the significant study by J. Carmignac, it has long been fashionable to divide that fifth category of prophetic exegetical works at Qumran into two groups, the continuous and the thematic.[2] Within the category of continuous exegetical works have normally been placed all those compositions that follow one scriptural work sequentially. All the extant continuous commentaries of this sort are clearly based on prophetic texts, whether prophetic oracles proper or the psalms viewed as prophecy.[3] Foremost amongst such compositions are the *Commentary on Habakkuk* (1QpHab) and the *Commentary on Nahum* (4QpNahum). Their structure is characterized by the presentation of the scriptural text in sequence without omissions, but divided up into short paragraphs each of which is given commentary, generally introduced by a formula which includes the word *pesher* (interpretation). In these continuous commentaries it appears as if the scriptural text in its original order controls the presentation of the commentary even though the message of the commentary may be based on a thematic theological or historical viewpoint, such as reflection on the experiences of the community of the commentator viewed eschatologically.

The significant difference in the group of commentaries which Carmignac labeled "thematic" is that the presentation of the commentary is no longer controlled by a long running sequence of the scriptural text, such as the whole of the first two chapters of Habakkuk or the whole of the book of Nahum. Rather, scriptural passages receive commentary and the whole seems to be organized on some principle other than the sequence of the scriptural text. This chapter is indeed concerned with the thematic commentaries on what may have been considered unfulfilled prophetic texts, but the main purpose of what is presented here is to draw the reader's attention to the very great diversity of the form of these exegetical works in the Qumran library and to suggest that the long-standing distinction between continuous and thematic commentaries no longer serves such a useful function as once it did. There are two obvious reasons for this. On the one hand it is clear that even amongst the so-called continuous *pesharim* there are varieties in the formal presentation of both prophetic scripture and exegesis. On the other hand some of the compositions that modern commentators include under the umbrella of "thematic commentary" are not exclusively based on unfulfilled prophecies.

---

2. J. Carmignac, "Le document de Qumrân sur Melkisédeq," *RevQ* 7 (1969-71): 360-61.

3. 11QPs[a] 27:11 describes how David composed all the psalms through "the spirit of prophecy" which was given to him by God.

The Variety of Thematic Scriptural Commentaries

Even if one is restricted to prophetic materials, an enormous variety of compositions can be designated as thematic commentaries. For the purposes of this chapter, it is necessary to attempt to delimit the literary corpus to be considered. Not to be considered here are those rewritten and reworked scriptural texts whose thematic exegesis of the underlying scriptural text is principally implicit. Into this category, as far as the prophets are concerned, fall many of the para-biblical compositions which concern prophetic figures: the *Apocryphon of Moses* (1Q22, 1Q29, 4Q375, 4Q376, 4Q408); 4QVisSam (4Q160; for Samuel); 4Qpap paraKings et al. (4Q382; for Elishah); the *Apocryphon of Jeremiah* (4Q383, 4Q384, 4Q385a, 4Q387, 4Q387a, 4Q388a, 4Q389, 4Q390); *Pseudo-Ezekiel* (4Q385, 4Q386, 4Q385b, 4Q388, 4Q391); and *Pseudo-Daniel* (4Q243-245).[4] These compositions belong with other para-biblical works amongst the Qumran library, the most well known of which are the so-called Reworked Pentateuch, those that preserve the book of *Jubilees,* and the several copies of the *Temple Scroll.* There are also similar para-biblical compositions dependent upon scriptural psalms and wisdom texts. Although the scriptural text is adjusted in many ways in these compositions, and sometimes exegetical comments have introductory formulae (such as involving the use of the demonstrative pronoun), the interpretation of scripture remains implicit in the rewriting, paraphrasing, or editing activity of the author. Nevertheless, it is noteworthy that the kinds of interpretation contained in these compositions can suitably be called "thematic," perhaps based on the need to present a harmonized and consistent scriptural text as in the Reworked Pentateuch, to argue for a particular reading of a prophetic oracle as in *Pseudo-Ezekiel,* or to reflect an overarching application of a halakic and calendrical perspective as in the book of *Jubilees.*

Also not to be considered here are those compositions from the Qumran library, sectarian or otherwise, which are essentially of a genre other than scriptural commentary but which refer, sometimes frequently, to prophetic passages to improve their argument. This is a demarcation that is difficult to define and may ultimately be indefensible, but for convenience' sake an example may illustrate what is in mind. In column 8 of the copy of the *Rule of the Community* from cave 1 (1QS) there is a brief description of the community that will separate itself from sinners and live in the desert. This

---

4. On some of the prophetic materials see G. J. Brooke, "Parabiblical Prophetic Narratives," in *The Dead Sea Scrolls after Fifty Years: A Comprehensive Assessment,* ed. P. W. Flint and J. C. VanderKam, 2 vols. (Leiden: Brill, 1998), 1:271-301.

move is justified by appeal to Isaiah 40:3: "In the desert, prepare the way of ****, straighten in the steppe a roadway for our God." The quotation is then given an explicit interpretation, "this is the study of the law which he commanded through the hand of Moses, in order to act in compliance with all that has been revealed from age to age, and according to what the prophets have revealed through his holy spirit."[5] This combination of prophetic quotation and interpretation is similar in form to that in many of the more overtly thematic commentaries, but in 1QS 8 it is an isolated instance of prophetic exegesis, and although it might be argued that the quotation and interpretation fit a theme of spiritual separation and preparation in the wilderness, in the immediate context of 1QS that theme is not worked through in a thoroughgoing way with multiple references to various prophetic passages that might have been deemed relevant.[6]

As a result, this chapter will consider briefly a wide range of commentaries which fall somewhere between the systematic (even thematic) reworkings and paraphrases found in such para-biblical compositions as the *Apocryphon of Jeremiah* and *Pseudo-Ezekiel,* and those works which cite and comment on prophetic texts from time to time but are not focused on scripture in an overarching way.

From Excerpted Texts to Excerpted Commentaries

For the purposes of this presentation the full range of thematic commentaries may be embraced within a spectrum that ranges from a consideration of an exegetical composition that lists four authoritative extracts within a very minimalist framework, but whose exegetical purposes seem more or less apparent, to the full-blown exegetical works such as the *Damascus Document,* one of whose traits is its use of prophetic passages in exegetical miniatures, almost certainly choicely picked from other exegetical works. Thus it is possible to characterize the range of thematic commentaries as spreading between those that are almost exclusively excerpts from authoritative texts to those which depend upon other commentaries of various kinds, using excerpts from them for their own exegetical purposes. For the most part in these the-

5. Trans. F. García Martínez, *The Dead Sea Scrolls Translated,* 2nd ed. (Leiden: Brill; Grand Rapids: Eerdmans, 1996), 12.

6. This example is given by D. Dimant in her programmatic article, "Pesharim, Qumran," in *ABD,* 5:245. Dimant calls this kind of exegetical example "isolated pesharim," which she defines as the "exposition of one or two biblical verses, within a work of a non-pesher genre."

matic commentaries prophetic texts form the basis of the commentary, but some intriguing exceptions will be noted briefly as the descriptive part of this chapter proceeds.

4QTestimonia

Four authoritative prophetic extracts make up this composition that is preserved on a single sheet of leather containing just one column of writing.[7] The four extracts have very brief nonscriptural introductions that can be understood as providing the reader with some guidance about the contents. The extracts are not followed by any explicit commentary, but the way they are presented in sequence is probably to be understood as an attempt to guide any preacher or commentator on the exegetical significance of the passages concerned.

The four excerpts are as follows. To begin with there is a quotation from the book of Exodus in the form known for a long time in the version of the Samaritan Pentateuch, but which was not necessarily exclusively Samaritan in all its readings. The proximity of many of the variant readings in the Reworked Pentateuch and in 4QpaleoExod[m] to the Samaritan version means that the sectarian character of the Samaritan Pentateuch should be defined in a restricted way by reference only to those few passages which privilege Mount Gerizim.[8] The multitude of minor improvements to the text of the Torah should not be seen as sectarian. In 4QTestimonia the use of Exodus 20:21 indicates an interest in the prophet like Moses who is to come.[9] The scriptural text is prophetic inasmuch as it refers to the as-yet-unfulfilled prediction that a prophet like Moses will one day arise.

The second extract is a quotation from the book of Numbers. Numbers 24:15-17 is part of the oracle of Balaam, self-evidently a prophetic text, and

---

7. See the full introductory description by A. Steudel, "Testimonia," in *Encyclopedia of the Dead Sea Scrolls*, ed. L. H. Schiffman and J. C. VanderKam (New York: Oxford University Press, 2000), 936-38.

8. On the Samaritan text-type in the Dead Sea Scrolls, see especially J. E. Sanderson, *An Exodus Scroll from Qumran: 4QpaleoExod[m] and the Samaritan Tradition*, HSS 30 (Atlanta: Scholars Press, 1986); E. Tov, "The Textual Status of 4Q364-367 (4QPP)," in *The Madrid Qumran Congress: Proceedings of the International Congress on the Dead Sea Scrolls, Madrid, 18-21 March 1991*, ed. J. Trebolle Barrera and L. Vegas Montaner (Leiden: Brill; Madrid: Editorial Complutense, 1992), 43-82.

9. The quotation corresponds with a combination of Deut. 5:28-29 and 18:18-19 in the MT.

speaks of the star that departs from Jacob and the scepter that arises from Israel. The scroll's editor probably understood this dual reference as an allusion to the royal messiah. It is noteworthy, however, that the same scriptural passage is used in the *Damascus Document* (CD 7:19-20) and the *War Scroll* (1QM 11:6-7); in the *Damascus Document* the star is identified with the Interpreter of the Law and the scepter alone with the prince of the whole congregation, in the *War Scroll* the commentary on the passage is more concerned with the motif of destruction than with identifying the star and scepter.[10] Whatever the case, it can be seen that this prophetic text is understood as concerning one or more eschatological figures.

In third place there is a quotation of Deuteronomy 33. This passage describes the figure of Levi (Deut. 33:8-11). In combination with the prophet who is to come and the oracular prediction of a royal figure, it is most likely that the extract from the Song of Moses is to be understood as an unfulfilled blessing of eschatological significance. These first three extracts thus seem to describe the three eschatological figures who will be on God's and the Qumran community's side when the time comes, in the last days. The interpretation is largely implicit, but as in several exegetical compositions found in the Qumran caves, the quotation of passages from what may have been understood as unfulfilled blessings and oracles urges the reader to understand that the figures referred to in the scriptural extracts are to be expected imminently.

The fourth extract is sometimes presented as a quotation of Joshua 6:26 with some kind of expansion.[11] However, we now know that there was a rewritten form of Joshua, recently relabeled the *Apocryphon of Joshua*,[12] which seems to be the source for the fourth authoritative excerpt in 4QTestimonia.[13]

---

10. See the comments on the similarities and differences between these uses of Num. 24 in G. J. Brooke, "*E Pluribus Unum:* Textual Variety and Definitive Interpretation in the Qumran Scrolls," in *The Dead Sea Scrolls in Their Historical Context,* ed. T. H. Lim, L. W. Hurtado, A. G. Auld, and A. Jack (Edinburgh: T&T Clark, 2000), 112-15.

11. Note, e.g., the way the text is printed with only Josh. 6:26 in italics in G. Vermes, *The Complete Dead Sea Scrolls in English* (London: Penguin Books, 1998), 496.

12. C. A. Newsom, "4Q378 and 4Q379: An Apocryphon of Joshua," in *Qumranstudien: Vorträge und Beiträge der Teilnehmer des Qumranseminars auf dem internationalen Treffen der Society of Biblical Literature, Münster, 25.-26. Juli 1993* (Göttingen: Vandenhoeck & Ruprecht, 1996), 35-85; C. A. Newsom, "Apocryphon of Joshua," in *Qumran Cave 4. XVII: Parabiblical Texts, Part 3,* ed. G. J. Brooke, et al., DJD 22 (Oxford: Clarendon, 1996), 237-88.

13. This is the standard view. It can also be argued that the *Apocryphon of Joshua* is citing from 4QTestimonia: H. Eshel, "The Historical Background of the Pesher Interpreting Joshua's Curse on the Rebuilding of Jericho," *RevQ* 15 (1991-92): 412 (of course, strictly speaking the extract is not a "*pesher*").

The text in both its full form in the *Apocryphon of Joshua* and in 4QTestimonia is preserved only in damaged sections of the respective manuscripts, so it is uncertain exactly what should be restored and read. However, the extract seems to be an unfulfilled curse on an evil man, "a man of Belial," and his two sons. If the first three extracts in the composition describe the three good figures of the eschatological period, so the fourth and final extract seems to describe three balancing bad figures.

Two points are worth noting here about 4QTestimonia. On the one hand, it is easy to see that the four extracts follow the sequence of the Pentateuch followed by Joshua. In this respect the excerpted texts look like some of the other thematic commentaries being considered here that also follow the sequence of scripture, not only within a single scriptural book, but also over a series of books. Secondly, the excerpts presented in 4QTestimonia, though provided with a minimum of exegetical framework and explanation, encourage the reader toward eschatological historicization. Just as in the so-called continuous *pesharim* the scriptural texts are explained in relation to the events experienced or expected by the community, so the excerpts presented in 4QTestimonia can be suitably read against a historical backdrop, though it is impossible to be certain exactly which historical events the composition may allude to.[14] In all likelihood the person who put the extracts together in this single column understood the texts as belonging to the latter days, the period running up to the eschaton, a period which had already begun in the experiences of the community. That is the overarching theme that lies behind the selection of prophetic passages.

4QpPsalms^a, 4QpIsa^b, 4QpIsa^c

It would be natural to follow the preceding comments on 4QTestimonia and its compiler's handling of scriptural texts in sequence, by referring to the commentaries that are concerned with a single scriptural book and that follow the sequence of that book as known from other witnesses to it. Those narrowly defined continuous commentaries have been discussed in closer detail in another chapter in this book. Nevertheless, it is important to point out that several of the commentaries that are generally ascribed to the group known as "continuous *pesharim*" contain features that might lead them to be

---

14. Steudel, "Testimonia," 937, lists the various options and herself sides with those who identify the "man of Belial" with John Hyrcanus I, though she also sees him as the referent of the first three extracts as well.

categorized differently. S. Berrin has suitably depicted the matter in the following way: "The continuity of continuous *pesharim* is not entirely consistent. Pesher Psalms[a] (4Q171) proceeds directly from Psalm 37 to Psalm 45. Pesher Isaiah[b] (4Q162) omits *Isaiah* 5.15-24. Pesher Isaiah[c] (4Q163) includes a citation from *Zechariah,* and apparently one from *Jeremiah,* and its current reconstruction presumes an irregular order of earlier and later chapters of Isaiah."[15] The point is that once the continuous sequence of scripture is broken, it is possible to surmise that scripture is no longer the dominant control in the commentary. Rather, scripture has given way to some other thematic control, such as a particular theological concern of the author.

A few comments are in order on some of these less than continuous *pesharim.* To begin with Pesher Psalms[a] (4Q171): out of the principal set of ten fragments, four columns of text can be reconstructed with a large measure of certainty. In column 4, after the interpretation of the last two verses of Psalm 37, there is a blank line. The superscription of Psalm 45 is then quoted in full and given interpretation, followed by the next few verses of the psalm before the manuscript becomes too broken for any further reconstruction. Why does the commentator move from Psalm 37 to Psalm 45?[16] One possibility is that he was basing his commentary on a Psalms manuscript that presented the psalms in that order. No such manuscript survives, but several versions of the Books of Psalms have come from the Qumran caves, and some of them contain the psalms in an order that differs from that later adopted as normative in the Masoretic Text. In fact, this possible explanation is not very likely, since it has become clear that nearly all the variations in the order of the psalms occur in Books Four and Five; the first three Books of Psalms seem to have retained a more or less stable content and order well before Qumran was occupied.[17]

It is far more likely that the commentator moved from Psalm 37 to Psalm 45 because he was engaged in an exercise of reading the Psalms histori-

---

15. Berrin, "Pesharim," in *Encyclopedia of the Dead Sea Scrolls,* 645.

16. It is noteworthy that the fullest modern commentary on 4QpPsalms[a] contains no discussion at all of why the ancient exegete moved straight from Ps. 37 to Ps. 45: see M. P. Horgan, *Pesharim: Qumran Interpretations of Biblical Books,* CBQMS 8 (Washington, D.C.: Catholic Biblical Association of America, 1979), 224.

17. The most thoroughgoing study of the various Psalms manuscripts from Qumran is that of P. W. Flint, *The Dead Sea Psalms Scrolls and the Book of Psalms,* STDJ 17 (Leiden: Brill, 1997). On the stabilization of the Psalter, see chap. 6; where the numbers of Psalms manuscripts are concerned, Flint's comments now need slight adjustment in light of the edition of all the cave 4 Psalms manuscripts in E. Ulrich et al., *Qumran Cave 4. XI: Psalms to Chronicles,* DJD 16 (Oxford: Clarendon, 2000).

cally in light of the experiences of the community of which he seems to have been a part. Psalms 38 to 44 are all variously prayers of healing and deliverance, and the commentator may have considered them unsuitable for his thematic historical purposes. Having applied the statements about injustice in Psalm 37 so that his readers might consider themselves vindicated and full of expectation for their just reward, he moved on to the next psalm that could also be readily applied to the experiences of the community. Psalm 45 seems to have suited his needs: he interprets its opening as concerning "the seven divisions of the returnees of Israel," and seems to identify the skilled scribe of Psalm 45:2 with the Teacher of Righteousness. Thus, Pesher Psalms[a] as a whole may have been a commentary on a set of chosen psalms presented sequentially but selected thematically.

In a similar fashion but apparently on a smaller scale, 4QPesher Isaiah[b] jumps from Isaiah 5:14 to 5:24. However, the matter is not straightforward. Superficially it seems as if the commentator has deliberately moved from the mention of the wicked in Judah (Isa. 5:11-14) to "those who have rejected the Law of the Lord" (5:24), and that through the move he is able to identify the two groups. Although that is indeed the case, the identification is done through a phrase that does not follow the regular pattern of the continuous *pesharim*. In place of an interpretative comment after the quotation of 5:11-14 introduced by a phrase including the word *pesher*, the commentator proceeds with "these are the scoffers who are in Jerusalem." He then adds that "they are the ones who rejected the Law of the Lord" and continues directly with the quotation of Isaiah 5:24-25, which is then given a similar interpretation without any *pesher* formula. In this way Isaiah 5:24-25 actually becomes subordinate to the quotation of Isaiah 5:11-14, rather than simply the continuation of the scriptural text.

How should the presentation of the content of this commentary in this structure be interpreted? M. Horgan has commented that the "phrases are clearly a sort of commentary, even though they do not follow the prevailing pesher form."[18] Earlier it had been suggested that this distinctive format was the way in which the commentator constructed his bridge between the two passages he was working with.[19] Whatever the case, it is clear that a process of reducing the amount of prophetic base text has resulted in a theme becoming clear as the matter that controls the abbreviation of the scriptural text. The commentator is concerned to identify the scoffers in Jerusalem as the object

18. Horgan, *Pesharim,* 92.
19. W. R. Lane, *"Pešer* Style as a Reconstruction Tool in 4Q *Pešer* Isaiah *b," RevQ* 2 (1959-60): 281-83.

of Isaiah's reproaches; he is not concerned with the exposition of every section of this part of Isaiah.

In the various fragments of 4QPesher Isaiah^c the text of Isaiah seems to be cited continuously. The variation in this commentary from the other continuous *pesharim* is to be found in the commentary. Although in all the continuous *pesharim* the commentary contains echoes of other scriptural passages as the principal prophetic text is applied to the circumstances or aspirations of the community, in Pesher Isaiah^c there are explicit quotations of other scriptural texts to support the comments being made on the running text of Isaiah. These supplementary quotations are from Isaiah itself, but also from Zechariah. The details of the fragmentary sections of the commentary where this takes place need not detain us, but the question to be asked is whether the quotation of supplementary prophetic texts compromises the continuous character of the handling of scripture in Pesher Isaiah^c. Does it suggest that at least in some parts of the commentary there is a thematic concern that breaks away from the narrow exegetical confines controlled by attention to the running text of Isaiah by itself? The answer to this question may never be known for sure because the contexts of the commentary where this happens are very broken. The point to be noticed, however, is that there is in the case of 4QPesher Isaiah^c some overlap in form of presentation and method with what is clear in the compositions which are readily assigned by scholars to the category of thematic commentary.

4Q174[20]

The principal fragment of 4Q174 was published by J. M. Allegro in 1958.[21] In the preliminary publication Allegro was trying to provide a suitable generic definition of the fascinating composition that had been assigned to his lot for publication, and his proposal was "eschatological *midrāšîm*." The designation has been much debated,[22] but 4Q174 has indeed become the touchstone for

---

20. Although Allegro eventually named this composition "Florilegium" (anthology), the title is not entirely suitable, since that term usually designates excerpts from other texts rather than excerpts interweaved with commentary. To avoid the problem of nomenclature in this section, the composition will be referred to solely by its catalogue number.

21. J. M. Allegro, "Fragments of a Qumran Scroll of Eschatological *Midrāšîm*," *JBL* 77 (1958): 350-54; four lines of this fragment were published earlier by Allegro in his study "Further Messianic References in Qumran Literature," *JBL* 75 (1956): 176-77.

22. See the brief discussion of the variety of alternatives that have been suggested in

the kind of thematic commentary that this chapter is considering; 4Q174 is the example that readily comes to mind when thematic commentaries are on the agenda. Although the comments that follow contain a brief description.of 4Q174, this section is chiefly an attempt to draw out some of the features of the composition as a whole which bear on the clarification of what might constitute a thematic commentary.

It is seldom remembered that the principal fragment of 4Q174 contains two rather different forms of commentary, though they also share some features. The first thirteen lines of the first column (now col. 4 of the reconstructed manuscript)[23] of the fragment continue and complete an interpretation of the oracle of Nathan in 2 Samuel 7. The distinctive features of this section of the composition can be described as follows. First, the text of 2 Samuel 7 is presented in its scriptural sequence, but the text does not all stand on the same level in the arrangement of the argument. The quotation of 2 Samuel 7:10, "[I will appoint a place for my people Israel and will plant them that they may dwell there and be troubled no more by their] enemies. No son of iniquity [shall afflict them again] as formerly, from the day that [I set judges] over my people Israel,"[24] is followed by an interpretation that is introduced by a demonstrative pronoun ("this is"). Within the interpretation there is a secondary use of Exodus 15:17-18 that is introduced by a formula identifying it clearly: "as it is written in the Book of Moses." In line 7 of the fragment 2 Samuel 7:11 is introduced with the phrase "and that he said to David." Since the subsequent quotation of a form of 2 Samuel 7:11-14 starts without introduction at the right-hand margin, it seems 2 Samuel 7:11 is being handled in a way similar to the quotation of Isaiah 5:24 in 4QPesher Isaiah[b]. A characteristic of the presentation in some thematic commentaries seems to be that not every section of the running scriptural text is always handled in the same way; sometimes subsequent verses can be cited as supporting a point made in the commentary, rather than as controlling a separate section of commentary for themselves.

A second feature of this thematic commentary is that not all the text of

---

G. J. Brooke, *Exegesis at Qumran: 4QFlorilegium in Its Jewish Context*, JSOTSup 29 (Sheffield: JSOT Press, 1985), 82-83.

23. The most thorough reconstruction of the composition has been provided by A. Steudel, *Der Midrasch zur Eschatologie aus der Qumrangemeinde (4QMidrEschat.[a.b])*: *Materielle Rekonstruktion, Textbestand, Gattung und traditionsgeschichtliche Einordnung des durch 4Q174 ("Florilegium") und 4Q177 ("Catena A") repräsentierten Werkes aus den Qumranfunden*, STDJ 13 (Leiden: Brill, 1994), 11-22.

24. This is the text as restored and presented by Vermes, *Complete Dead Sea Scrolls*, 493.

2 Samuel 7 is cited. Whereas in 7:11-12 it is clear that the offspring referred to is Solomon, and the house to be built is both the royal lineage from Solomon onward as well as the temple Solomon will build, in 4Q174 the citation is abbreviated so that the phrase concerning the building of the house need not be understood exclusively as a reference to the Davidic dynasty, but rather to the fact that God himself will one day establish the temple. Furthermore, the clear reference to David's immediate heir is dropped so that the commentary speaks only of an undesignated son whose throne God will establish. As the commentary makes clear, this is no reference to the house of David established by Solomon, but rather a way of introducing the shoot of David, the replacement of the old dynasty that has fallen by the new growth who will arise with the Interpreter of the Law to save Israel. From this it is evident that the thematic content of the commentary, concerning what will happen in the latter days, is controlling the presentation of the scriptural text that is being cited. There is no need in this kind of thematic commentary for every word of a scriptural passage to be cited; citations can be suitably edited so that they fit the comment that follows afterward with all the more clarity, and problematic issues or challenges for the interpretation can be neatly sidestepped. In this way 4QPesher Isaiah[b] with its jump from Isaiah 5:14 to Isaiah 5:24 is very similar to the presentation of 2 Samuel 7 in 4Q174.

A third distinctive mark of the commentary on 2 Samuel 7 is the notable absence of the technical term *pesher*. In many exegetical passages outside the so-called continuous *pesharim*, the interpretation is commonly introduced by the term *pesher*, but in the interpretation of 2 Samuel 7 in 4Q174 the interpretation is governed by demonstrative pronouns and other linguistic signals and devices. What is the significance of this? An answer is not readily available. There does not seem to be anything out of the ordinary in 2 Samuel 7. Like the sayings of Habakkuk or Nahum, it is a prophetic oracle. As in the commentaries on Habakkuk and Nahum, the oracle is given an interpretation which relates the true meaning of the oracle to the eschatological period, the beginnings of which the community identified as having already started in their own experiences; *pesher*-type interpretation seems to have been commonly applied to what might have been understood to be unfulfilled blessings, curses, and prophetic oracles.

Two possibilities emerge for the most suitable understanding of what is taking place in this section of 4Q174. On the one hand, it is noticeable that secondary or supplementary quotations of scriptural texts as part of the argument of *pesher* interpretations are not themselves interpreted by means of a formula including the technical term. This might have been because often such subsidiary citations are not themselves from unfulfilled oracles, but even when such is the case the term is not used — as with the use of Amos 9:11 in 4Q174 4:12-13 or Isaiah 5:24 in 4QPesher Isaiah[b]. On the other hand, if the use of 2 Samuel 7 in some subsidiary way does not explain the absence of the technical term *pesher,* then possibly the explanation for the difference in formulation is the result of this section of 4Q174 being an excerpt from a commentary of a different kind or from a slightly different school of thought. The use of the label "sons of light" in this section of the commentary would still strongly suggest that this school of thought belonged within the community, at least part of which was identified with the Qumran site, so perhaps the absence of the technical term *pesher* should not be overinterpreted.

The second major section of the principal fragment of 4Q174 contains the interpretation of a series of Psalms in the order known from various scriptural sources. Three additional features of what may constitute thematic commentary are discernible in this section of 4Q174. To begin with, over against the earlier sections of commentary on 2 Samuel 7 which lack any use of the term *pesher,* the section on the Psalms not only uses the term to introduce each major section of interpretation, but also the whole unit of commentary on the Psalms begins with the phrase "midrash on" *(midrash min).* It is widely agreed that this term should not be taken in its later rabbinic sense as designating an overarching category of formal commentaries,[25] but it is not quite clear whether the term does indeed have a quasi-technical function, such that with an introductory phrase like this all such thematic analyses of prophetic texts might be understood as examples of the formal searching of the scriptures, the kind of interpretative exercise which could be written up and presented for particular thematic purposes.

A second feature of the section of commentary on the Psalms is intriguing: only the opening verses of the psalms are cited. As a result, some aspects of the interpretations given have to be related by the hearer to parts of the Psalms they have not heard. This need not cause alarm, for the citations given can be understood as functioning as incipits. It is noteworthy, however, that even though the citation of 2 Samuel 7:11-12 has resulted in a comment about the shoot of David, the opportunity for talking about the Davidic messiah on the basis of a messianic understanding of Psalm 2:7 is not taken up. Rather the whole psalm is related to "the elect of Israel in the latter days" (4Q174 4:19); what in other traditions has provided a basis for individual messianic

---

25. See the comments on this phrase and the term "midrash" in the sectarian scrolls by T. H. Lim, "Midrash Pesher in the Pauline Letters," in *The Scrolls and the Scriptures: Qumran Fifty Years After,* ed. S. E. Porter and C. A. Evans, JSPSup 26 (Sheffield: Sheffield Academic Press, 1997), 282-90.

exegesis is turned into a reference to the whole community. Although the content of the commentary may fascinate the modern reader, it should be noticed that whereas in the presentation of 2 Samuel 7 some phrases are deliberately omitted so as not to detract from the force of the commentary, in the section on the Psalms important comments are made that make best sense in relation to parts of the scriptural text which have not been cited. In thematic commentaries it is always necessary to consider how much the commentator wishes the reader or hearer to take account of the wider context of what is cited and how much he is requiring the reader or hearer to focus only on the phrases quoted.

A third feature of the thematic commentary on the Psalms is apparent in the introduction to one of the supplementary quotations of scriptural texts that are used to reinforce the argument and demonstrate the authority of the exegesis. Whereas the quotation of Ezekiel 37:23 is introduced by the phrase "what was written concerning them in the Book of Ezekiel the prophet" (4Q174 4:16), the quotation of Isaiah 8:11 is introduced by an extended formula: "that is written in the Book of Isaiah the prophet for the latter days" (4Q174 4:15). In the supplementary quotation of Isaiah the introductory formula makes it clear that the passage is being used to support an interpretation of the Psalms for "the latter days": at this point the character of the thematic commentary is made completely clear. In continuous *pesharim* there is generally no room for such introductory formulae; in thematic commentaries the introductory formulae to scriptural quotations can give away in a nutshell the very purpose of the commentary.

In addition to the six features of the thematic commentary of 4Q174 mentioned above, a further characteristic may result from the convincing reconstruction of 4Q174 by A. Steudel. Whereas Allegro had presented the fragments assigned to the manuscript in order of size, with the relatively small fragments containing parts of Deuteronomy 33 designated as fragments 6-11,[26] Steudel's analysis of the damage patterns in the manuscript has shown that it is very likely that these fragments preceded the section of the commentary where there was discussion of 2 Samuel 7 and then the Psalms. One outcome of this analysis has been the proposal that the various sections of the commentary presented in 4Q174 are deliberately ordered in the sequence of Torah, Prophets, and Psalms, indicating an understanding of the constituent parts of the emerging canon such as might be hinted at in 4QMMT. In the composite text, the editors have reconstructed the phrase

26. J. M. Allegro, *Qumrân Cave 4.I (4Q158-4Q186)*, DJD 5 (Oxford: Clarendon, 1968), 53-57.

"in the book of Moses, and the books of the Prophets and (the writings of) David."[27] There is ongoing debate about the suitability of this restoration and about whether there is reference to two, three, or even four sets of written works. Whatever the case, there is apparently some ordering of authoritative texts as in the Greek preface to Ben Sira: "the Law and the Prophets and the other books of our ancestors." It thus becomes possible to surmise, as E. Puech has done,[28] that the principal scriptural texts being commented upon in 4Q174 are in the order they are in because of a known way of ordering the scriptures. Since it is clear that the scriptural citations in 4QTestimonia are also in the order later confirmed for the canon, so it might be that there is a general preference in thematic commentaries for ordering their selective interpretative sections on the basis of such an order.

Was there any other reason for the commentary taking the shape that its few surviving fragments seem to indicate? I have wondered elsewhere whether the combination of Deuteronomy 33, 2 Samuel 7, and some of the Psalms might rest upon some liturgical celebration; the use of the term "sukkath" or "sukkoth" in 4Q174 4:12, on the basis of Amos 9:11, might suggest the Feast of Tabernacles, but there is no external evidence to support the proposal.[29] If the model of 4QTestimonia is followed, then it could be supposed that the combination of Deuteronomy 33 and 2 Samuel 7 is based on the commentator's wish to talk about the two eschatological messianic figures, an anointed Levitical priest and a shoot of David. Such explicit messianism, however, seems to be combined with some mature reflection on the suffering and persecution that the community is undergoing, suffering which is possibly tempered somewhat by exegesis which identifies the anointed of Psalm 2:7 with the community of the elect in the latter days.

In sum, 4Q174 may suggest that the character of thematic commentary on unfulfilled prophetic texts, including the Psalms, is rich indeed. Perhaps ordered in a sequence later to be established for the Jewish canon, the commentary does not shirk from presenting scriptural passages in a variety of ways. Sometimes the scriptural passages are abbreviated, sometimes assumed. Sometimes the structure reveals that the base text is supporting the interpretation being given, rather than generating it. Sometimes the introductory formulae for supporting quotations contain key phrases that allow the reader or

27. E. Qimron and J. Strugnell, *Qumran Cave 4.V: Miqṣat Maʿaśe Ha-Torah*, DJD 10 (Oxford: Clarendon, 1994), 58-59.

28. E. Puech, *La croyance des Esséniens en la vie future: immortalité, résurrection, vie éternelle? Histoire d'une croyance dans le Judaïsme ancien*, EB 22 (Paris: J. Gabalda, 1993), 573 n. 20.

29. Brooke, *Exegesis at Qumran*, 161-66.

hearer to grasp the essential point of the thematic interpretation. In the formal detail of its presentation sometimes the commentary proper is introduced by a formula including the word *pesher,* sometimes by some other formulaic device.

4Q177

Only a few comments are needed on 4Q177. The character of the content as reconstructed by A. Steudel closely resembles that of 4Q174.[30] In fact, so closely do the two thematic commentaries resemble each other that Steudel has become convinced that they are part of the same literary work. She has also suggested that there may be other examples of the same work in the Cave 4 collection: 4Q182, 4Q178, and 4Q183. There is no way of knowing whether Steudel is correct, since there is no overlap between the two compositions, but it is clear that in both form and content they are very similar.

In what Steudel reconstructs as column 8,[31] there appears to be a thematic commentary on Psalms 11 and 12. In each section of commentary supplementary scriptural citations occur, also from the Prophets (Isa. 37:30; 32:7; Mic. 2:10-11; and Isa. 22:13), as in each section of commentary in 4Q174. The same is observable in Steudel's column 9: quotations of Psalms 12 and 13 with commentary introduced by a formula including the word *pesher* as for Psalms 1 and 2 in 4Q174, and each section of commentary contains supplementary prophetic citations (Zech. 3:9; Ezek. 25:8). And the same is the case in Steudel's column 10: Psalms 16 and 17 are cited and the commentary concerns the fulfillment of the Psalms in "the latter days" with the supplementary quotation of Hosea 5:8 in what survives. In Steudel's column 11, her placement of the fragments most suitably according to her rigorous method of reconstruction results in the appearance of Psalm 6, out of order. Beyond reflecting on the different order of some psalms in some of the scriptural manuscripts from Qumran, Steudel does not offer any detailed explanation for the order of the psalms as presented in her reconstruction of 4Q177. It appears that for one reason or another, from time to time, thematic commentaries do not follow the sequential order of the scriptural passages that form the basis of the commentary. In most other respects, 4Q177 shares the same features as have been highlighted in more detail in the discussion of 4Q174.

---

30. Steudel, *Der Midrasch zur Eschatologie aus der Qumrangemeinde,* 57-124.
31. Presented as col. I in the translation by García Martínez, *Dead Sea Scrolls Translated,* 209.

11QMelchizedek

Along with 4Q174, 11QMelchizedek is most commonly cited as the clearest example of a thematic commentary.[32] Parts of three columns of this commentary have been preserved. The editors of the principal edition describe its contents as follows: "The preserved text of col. II gives an eschatological description of the end of days, the tenth and last jubilee. The events of this period are described by means of thematic *pesharim;* Leviticus 25, Deuteronomy 15, Isaiah 52:7 and 61:1-3, Psalms 7:8-9 and 82:1-2 are quoted or alluded to, and explained with regard to the tenth jubilee."[33] In some ways the commentary in 11QMelchizedek is more intricate than those found in the various sections of 4Q174 or 4Q177. In the principal section that survives, there is a set of thematic interpretative developments more like the interwoven themes of a fugue than the more straightforward playing of one melody after another. Two texts provide point and counterpoint and then are variously returned to during the course of the exegesis. The two texts are Leviticus 25 and Isaiah 61.

Proper literary appreciation of 11QMelchizedek rests in discerning the organization of its use of scriptural texts. In what remains of column 2 there appear to be four sections. Each contains an opening set of statements that are followed by scriptural citations. Each citation is introduced with a formula such as "and as for what he said." Each citation or set of citations is then followed by an interpretation, again formulaically introduced: in what is extant, twice such formulae include the technical term *pesher.*

For the first section (11QMelch 2:1-8) there is hardly anything remaining of the opening statement. Then follow consecutive explicit quotations of Leviticus 25:13 concerning the year of the jubilee and Deuteronomy 15:2 concerning the year of release. The formulaically introduced interpretation makes the texts refer to the eschatological period, the latter days, when liberty will be proclaimed by Melchizedek. In all the other examples of thematic commentaries in this brief study, *pesher* interpretation is given exclusively to unfulfilled prophetic texts, blessings, curses, or promises, but in this section of 11QMelchizedek passages from Leviticus and Deuteronomy receive the same treatment. Chronology plays a major part in the interpretation; the commentator seems concerned to point out that all the events described be-

---

32. The most recent version of 11QMelch is the new principal edition presented by F. García Martínez, E. J. C. Tigchelaar, and A. S. van der Woude, *Qumran Cave 11. II: 11Q2-18, 11Q20-31,* DJD 23 (Oxford: Clarendon, 1998), 221-41.

33. García Martínez, Tigchelaar, and van der Woude, *Qumran Cave 11. II: 11Q2-18, 11Q20-31,* 222.

long in the tenth jubilee and that the ultimate Day of Atonement occurs at the end of that jubilee period.

The second section (11QMelch 2:8-13) seems to start with a statement about Melchizedek, who was spoken about in the interpretation of the previous section. The section is concerned to define the judgment he exercises. The scriptural quotations are from Psalms 82:1, 7:8-9, and 82:2. Melchizedek is represented as chairing the divine council, exercising judgment on God's behalf. The interpretation is introduced by a formula including the word *pesher*. It is concerned with Belial and those of his lot against whom the judgment falls and from whom Melchizedek seeks to deliver those he enslaves.

The third section (11QMelch 2:14-25) opens with a statement about those who help Melchizedek at this time. The circumstances of the time are then elucidated through another scriptural quotation, Isaiah 52:7, which is then interpreted phrase by phrase. This variation in the style of the interpretation leads to a different organization of the material. Within the interpretation of the various parts of Isaiah 52:7 are supporting secondary quotations, Daniel 9:25, Isaiah 61:2-3, and Isaiah 8:11. The quotation of Daniel 9 tells when and by whom the proclamation of Isaiah 52:7 will be made. It seems to suggest an addition to the periodization of the tenth jubilee of the column's opening section: after another seven weeks an anointed one will come. The subsidiary quotation of Isaiah 61:2-3 makes explicit the content of what is to be proclaimed to Zion according to Isaiah 52:7. The citation of Isaiah 61 also picks up the earlier allusions to the same text and its context in 11QMelch 2:4 ("to proclaim liberty to the captives"), in 11QMelch 2:9 ("the year of favour"), and 11QMelch 2:14 ("righteousness").

The last section (11QMelch 2:25ff.), the start of which is indicated by a space in the manuscript, begins directly with a quotation of Leviticus 25:9. The fragmentary interpretation at the top of column 3 seems to imply that the law is in favor of those whom the text addresses and that the judgment which will take place on the great Day of Atonement, when Belial will be consumed by fire, is assured. The section seems to recapitulate some motifs already mentioned in earlier sections.

Three features of 11QMelchizedek are worth highlighting in this overall discussion of thematic commentaries. First, the structure of the commentary differs from the others considered here inasmuch as opening comments are made and the scriptural citations follow in a complex schematic way. Rather than citing a scriptural text first and providing interpretation for it, the theme controls the commentary throughout. Second, it is noteworthy that scholars have been unable to identify convincingly which scriptural text is acting as the control in any one section of the commentary.[34] This may be partly reflected in the very organization of the commentary: it is the theme that is the control rather than any particular text, but scriptural passages are also interwoven throughout the commentary, making it difficult for any single scriptural text to inform, let alone control, any particular section of commentary. A third feature of 11QMelchizedek is its interest in chronology. Although little more than a single column of text survives, it could well be argued that the commentary's attention to the jubilee periods acts as the guiding principle upon which the whole interpretation hangs. Two more examples of thematic commentaries that have major chronological concerns will indicate this as a common concern in greater detail. It is not just a matter of reflecting on what will be fulfilled in "the latter days," but of identifying more precisely the period in which the community stands and the precise circumstances which belong to each period in an overall scheme of history which is understood to be coming to its climax.

4QAges of Creation (4Q180-181)

Little need be said about the fragments that belong to these two manuscripts that probably contain independent but related compositions. J. T. Milik considered not only that they were two versions of the same composition and so could readily be used to restore each other, but also that 4Q180 in particular contained the opening of the composition that was nearing its end in what survived in 11QMelchizedek.[35] Closer analysis by D. Dimant has suggested that all three manuscripts should be treated as containing discrete compositions.[36]

What remains of these two manuscripts contains very little by way of explicit scriptural quotation. 4Q180 opens with the phrase "Pesher concerning the periods made by God, (each) period in order to complete (all that is) and all that will be." It thus purports to contain some kind of interpretative

---

34. The two major options are Lev. 25 represented by J. A. Fitzmyer, *Essays on the Semitic Background of the New Testament* (London: Chapman, 1971), 251 ("The thread which apparently runs through the whole text and ties together its various elements is Lv 25"), and Isa. 61 represented by M. P. Miller, "The Function of Isa 61:1-2 in 11Q Melchizedek," *JBL* 88 (1969): 467 ("the passage stands behind our document and appears in the form of Stichwörter at crucial points").

35. J. T. Milik, "Milkî-ṣedeq et Milkî-reša' dans les anciens écrits juifs et chrétiens," *JJS* 23 (1972): 109-26.

36. D. Dimant, "The 'Pesher on the Periods' (4Q180) and 4Q181," *Israel Oriental Studies* 9 (1979): 77-102.

commentary. However, the commentary is not directly on scripture but on scripture summarized into a periodic scheme of some kind. Whereas the chronological concerns of 11QMelchizedek are commented upon with several interwoven scriptural quotations, the chronological concerns of 4Q180 and 4Q181 are reflected more in a summary retelling of scripture. These two compositions thus resemble some forms of para-biblical composition more than they form sound examples of thematic commentary. It is certainly the case that no unfulfilled prophetic text of any kind is discernible as the basis for the composition of either 4Q180 or 4Q181.

4QCommentary on Genesis A (4Q252)

As with 4Q180 and 4Q181, a similar question has arisen concerning the most suitable classification of 4QCommentary on Genesis A. Small fragments of several commentaries on Genesis have survived. The most complete is 4QCommentary on Genesis A. It originally had six columns of somewhat unequal width, written on a single sheet of leather. Its opening column is well preserved and there are substantial extant portions of columns 2, 5, and 6. The rest is very fragmentary. The Commentary contains interpretations of several different sections of Genesis, presented in the order of the scriptural text.

At the outset (1:1–2:5) there is a rewriting of the flood narrative from Genesis 6:3–8:18. The purpose of the rewriting is to align the dates of the Genesis narrative with the 364-day calendar that the narrative might be read as reflecting. The commentary, identifying the various events of the flood account with particular days of the months and days of the week, is done through the same kind of implicit exegesis found in the *Reworked Pentateuch* and the book of *Jubilees*. This opening section is closer to rewritten Bible than to commentary in the form of quotation with interpretation. A second section (2:5-8) is a bridging passage from Noah to Abraham; it contains three poetic half-lines that may well come from a source. In a third section there is attention to the chronology of events surrounding Abram. In column 3 there are fragmentary remains of at least three further sections: the first is an adaptation of the Sodom and Gomorrah episode to which is applied the law concerning the idolatrous city (Deut. 13:13-19), the second is an abbreviation of the narrative of the binding of Isaac with no apparent comment, and the third a probable use of Isaac's blessing of Jacob for some purpose. Column 4 contains the quotation of Genesis 36:12 together with an interpretation which is formulaically introduced; the interpretation is reminiscent of similar passages in 1 Samuel 14:48, 15:3 and 7. Columns 5 and 6 contain the quotation of portions of the blessings of Jacob together with interpretations that are introduced with formulae using the word *pesher*.

Is this collection of interpretative materials a thematic commentary? The materials have been organized in the running order of Genesis itself, from Genesis 6 to Genesis 49, but the varying forms of the individual sections and their likely purposes make the question difficult to answer. On the one hand are those who incline toward seeing some kind of unity behind the compilation of interpretative pericopae.[37] Amongst the thematic possibilities, at least for some sections, are the concerns with unfulfilled blessings and curses: the curse of Canaan and exclusion of Japhet, the unfulfilled curse of the Amalekites, the blessing of Jacob, and Jacob's blessing of his sons. Many of these passages also seem to be linked to the promise of the land; perhaps the author or compiler viewed himself as having the right credentials to take possession of the land. Sexual misdemeanors lie behind several of the pericopae too, as do various calendrical and chronological issues. On the other hand, it has been demonstrated by M. J. Bernstein not only that the variety of interpretative forms is somewhat inconsistent with a thematic commentary with some kind of overarching message, but also that several of the individual sections can be read as offering solutions to conundrums in the plain meaning of the text of Genesis, thus apparently rendering the search for an overall theme redundant.[38]

It is clear that 4QCommentary on Genesis A is not a thematic commentary like 4Q174 or 11QMelchizedek. However, several features make its consideration here worthwhile. To begin with, like most of the compositions considered in this chapter, its units of interpretation follow the sequence of the scriptural text; scripture is acting as some kind of control. Second, it is clear that 4Q252 makes no attempt at providing comments on every part of Genesis; some kind of process of selection has taken place. Third, it is highly likely, given the range of genres within this interpretative collection, that whoever compiled 4Q252 did so from a number of other literary sources. This obser-

---

37. The strongest advocates of some kind of thematic interpretation of 4Q252 are G. J. Brooke, "The Thematic Content of 4Q252," *JQR* 85 (1994): 33-59; and I. Fröhlich, "'Narrative Exegesis' in the Dead Sea Scrolls," in *Biblical Perspectives: Early Use and Interpretation of the Bible in Light of the Dead Sea Scrolls. Proceedings of the First International Symposium of the Orion Center for the Study of the Dead Sea Scrolls and Associated Literature*, ed. M. E. Stone and E. G. Chazon, STDJ 28 (Leiden: Brill, 1998), 81-99.

38. M. J. Bernstein, "4Q252: From Re-Written Bible to Biblical Commentary," *JJS* 45 (1994): 1-27; M. J. Bernstein, "4Q252: Method and Context, Genre and Sources," *JQR* 85 (1994): 61-79.

vation seems to be confirmed by the way in which the opening sentence of the commentary contains a pronominal suffix with no apparent antecedent. Fourth, at least some of the interpretative sections of 4Q252 involve unfulfilled blessings and curses; in fact, those sections that do so most closely resemble in format sections of 4Q174. Each of these characteristics overlaps with features that belong to one or more of the other commentaries discussed briefly in this chapter.

The Damascus Document

The *Damascus Document* is not a thematic commentary on a set of prophetic texts. The kind of scriptural interpretation it contains, for the most part, is of an exhortatory kind, appealing to scriptural passages to encourage a particular attitude or mode of behavior. For the section of the composition known as the Admonition, J. G. Campbell has provided the most thorough and convincing analysis of the place of scripture in the overall argument of the work. He has proposed that a body of scriptural passages underlies most of the Admonition. Although this argues for the literary coherence of the Admonition, it does not exclude the possibility that the author or compiler of the Admonition used sources as he worked.

It is the possibility of the use of sources that makes it worthwhile including the *Damascus Document* in this description of some of the features of the thematic commentaries. Two short sections in the Admonition are very close in format to what is found in 4Q174, 4Q177, and 11QMelchizedek. The so-called "well midrash" in column 6 is an interpretation of the song (possibly understood as oracular) in Numbers 21:18 through the use of Isaiah 59:20, 54:16, and Hosea 10:12. The so-called "Amos-Numbers midrash" in column 7 is similarly complex in its construction and uses Isaiah 7:17, Amos 5:26-27, Amos 9:11, and Numbers 24:17 (from Balaam's oracle). The compact argumentation in both these short sections and their evident use of prophetic texts render it possible that use is being made of some kind of thematic commentary as the author of the *Damascus Document* constructs his overall argument.

Conclusion

What do we have overall? An enormous range of scriptural exegesis has been considered in this short chapter, and many other fragmentary compositions might have deserved a place. A set of characteristics emerges from this summary analysis of some key texts.

Thematic commentaries on prophetic scriptures are commonly organized with attention to the sequence of the scriptural texts themselves. This is clear in 4QTestimonia, highly likely in 4Q174, visible in 4QCommentary on Genesis A, but less obvious in a work like the *Damascus Document,* which is not a thematic commentary but may be using extracts from one or more such compositions.

Thematic commentaries are constructed selectively. Not only is the selection of scriptural passages for interpretation determined by the theme, but also the choice of passages may be influenced by a range of sources. The excerpts cited in 4QTestimonia were not all taken from a single scriptural scroll. The exegetical sections of 4Q174 may have been taken from a range of other exegetical works in which formulae were used in different ways. The amazing variety of genres in 4QCommentary on Genesis A strongly suggests that several sources have played a part in the compilation of the commentary.

The thematic commentaries on prophetic scriptures from Qumran appear to focus on unfulfilled blessings, curses, promises, oracles, and visions. The range of authoritative material that can be used as the basis for thematic comment is thus far wider than the oracles of the literary prophets. It is not uncommon to find sections from the Law and from the historical books. Special recognition is also given to the Psalms and possibly to other songs; they are viewed as prophecy.

The thematic commentaries take a variety of forms and use a wide range of interpretative formulae. Sometimes the prophetic text is cited first and then given commentary, often with the use of supplementary prophetic passages. Sometimes the scripture is briefly introduced (4QTestimonia; the psalms in 4Q174) or preceded by an elaborate comment that demonstrates how the prophetic text is to be viewed (11QMelchizedek). In the interpretative sections there does not seem to be any necessary privileging of formulae that contain the word *pesher;* many other formulaic devices are used, as indeed is the case in many of the so-called continuous *pesharim,* especially when sections of prophecy are requoted and their constituent elements identified.

Not surprisingly, thematic commentaries on prophetic scriptural passages are commonly concerned with eschatological matters. The prophecies are understood as being fulfilled in the experiences of the readers or hearers, or very shortly so to be fulfilled. However, alongside this interest in fulfillment runs an entirely compatible concern with chronology. The counting of periods or jubilees or weeks enables the commentator to demonstrate where his readership stands in relation to the end. This two-sided interest in the end times or the latter days that lead up to the end and anticipate it results in many prophetic images receiving narrow historical interpretations. A general motif is commonly historicized, though often not to the point where ongoing nonfulfillment would render the commentary or its author redundant.

The thematic commentaries discussed here do not seem to contain any special interpretative techniques. The same kinds of interpretative processes as have been variously described for the continuous *pesharim* and other exegetical works are also used in these thematic commentaries. The general process of atomistic interpretation is achieved through a large number of hermeneutical devices.

All the compositions considered here are sectarian. They reflect the concerns, the ideology, and the language of the principal sectarian texts. Nevertheless, they may reflect exegetical activity far beyond the narrow confines of their own community. These thematic commentaries reveal a diverse richness in exegetical form, content, and method.

The Prophet David at Qumran

PETER W. FLINT

The figure of David in the Hebrew Bible/Old Testament brings distinctive qualities to mind. The biblical references may be grouped in several categories: David as Israel's greatest king, the ancestor of the Messiah, a righteous example, a repentant sinner, the man after God's own heart, the psalmist par excellence.

An examination of the nonbiblical scrolls found at Qumran reveals several of the same qualities. In the *Commentary on Genesis A* (4Q252), for example, we read of the *Righteous Messiah*, the *Branch of David* (col. 5:3); and in the *Florilegium* (4Q174) the Messiah is described as the *Shoot of David*:

> 10"Moreover the LORD decl[ares] to you that He will make you a house," and that "I will raise up your offspring after you, and establish the throne of his kingdom 11[fore]ver. I will be a father to him, and he will be My son" (2 Sam 7:11c, 12b, 13b-14a). This passage refers to the *Shoot of David*, who is to arise with 12the Interpreter of the Law, and who will [arise] in Zi[on in the La]st Days. . . .[1]

David is also presented as a righteous example and a man of virtue: for example, in 4QMMT (4Q397-399), which describes him as "a man of pious works who was saved from many sufferings" (section C: 25-26).

The present paper considers whether David was also viewed or interpreted prophetically in some of the Qumran scrolls. Investigation shows that David is not called a prophet or said to prophesy in the Qumran corpus, which is somewhat surprising since he is clearly viewed as such in several writings from the early part of the common era.

---

1. Translation from M. Wise, M. Abegg, and E. Cook, *The Dead Sea Scrolls: A New Translation* (San Francisco: Harper San Francisco, 1997), 227-28.

David Called a Prophet or Said to Prophesy in Other Writings

Some New Testament texts describe David as a prophet or associate him with prophecy, most notably Peter's Pentecost sermon in Acts 2:25-30:

> 25For David says concerning him, "I saw the Lord always before me, for he is at my right hand so that I will not be shaken. . . ." 29Fellow Israelites, I may say to you confidently of our ancestor David that he both died and was buried, and his tomb is with us to this day. 30Since he was *a prophet,* he knew that God had sworn with an oath to him that he would put one of his descendants on his throne.

Several comparable passages are found in Josephus's *Antiquities,* although the Jewish historian prefers to use the verb over the noun: "So Samuel, when he had given him these admonitions, went away. But the Divine Power departed from Saul, and removed to David; who, upon this removal of the Divine Spirit to him, *began to prophesy*" (6.8.2 166).

The Psalms Targum also uses prophetic language with respect to David, with an apparent emphasis on the noun "prophecy." In the following examples,[2] the Targumist pointedly adds that David speaks in the spirit of prophecy:

Masoretic Text (NRSV)	*Psalms Targum (trans. E. Cook)*[3]
You are the most handsome of men; grace is poured upon your lips; therefore God has blessed you forever. (Ps. 45:2)	Your beauty, O King Messiah, is greater than the sons of men; *the spirit of prophecy* has been placed on your lips; because of this the Lord has blessed you forever. (Tg. Ps. 45:3)
But God will ransom my soul from the power of Sheol, for he will receive me. (Ps. 49:15)	David said in *the spirit of prophecy,* Truly God will redeem my soul from the judgment of Gehenna, for he will teach me his Torah forever. (Tg. Ps. 49:16)

2. Although the first example is addressed "O King Messiah," the previous verse in both the Masoretic Text and the Psalms Targum indicates that the Psalms are addressed to the king.

3. Published on the Internet at http://www.tulane.edu/%7Entcs/pss/tg_s_ps_index .htm.

David is also seen as a prophet or associated with prophecy in some rabbinic writings. In a passage from the Babylonian Talmud, for example, he is specifically called a prophet: "Who are the first prophets? Rabbi Huna said: 'They are David, Samuel, and Solomon'" (*b. Soṭa* 48b).

Prophesying and Prophets in the Hebrew Bible

In order to understand the use of terms denoting prophets and prophecy at Qumran, a brief survey of prophets and prophesying in the Hebrew Bible is required. The later texts reveal that several writers viewed the main term for prophet with some uneasiness or suspicion.

The verb "to prophesy" (נבא) is found some 103 times in the Hebrew Bible (e.g., 1 Sam. 10:13). The less common noun is "prophecy" (נבואה), which occurs only four times in late biblical texts (2 Chron. 9:29; 15:8; Ezra 6:14; Neh. 6:12). By far the most frequent term is the noun "prophet" or *nabi'* (נביא), which is found 291 times. According to Robert W. Wilson, the *nabi'* is "a person who serves as a channel of communication between the human and divine worlds."[4] However, this is not the preferred term throughout Israel's history.

In the Deuteronomistic History and the literature influenced by it (i.e., Deuteronomy, Joshua, Judges, Samuel, Kings, Hosea, Jeremiah), *nabi'* is the preferred title for denoting a prophet. But the term is used less frequently in writings that originated in Judah and Jerusalem (especially Amos, Micah, Isaiah, Chronicles), and often occurs in negative contexts. In these southern writings the preferred term is "visionary" or *hozeh* (חזה).[5]

There are three other, less common, titles used for prophets in the Hebrew Bible. The "seer" (ראה) is found in 1 Samuel in reference to Samuel (e.g., 9:9). This term seems to have disappeared in the early monarchical period. The "man of God" is used especially in prophetic stories set in the time of Elijah and Elisha (1 Kings 17–2 Kings 10). Finally, the term "sons of the prophets" was used to describe hierarchically structured prophetic groups or guilds.

---

4. Wilson, "Prophet," in *HarperCollins Bible Dictionary,* ed. P. Achtemeier et al., rev. ed. (New York: HarperCollins, 1996), 884-89, esp. 884.

5. Wilson, "Prophet," 885.

Prophesying and Prophets in the Scrolls

The verb "to prophesy" (נבא) is very rare in the scrolls (with only nine instances in the Cave 4 material). Eight of these are in the *Pseudo-Ezekiel Text* (4Q385-386), which essentially paraphrases Ezekiel's vision of the dry bones in chapter 37. More significant is the ninth example, a section from the *Damascus Document* that refers to the prophets of Israel as "the holy anointed ones" (משיחי הקודש, CD 5:21–6:1). In this passage the author condemns their opponents, because "they prophesy falsehood in order to turn Israel from God" (CD 6:1).

The noun "prophecy" (נבואה) occurs only once in the Qumran corpus: in the prose epilogue of the Great Psalms Scroll (11QPs^a 27:11) as the means by which David composed his liturgies, and which is given to him by God. This important passage will be discussed in further detail below.

As in the Hebrew Bible, the most common term in the present context is "prophet" or *nabi'* (נביא). However, while it occurs more often than the verb (some thirty-three cases in the Cave 4 scrolls), this noun is quite infrequent. The term is used in at least seven ways. (1) The most common occurrence is for classical prophets, who are named: for example, Ezekiel the prophet (CD 3:21); Isaiah the prophet (CD 4:13); Jeremiah the prophet (4Q385 frg. 16 i 2); the prophet Habakkuk (1QpHab 1:1); and the prophet Zechariah (CD 19:7). (2) "Prophet" or *nabi'* is also used for the prophets in general. In the *Rule of the Community*, for example, Isaiah 40:3 is explained as "the expounding of the Law, decreed by God through Moses for obedience, that being defined by what has been revealed for each age, and by what the prophets have revealed by his holy spirit" (1QS 8:15-16).[6] (3) The term also features in the phrase "My/his servants the prophets," for example, "just as he commanded through Moses and all His servants the prophets" (1QS 1:2-3; see also 1QSb 1:27). (4) This noun also denotes the written books of the prophets, whether alone or in combination with other groups of scriptures. In the *Damascus Document*, for example, the "foundation of your images" found in Amos 5:26 denotes the books of the prophets (CD 7:17); a passage in 4QMMT speaks of "Moses and the [books of the prophet]s" (4Q397 frgs. 14-21.15 [C17]); a few lines earlier, the same text refers to "the book of Moses, the book[s of the Pr]ophets, and Davi[d" (4Q397 frg. 14-21.10 [C10]). (5) The *nabi'* will be the Qumran community's end-time prophet "until there come the Prophet and the Messiahs of Aaron and Israel" (1QS 9:11). (6) The term is used for a new Mosaic prophet: "I will raise up for them a prophet like you

---

6. Wise, Abegg, and Cook, *The Dead Sea Scrolls*, 138.

from among their own people . . ." (4Q175 1:5). (7) Finally, this noun denotes modern-day prophets, most often in a pejorative sense: "the words of lying prophets corrupted by error" (1QHod 12:16), and in the phrase "prophet" or "interpreter of dreams" (11QT^a 54:8). This negative sense is especially evident in a passage from the *Temple Scroll* that deals with a false prophet:

> (The prophet who presumes) to de[clare something] in [My na]me [that I have n]ot commanded [him to] declare, or who [speaks in the name of ot]her go[ds] — 2that prophet must be put to death. You may say to yourselves, "How shall we recognize that 3which the Lord has not spoken?" When a prophet speaks in the name of the Lord but the prophecy is not fulfilled 4and does not come to pass, that is a prophecy I have not spoken. The prophet spoke rebelliously; do not fear 5him. (11QT^a 61:1-5)[7]

This brief survey indicates that, as in the several later texts from the Hebrew Bible, the Qumran writers viewed the main term for prophet in a rather negative light. A more positive view, however, is evident where the classical prophets or their written books are being referred to.

David as Prophet or Associated with Prophecy in the Scrolls

In light of the previous section, it is not surprising that the Qumran writers were coy or reluctant to name David directly as a prophet. Other evidence, however, indicates that they nevertheless regarded David as having a prophetic function or qualities.

David's Compositions

The most significant passage is "David's Compositions," which is preserved in column 27 of 11QPs^a (11Q5). There we read that David composed his psalms and songs through "prophecy" (נבואה):

> 2And David, the son of Jesse, was wise, and a light like the light of the sun, and literate, 3and discerning and perfect in all his ways before God and men. And the LORD gave 4him a discerning and enlightened spirit. And he wrote 53,600 psalms; and songs to sing before the altar over the whole-burnt 6perpetual offering every day, for all the days of the year, 364; 7and for the offering of the Sabbaths, 52 songs; and for the offering of the New

7. Wise, Abegg, and Cook, *The Dead Sea Scrolls*, 488.

8Moons and for all the Solemn Assemblies and for the Day of Atonement, 30 songs. 9And all the songs that he spoke were 446, and songs 10for making music over the stricken, 4. And the total was 4,050. 11All these he composed through prophecy which was given him from before the Most High. (col. 27:2-11)[8]

This passage has rich implications: David is endowed with wisdom ("wise, . . . discerning. . . . And the LORD gave him a discerning and enlightened spirit"), perfect in his ways, and the composer of psalms and other songs. As has often been noted, the numbers of these psalms and songs reflect the solar calendar that was followed by the Qumran covenanters.[9]

In my earlier monograph, the chapter titled "David's Solar Psalter: The Structure and Provenance of 11QPs[a]" maintains that one key for understanding the structure of 11QPs[a] is the solar calendar, which contains 364 days and fifty-two weeks. Although only forty-nine compositions are represented in 11QPs[a], the proposed structural outline of the original scroll incorporates fifty-six compositions. I suggest that 11QPs[a] originally contained fifty-two psalms, which correspond with the weeks of the solar year, plus an additional four pieces that serve to assert Davidic authorship of the entire collection.[10] These are David's Last Words and David's Compositions, which together form an extended epilogue, and the (only) truly autobiographical psalms, 151A and 151B, whose function is to assert Davidic authorship of the 11QPs[a]-Psalter.

Michael Chyutin holds a related but more elaborate viewpoint: the redaction of the book of Psalms is connected to the "wars of the calendars," and is found in two forms: 11QPs[a] based on the solar calendar of 364 days, and the "traditional" book of Psalms based on the lunar calendar of 354 days. The Israeli scholar understands the "Qumranic Book of Psalms" as comprising a sample collection of David's songs in a calendrical sequence:[11] 25 percent of the Psalms for every day, 50 percent of the Sabbath Psalms, all the Psalms for the New Moons and Festivals, and all for the intercalary days.[12] In accordance with these figures, the number of compositions found in this Psalter totals 151:

8. Translation: J. Sanders, *The Dead Sea Psalms Scroll* (Ithaca, N.Y.: Cornell University Press, 1967), 87.

9. For example, Sanders, *Dead Sea Psalms Scroll*, 134.

10. P. W. Flint, *The Dead Sea Psalms Scrolls and the Book of Psalms*, STDJ 17 (Leiden: Brill, 1997), 172-201.

11. Chyutin, "The Redaction of the Qumranic and the Traditional Book of Psalms as a Calendar," *RevQ* 63 (1994): 367-95, esp. 367.

12. Chyutin ("Redaction," 370) interprets the "Four Songs for making music over the Stricken (הפגועים)" as days of "meeting," and thus as intercalary days. For the sense of "to meet" for the root פגע he cites Josh. 19:11-34, esp. vv. 11, 22, 26, 27, and 34.

Psalms for every day	91 (= 25% of 364)
Psalms for Sabbaths	26 (= 50% of 52)
Psalms for New Moons and Festivals	30
Psalms for intercalary days	4
Total number of Psalms	151

Chyutin adds that David's Last Words and David's Compositions together form a prose conclusion to the calendrical portion, and explains the problematic position of the final four psalms in 11QPs^a (140, 134, 151A, 151B) by classifying them as "additional."[13] For him these pieces were not included in the Qumranic Book of Psalms because they deal with war and victory — specifically the victory of the Sons of Light over the Sons of Darkness in the future, which would be a unique and noncalendrical event.[14] (I have provided a critique of Chyutin's work elsewhere.)[15]

Although much more could be said concerning the calendar, the point made here is that David's Compositions claims David to have composed a great number of psalms and other songs "through prophecy which was given him from before the Most High." The key term "prophecy" confirms that for the compiler and his audience, (a) the form of the Psalter preserved in 11QPs^a is authoritative and from God himself; (b) that this Psalter has been compiled in accordance with the solar calendar; and (c) that David composed many psalms and songs in addition to those found in the book of Psalms. The author of David's Compositions falls shy of actually calling David a prophet, but implies this by his use of the word "prophecy."

David's Compositions was probably not written by the Qumran community; there is also no evidence that the collection (the 11QPs^a-Psalter) in which it is found was compiled at Qumran.[16] Nevertheless, this was the main edition of the book of Psalms used at Qumran, and was authoritative for the community.[17]

13. Compare the superscription to Ps. 151 in the Septuagint, denoting that this psalm is "outside the number" (ἔξωθεν τοῦ ἀριθμοῦ).
14. Chyutin, "Redaction," 381-82.
15. Flint, Dead Sea Psalms Scrolls, 182-86.
16. Flint, Dead Sea Psalms Scrolls, 198-200.
17. For this proposal and opposing views (with bibliography), see the chapter "True Psalter or Secondary Collection?" in Flint, Dead Sea Psalms Scrolls, 202-27.

The Pesharim

A number of *pesharim* (commentaries) were written on the psalms of David: 1QpPs (1Q16), 4QpPs^a (4Q171), and 4QpPs^b (4Q173). Virtually all the other *pesharim* were written on prophetic books: Isaiah,[18] Hosea,[19] Micah,[20] Nahum,[21] Habakkuk,[22] Zephaniah,[23] and Malachi.[24] In general, the *pesharim* deal with central issues in the life of the Qumran community, with several containing references to the Teacher of Righteousness, the Wicked Priest, and the Man of the Lie.

The largest surviving pieces of 4QpPs^a (4Q171) preserve a running commentary on Psalm 37. The righteous are to keep faith in God despite the successes of the wicked. God will ensure that both righteous and wicked get their due: the righteous will receive a reward for their faithfulness; the wicked will receive punishment. The men of the *Yaḥad* and their leader, the Teacher of Righteousness, represent the righteous, while their enemies, the Wicked Priest and the Man of the Lie, who have persecuted them, represent the wicked. In column 1:17–2:5, for instance, Psalm 37:7-9 is interpreted as referring to the Man of the Lie and those who return to the Law:

> 17*[Be] silent before [the Lord and] wait for him, and do not be jealous of the successful man* 18*who does wicked deeds.* (Ps. 37:7)

> [This refers] to the Man of the Lie who led many people astray with deceitful 19statements, because they had chosen trivial matters but did not listen to the spokesmen for true knowledge, so that Col. 2:1they will perish by sword, famine, and pestilence.

> *Renounce your anger and abandon your resentment, don't* 2*yearn to do evil, because evildoers will be wiped out.* (Ps. 37:8-9)

> This refers to all who return 3to the Law and do not hesitate to repent of their sin, because all who refuse 4to repent of their faults will be wiped out.

> *But those who trust in the Lord are the ones who will inherit the earth.* (Ps. 37:9)

18. 3QpIsa^a (3Q4), 4QpIsa^{a-e} (4Q161-165).
19. 4QpHos^{a,b} (4Q166-167).
20. 1QpMic (1Q14), 4QpMic? (4Q168).
21. 4QpNah (4Q169).
22. 1QpHab.
23. 1QpZeph (1Q15), 4QpZeph (4Q170).
24. 5QpMal? (5Q10).

This refers 5to the company of his chosen, those who do his will.[25]

In column 4 of the same text, Psalm 37:32-33 is interpreted as indicating the Wicked Priest's desire to kill the Teacher. The commentary also refers to the Law that the Teacher sent to the Priest, which some scholars have identified with 4QMMT. The broken text later appears to understand Psalm 37:35-36 as referring to the end of the Man of the Lie:

> 7*The wicked man observes the righteous man and seeks [to kill him. But the Lo]rd [will not leave him in his power and will not co]ndemn him when he comes to trial.* (Ps. 37:32-33)

> 8This refers to the Wicked [Pri]est who ob[serv]es the [Teach]er of Righteous[ness and seeks] to kill him [. . .] and the Law 9that he sent to him, but God will not le[ave him in his power] and will not [condemn him when] he comes to trial. But to the [wicked God will give] his just [de]serts, by putting him 10into the power of the cruel Gentiles to do with him [what they want]. . . .

> 13*[I once saw] a wicked man, cruel, and stretched [out like a stately tree. But] when I passed by his home again, he was gone. I [looked for him] but he was* 14*[nowhere to be found].* (Ps. 37:35-36)

> [This refers to] the Man of the Lie, [who . . .] against God's chosen people [and sou]ght to put an end to [. . .] 15[. . .] judgment [. . .] he defiantly presumed 16[. . .][26]

Conclusion

Although some New Testament texts, the Psalms Targum, and some rabbinic writings describe David as a prophet or associate him with prophecy, this aspect is relatively rare in the Qumran corpus. The verb "to prophesy" (נבא) is very infrequent, the noun "prophecy" (נבואה) occurs only once, and the noun "prophet" or *nabi'* (נביא) occurs some thirty-three times in the Cave 4 scrolls. In the case last mentioned, however, the Qumran writers viewed *nabi'* in a negative light, except where the classical prophets or their written books are being referred to.

This uneasiness is understood with reference to the Hebrew Bible itself,

25. Translation: Wise, Abegg, and Cook, *The Dead Sea Scrolls*, 220-21.
26. Wise, Abegg, and Cook, *The Dead Sea Scrolls*, 223.

where writings that originated in Judah and Jerusalem show that several writers viewed the term *nabi'* with some suspicion. In these southern writings the preferred term is "visionary" or *ḥozeh* (חזה).

Nevertheless, there is evidence that at least some of the Qumran community regarded David as a prophet or as having prophetic qualities. Evidence includes David's Compositions, which tells us that David composed his psalms and songs through prophecy (נבואה). David's Compositions was probably not written by the Qumran community, but was authoritative to them as part of the 11QPsᵃ-Psalter, which was the main edition of the book of Psalms used at Qumran.

David's association with prophecy is also seen in the three *pesharim* written on the Psalms of David: 1QpPs (1Q16), 4QpPsᵃ (4Q171), and 4QpPsᵇ (4Q173). Almost all the other *pesharim* were written on prophetic books, which strongly suggests that these three *pesharim* associate David with prophecy or indicate that he was viewed as a prophet. The *Psalms Pesharim* (notably 4QpPsᵃ) interpret several passages from the Psalms as referring to central issues in the life of the Qumran community, including the men of the יחד and the Teacher of Righteousness as representing the righteous, and the Wicked Priest and the Man of the Lie as representing the wicked. These commentaries indicate that for the men of the יחד, the psalmist David was viewed as a prophet to whom God revealed later and significant events in their lives and community.

Psalm 91 in Premodern Interpretation and at Qumran

MATTHIAS HENZE

Hardly any book of the Hebrew Bible has had so great an impact on early Judaism and early Christianity as the book of Psalms. Its hymns and prayers have been incorporated into, indeed have shaped Jewish and Christian liturgies for over two millennia. Since late antiquity the mere recitation of individual psalms has been regarded as an act of piety. In some Jewish circles the Psalter was viewed as the divinely ordained book of mandatory prophetic prayers, while elsewhere it was seen as a book of divine revelation comparable to the Torah.[1] The psalms played an equally important role in early Christianity. Throughout the first three centuries of the common era the book of Psalms, together with Isaiah, remained the prophetic book most used for apologetic and pastoral purposes. It was the desire of early Christians "to understand Christ's prayer and to participate in it as a church."[2]

The community at Qumran shared the same appreciation of the book

---

1. Jewish conceptions of the Psalter since late antiquity are discussed by U. Simon, *Four Approaches to the Book of Psalms: From Saadiah Gaon to Abraham Ibn Ezra* (New York: SUNY, 1991; Hebrew ed., Ramat Gan: Bar Ilan University Press, 1982); see also J. L. Kugel, "Topics in the History of the Spirituality of the Psalms," in *Jewish Spirituality: From the Bible through the Middle Ages*, ed. A. Green (New York: Crossroad, 1994), 113-44.

2. J. Gribomot, "Psalms, Book of," in *Encyclopedia of the Early Church* (New York: Oxford University Press, 1992), 2:722. For a formidable survey of early Christian commentaries on the Psalter, see Marie-Josèphe Rondeau, *Les commentaires patristiques du psautier, IIIe-Ve siècles*, Orientalia Christiana Analecta 219-20 (Rome: Pont. Institutum Studiorum Orientalium, 1982).

of Psalms. The three books in the Hebrew Bible most often quoted in the New Testament — the Psalms, Isaiah, and Deuteronomy — are also among the most frequently attested biblical books among the Dead Sea Scrolls, surely an indication of their importance to the community.[3] Leading the list with thirty-nine manuscripts is the book of Psalms.[4] The discovery of the Dead Sea Scrolls has furthered greatly our understanding of the role the psalms played in early Judaism and Christianity in several areas. The scrolls provide invaluable information about the formation of the biblical Psalter, the early history of interpretation of the psalms, as well as about the psalms' liturgical employment, i.e., the use of the psalms in the liturgies of the late Second Temple period.

The subject of this paper is Psalm 91. Following a brief review of psalms scholarship, I will turn to Psalm 91 first and then discuss its reception history in early Judaism and Christianity, particularly in the New Testament. We will see that the overwhelming majority of premodern interpreters read Psalm 91 as an apotropaic hymn believed to possess antidemonic powers. Of the fragments from Qumran, at least one scroll, 11QApocryphal Psalms, used the psalm in precisely this context. It is questionable, however, whether this scroll was composed at Qumran. Another group of apotropaic songs, 4Q510 and 4Q511 in particular, include several elements of distinct sectarian teaching and hence were almost certainly written at Qumran. Unlike 11QApocryphal Psalms, they never refer to Psalm 91 in any explicit way.

Recent Scholarship on the Psalms at Qumran

The discovery of the psalm fragments from the Dead Sea Scrolls has spurred the debate on the stabilization of the biblical Psalter. The discussion has focused primarily on the Psalms Scroll from Cave 11 (11QPs[a], or 11Q5), first edited by James A. Sanders in 1965.[5] Copied in circa 50 c.e., it is the largest of the

---

3. The most recent list published in J. C. VanderKam and P. W. Flint, *The Meaning of the Dead Sea Scrolls: Their Significance for Understanding the Bible, Judaism, Jesus, and Christianity* (San Francisco: Harper San Francisco, 2002), has the book of Psalms lead the list with 39 manuscripts, followed by Deuteronomy (33), Genesis (24), and then Isaiah (18).

4. See P. W. Flint, "Psalms, Book of: Biblical Text," in *Encyclopedia of the Dead Sea Scrolls,* ed. L. H. Schiffman and J. C. VanderKam (New York: Oxford University Press, 2000), 702.

5. J. A. Sanders, *The Psalms Scroll of Qumran Cave 11 (11QPs[a]),* DJD 4 (Oxford: Clarendon, 1965); Sanders, *The Dead Sea Psalms Scroll* (Ithaca, N.Y.: Cornell University Press, 1967).

extant psalm collections from Qumran. The Psalms Scroll includes forty biblical psalms, mostly from Books IV and V of the Psalter, and arranged in an order that diverges at times significantly from that found in the Masoretic Psalter. Notably, the 11Q5 arrangement is confirmed by two other scroll fragments, 4Q87 and 11Q6.[6] Furthermore, there are a total of nine nonbiblical compositions interspersed with the psalms, four of which had previously been known from ancient translations, four that were unknown, plus one prose composition. Sanders, followed by Wilson,[7] has argued in a number of publications that the large Psalms Scroll served as a *canonical* collection of psalms at Qumran, that it was regarded as a true Davidic Psalter, and that it thus represents a fairly late stage in the canonical process of the stabilization of the Psalter. "[T]he Qumran Psalter, represented by 11QPs[a] but also by other more fragmentary Psalter manuscripts from Caves 4 and 11, was revered at Qumran as authoritative as any other Psalter present there: it was 'canonical' at Qumran though by no means closed; on the contrary, it was, while authoritative, still open-ended."[8]

Sanders's assessment of the status of 11Q5 at Qumran was challenged by a number of scholars. Following the early lead of Shemaryahu Talmon[9] and Moshe H. Goshen-Gottstein,[10] Patrick W. Skehan in particular repeatedly argued for the nonbiblical, or secondary, status of the large Psalms Scroll. According to Skehan, 11Q5 is an "instruction book" that is dependent on an already existing MT–150 Psalter. In his own words, "what we have basically in 11QPs[a] is a collection of Pss 101–150 with liturgical regroupings and 'library edition' expansions."[11]

6. P. W. Flint, *The Dead Sea Psalms Scrolls and the Book of Psalms*, STDJ 17 (Leiden: Brill, 1997), 155-71.

7. G. H. Wilson, *The Editing of the Hebrew Psalter*, SBLDS 76 (Chico, Calif.: Scholars Press, 1985).

8. J. A. Sanders, "The Qumran Psalms Scroll (11QPs[a]) Reviewed," in *On Language, Culture, and Religion: In Honor of Eugene A. Nida*, ed. M. Black and W. A. Smalley (The Hague: Mouton, 1974), 98; see also his "*Variorum* in the Psalms Scroll (11QPs[a])," *HTR* 59 (1966): 83-94.

9. Talmon, "Pisqah Be'emsa' Pasuq and 11QPs[a]," *Textus* 5 (1966): 11-21.

10. Goshen-Gottstein, "The Psalms Scroll (11QPs[a]): A Problem of Canon and Text," *Textus* 5 (1966): 22-33. More recently see Ben Zion Wacholder, "David's Eschatological Psalter: 11QPsalms[a]," *HUCA* 59 (1988): 23-72; and M. Haran, "11QPs[a] and the Canonical Book of Psalms," in *Minhah le-Nahum: Biblical and Other Studies Presented to Nahum M. Sarna in Honour of His Seventieth Birthday*, ed. M. Brettler and M. Fishbane, JSOTSup 154 (Sheffield: JSOT Press, 1993), 193-201.

11. Skehan, "A Liturgical Complex in 11QPs[a]," *CBQ* 34 (1973): 201 n. 24. Elsewhere Skehan emphasizes that 11Q5 "is not simply a liturgical composition, but what I have called a library edition of the putative works of David, whether liturgical or not." Skehan

The most comprehensive analysis to date of the psalms material from the Dead Sea Scrolls comes from Peter W. Flint. In a series of publications Flint has carefully examined the evidence and has presented his own view, which largely corroborates Sanders's general assessment, albeit with some variation.[12] Building largely on Sanders's work, Flint makes four principal claims. He argues that the stabilization of the Psalter did not happen gradually but in two distinct phases. Psalms 1–89, or roughly the equivalent of Books I-III of the Psalter, were fixed well before the second century B.C.E., while Psalms 90–150, or Books IV-V, were still in a state of flux at that time and only became stable by the end of the first century C.E. Secondly, Flint proposes that there existed at Qumran side by side two — or quite possibly even more — variant editions of the Psalter. Another arrangement could be preserved in fragment 4QPs^f, though the evidence does not allow for any certainty. There is virtual agreement among the manuscripts regarding the arrangement of Psalms 1–89, i.e., in what Flint calls the "early Psalter," whereas there exist at least two different psalm groupings of the remaining psalms, Psalms 90–150. These two arrangements are the Masoretic Text–150 Psalter and the alternate collection represented mainly by the large Psalms Scroll. It is important to note that according to Flint the former is not chronologically prior to the latter but that the two developed independently of each other. Thirdly, while Sanders had originally suggested that the large Psalms Scroll was composed at Qumran yet later modified his view to assume that the scroll was brought there from the outside,[13] Flint asserts that the 11Q5 collection was used by a wider circle of Jewish groups and, in all likelihood, originated before the Qumran period. The fourth and final claim concerns the status of the large Psalms Scroll already discussed above. Flint has been adamant in arguing that the large Psalms Scroll was used at Qumran as Scripture. "[I]t may be stated with some confidence that the 11QPs^a-Psalter is the foremost

---

insists that this collection is secondary to the MT–150 Psalter. "I would restate it as my judgment, that from the way it begins, from the way it ends, and from a number of indications in between, 11QPs^a shows its dependence on the standard collection of 150 Psalms." Skehan, "Qumran and Old Testament Criticism," in *Qumrân: Sa Piété, sa théologie et son milieu*, ed. M. Delcor (Paris-Gembloux: Duculot; Leuven: University Press, 1978), 169 and 172, respectively.

12. In addition to his monograph on the subject see, for example, "The Book of Psalms in the Light of the Dead Sea Scrolls," *VT* 48 (1998): 453-72; and "Psalms and Psalters in the Dead Sea Scrolls," in *The Hebrew Bible and Qumran*, ed. J. H. Charlesworth, The Bible and the Dead Sea Scrolls 1 (North Richland Hills: BIBAL Press, 2000), 307-59.

13. Sanders, "Psalm 154 Revisited," in *Biblische Theologie und gesellschaftlicher Wandel: Für Norbert Lohfink*, ed. G. Braulik et al. (Freiburg: Herder, 1993), 301-2.

representative of the Book of Psalms in the Dead Sea Scrolls. As such it must have been used as Scripture."[14]

Flint's work marks a significant advance in the debate. His comprehensive examination of the evidence has provided a firm basis for further discussion. Sanders and Flint are certainly correct in arguing that there is no compelling reason to ascribe priority, either chronological or canonical, to the Masoretic Text–150 Psalter. Such an assumption is anachronistic and is not borne out by the evidence. We must not assume, furthermore, that the liturgical use of the psalms or the compilation of a liturgical psalm collection *required* a fixed book of Psalms in place, let alone that this book was identical in form with the Masoretic Text–150 Psalter. Even if there existed a fixed book of Psalms, this would not exclude the existence of other psalm collections which were still in a state of flux. Finally, "canonical" and "liturgical" are not mutually exclusive categories. The observations of Skehan and others regarding the redactional and, in particular, liturgical aspects of 11QPs[a] are "extremely helpful," as Sanders himself readily acknowledged,[15] particularly as they explain the arrangement of the Qumran Psalter.[16] But liturgical observations do not necessarily imply that the scroll as a whole was of secondary status.

The other two areas of psalms studies for which the scrolls provide invaluable information, the interpretation of the psalms and their use in the liturgy, are intertwined with one another. The study and interpretation of Scripture on the one hand and the community's liturgical practice on the other were closely related. A revealing passage from the *Community Rule* tells of an institutionalized common Bible study as part of the community's everyday life. "And where there are ten (members) there must not be lacking there a man who studies the Torah day and night continually, each man relieving another. The Many shall spend the third part of every night of the year in unity, reading the Book, studying judgment, and saying benedictions in unity" (1QS 6.6-8).[17] Each member, the text stipulates, is required to devote one-third of each night to the common study. The nocturnal curriculum consisted of three parts. It began with the study of Torah (literally, "to read in the book"), which was followed by lessons in the esoteric teachings of the community, here simply referred to as the studying of "judgment" (מׁשׁפט), and concluded with the

14. Flint, *Dead Sea Psalms Scrolls,* 223.

15. Sanders, "Psalms Scroll (11QPs[a]) Reviewed," 96.

16. Wacholder, "David's Eschatological Psalter: 11QPsalms[a]," 23-72.

17. The translation of the *Community Rule* is that of E. Qimron and J. H. Charlesworth, "Rule of the Community," in *The Dead Sea Scrolls: Hebrew, Aramaic, and Greek Texts with English Translations,* vol. 1, *Rule of the Community and Related Documents,* ed. J. H. Charlesworth (Tübingen: J. C. B. Mohr; Louisville: Westminster, 1994), 27.

common "recitation of blessings." The Hebrew describing the latter compo-
nent of the curriculum, "saying the benedictions in unity" (לברך ביחד), is
ambiguous and could be interpreted either to imply the recital of "benedictions in unity" or, taking יחד as a technical term, "to pray as a Community."
Precisely what these blessings are the text does not say, but it seems likely that
the recital of psalms was at least part of them.[18] The passage succinctly captures the close connection between scriptural study and devotion at Qumran,
in which the psalms occupied a central role. As one scholar of the scrolls has
put it, "[T]his concluding of the nightly study sessions with a liturgical practice suggests that communal study was itself a religious performance."[19]

The continuous encounter with the Psalter in study and devotion left its
mark on the community's own writings. This becomes especially evident in
the liturgical and poetic texts from Qumran.[20] The sectarian liturgies and
prayers in particular show a strong tendency to draw extensively on Scripture,
particularly on the psalms as well as on poetic texts from the Bible found outside the Psalter. Conversely, much can be learned about a document by identifying the scriptural passages it reflects. A good example is the poetic texts of
4Q500-504.[21] 4Q500 (4QBenediction), a highly fragmented text, contains a

18. The same verb, ברך, occurs a few lines earlier in the same column, "Wherever
they [the members of the Community] are found each one with respect to his fellow: the
lesser one shall obey the greater with respect to work and money. And they shall eat (in)
unity, say the benedictions (in) unity, and give counsel (in) unity" (1QS 6:2-3). J. Licht, *The
Rule Scroll: A Scroll from the Wilderness of Judea 1QS 1QSa 1QSb* (Jerusalem: Bialik Institute, 1965 [reprint 1996]; Hebrew), 140, observed that the reference to benedictions is
equally unspecific in either place and simply denotes communal prayer in general. Later in
the *Community Rule* we read about the duties of the "wise leader" or *Maskil:* "He shall
bless (ברך) him [God] (in accord) with the times which he has decreed: at the beginning
of the dominion of light, at its turning-point when it withdraws itself to its assigned dwelling, at the beginning of the watches of darkness when he [God] opens its treasure and
spreads it over [the earth], and at its turning-point when it withdraws itself before the
light, when luminaries shine forth from the realm of holiness" (1QS 9:26–10:3; cf. 1QH
20:4-11, but there the recitation of blessings is omitted). There follows a liturgical calendar
of fixed sacred times for prayer for each day.

19. S. D. Fraade, "Interpretive Authority in the Studying Community at Qumran,"
JJS 44 (1993): 57-58.

20. See the overviews by E. G. Chazon, "Prayers from Qumran and Their Historical
Implications," *DSD* 1, no. 3 (1994): 265-84, and more recently by D. K. Falk, "Prayer in the
Qumran Texts," in *The Cambridge History of Judaism,* vol. 3, *The Early Roman Period,* ed.
W. Horbury et al. (Cambridge: Cambridge University Press, 1999), 852-76.

21. M. Baillet, *Qumrân Grotte 4, III (4Q482-4Q520),* DJD 7 (Oxford: Clarendon,
1982). On the examples that follow see G. J. Brooke, "Psalms 105 and 106 at Qumran," *RevQ*
14, no. 54 (1989): 271-72.

blessing. The terminology throughout is reminiscent of Isaiah 5, while the phrase in line 4, "at the gate of the holy height," is not attested in Isaiah 5 but reflects Psalm 102:20.[22] 4Q501 (4QApocryphal Lamentations B) is a lamentation not unlike chapter 5 of the book of Lamentations. A group of people call on God to deliver them from their current oppressors who are identified as "foreigners" (line 1) and as "the wretched ones of your people" (line 4). The use of the first-person plural suggests that 4Q501 is a communal lament, a genre known from the biblical Psalter (e.g., Pss. 44; 74; 79; 80). It was most likely intended for communal recitation.[23] The language of the lament is again similar to that of the psalms, for example of Psalms 145 and 146. The plea in line 2, "Remember the sons of your covenant," is a direct echo of Psalm 106:45-46.[24] 4Q502 (4QRitual of Marriage) pertains to a ritual of celebration, though the exact nature of the celebration remains elusive. This may be a ritual of marriage as initially proposed by Baillet, a rite for already-married couples who enter the celibate community, or, even though this seems less likely, a New Year celebration.[25] 4Q502 7-10, lines 4-9 contain a joyful psalm, praising God's creation, including rams, flocks, reptiles, and birds. The language is borrowed from Genesis 1 and Psalm 148, "louange cosmique, où la série de créatures invitées à louer Dieu rappelle celle du Ps 148."[26]

4Q504 (4QWords of the Luminaries[a]), finally, is the oldest and most intact copy of the Words of the Luminaries, a work probably of pre-Qumranic origin and attested in two copies.[27] The Words of the Luminaries is a collection of prayers for the consecutive days of the week, consisting of six weekday prayers and ending with two (or possibly more) short prayers for the Sabbath. The consecutive prayers for the days of the week include lengthy historical sections, beginning with the creation of Adam on the first day of the week and culminating on the sixth day in the postexilic period, with the liturgy for the Sabbath standing apart from the chronological scheme. Each of the week-

---

22. Baillet, *Qumrân Grotte 4, III*, 78. J. M. Baumgarten, "4Q500 and the Ancient Exegesis of the Lord's Vineyard," *JJS* 40 (1989): 1-6.

23. J. R. Davila, *Liturgical Works*, Eerdmans Commentaries on the Dead Sea Scrolls 6 (Grand Rapids: Eerdmans, 2000), 178.

24. Brooke, "Psalms 105 and 106," 272.

25. Davila, *Liturgical Works*, 181-207; J. M. Baumgarten, "4Q502, Marriage or Golden Age Ritual?" *JJS* 34 (1983): 125-35; M. L. Satlow, "4Q502 a New Year Festival?" *DSD* 5 (1998): 57-68.

26. Baillet, *Qumrân Grotte 4, III*, 84.

27. 4Q504 and 4Q506. Another fragment, 4Q505, originally believed to be a third copy of the *Words of the Luminaries*, is now thought to be part of 4Q509, *Festival Prayers*; see D. K. Falk, *Daily, Sabbath, and Festival Prayers in the Dead Sea Scrolls*, STDJ 27 (Leiden: Brill, 1998), 59-68.

day prayers includes several formal elements that connect the prayers with each other and suggest that the work as a whole is a deliberate literary composition intended for liturgical use by the community. The same elements are also found in the *Daily Prayers* (4Q503), and in the *Ritual of Marriage* (4Q502) mentioned above.[28]

The connections between the *Words of the Luminaries* and the biblical Psalms are numerous. In the early history of the Jewish liturgy the *Words of the Luminaries* occupies an important place in that it testifies to the existence of set petitions for deliverance for each day of the week that were composed possibly as early as during pre-Qumranic times. Moreover, the custom of assigning a prayer to a particular day of the week is not without precedent. The superscriptions of the Greek Psalter already assign several psalms to specific days: Psalm 24 (LXX 23) to Sunday, Psalm 38 (LXX 37) to the Sabbath, Psalm 48 (LXX 47) to Monday, Psalm 93 (LXX 92) to Friday, and Psalm 94 (LXX 93) to Wednesday. The MT and LXX both assign Psalm 92 (LXX 91) to the Sabbath.[29]

There are also several parallels in language and content between the *Words of the Luminaries* and the biblical psalms. Indeed, the text is "a collage of scriptural quotations and allusions,"[30] with the psalms occupying a prominent role. Like 4Q501, the prayers for the six weekdays fall into the genre of communal lament known from the Bible (see above). The petitions that stand at the heart of each prayer are preceded by historical reviews. Similar reviews are also found in the psalms. For example, the prayer for Thursday begins with an allusion to the exodus, which may be compared with Psalm 78:12, 15, 32, and Psalm 106:7, 9, 14, 22.

In sum, the liturgies and prayers from Qumran are fully immersed in biblical literature and heavily draw on it. This is evident in their genres, themes, compositions, and above all in their language, which closely follows that of the Bible and, in particular, that of the Psalms.

---

28. E. G. Chazon, "*4QDIBHAM*: Liturgy or Literature?" *RevQ* 15, no. 57-58 (1991): 447-55; "*Dibre Hamme'orot*: Prayer for the Sixth Day (4Q504 1-2 v-vi)," in *Prayer from Alexander to Constantine: A Critical Anthology*, ed. M. Kiley (London: Routledge, 1997), 23-27; L. H. Schiffman, "The Dead Sea Scrolls and the Early History of Jewish Liturgy," in *The Synagogue in Late Antiquity*, ed. L. I. Levine (Philadelphia: American Schools of Oriental Research, 1987), 33-48, esp. 41.

29. In addition, the Old Latin assigns Ps. 81 to Thursday. See Davila, *Liturgical Works*, 241; Falk, *Daily, Sabbath, and Festival Prayers*, 72 n. 77.

30. Davila, *Liturgical Works*, 242.

Psalm 91

Psalm 91 is the second psalm in Book IV of the biblical Psalter. Preceding it is Psalm 90, a prayer of Moses that combines a hymn praising the eternity of God and a lament over the transitoriness of human existence. The poignant contrast between the brevity of human life, a theme already found in the preceding psalms, and the eternity of God makes Psalm 90 an especially appropriate opening for Book IV of the Psalter.[31] Psalm 91, which lacks a superscription,[32] has variously been called a wisdom psalm,[33] a royal psalm,[34] a psalm of conversion,[35] and a psalm of asylum.[36] God appears as the protector

---

31. The latter part of the Psalter, divided into Book IV (90–106) and Book V (107–150) and sometimes called the "Moses-Psalter" based on Ps. 90:1, bears several distinct characteristics. It consists of smaller collections such as the Enthronement Psalms (93; 95–99), Psalms of David (108–110), the so-called *Hallel* (113–118), and several "Twin Psalms": "New Songs" (96/98), liturgical formulas (101/102), Hymns of Creation (103/104), and Wisdom Psalms (111/112). Pss. 90 and 91, too, have several elements in common: they both are reminiscent of the wisdom tradition, and both affirm God's protective powers. Ps. 91 continues the theme of God's faithfulness already voiced in Ps. 90. Particularly striking in this respect is the final promise in Ps. 91:16 of human longevity (v. 16a, "With a long life I will satisfy him"), in contrast to the meditation on the ephemerality of life in Ps. 90:4-6 and 9-10. See, e.g., D. M. Howard, "A Contextual Reading of Psalms 90-94," in *The Shape and Shaping of the Psalter*, ed. J. Clinton McCann (Sheffield: JSOT Press, 1993), 11-12. Premodern interpreters, too, have pointed to the prominent position of Ps. 90 at the beginning of Book IV. See in particular R. E. Heine, ed., *Gregory of Nyssa's Treatise on the Inscriptions of the Psalms* (Oxford: Clarendon, 1995), 101-8. Only a few psalms in Book IV have superscriptions, a deficiency the LXX often "amends" by providing a Davidic heading. There are a number of liturgical and hymnic texts in Books IV and V, of which several may have originated in the cult.

32. The LXX attributes the psalm to David and provides a superscription similar to that in Pss. 93ff., "A Song. A Psalm of David."

33. H. Gunkel, *Einleitung in die Psalmen*, 4th ed. (Göttingen: Vandenhoeck & Ruprecht, 1985), 385.

34. M. Dahood, *Psalms II: 51–100*, AB 17 (New York: Doubleday, 1968), 329: "A royal psalm of trust or confidence composed by a court poet who here recites it before the king."

35. O. Eißfeldt, "Jahwes Verhältnis zu 'Eljon und Schaddaj nach Psalm 91," *Die Welt des Orients* 2 (1954-59): 343-48, reprinted in Eißfeldt, *Kleine Schriften: Dritter Band*, ed. R. Sellheim and F. Maass (Tübingen: J. C. B. Mohr, 1966), 441-47.

36. L. Delekat, *Asylie und Schutzorakel am Zionheiligtum: Eine Untersuchung zu den privaten Feindpsalmen. Mit zwei Exkursen* (Leiden: Brill, 1967), 235-39. Delekat's analysis of the genre is based primarily on his understanding of the word סתר in v. 1 to mean "asylum" ("Heiligtumsasyl," p. 237). He also claims that the expression "to find refuge under God's wings" (v. 4) ought to be understood to mean "to seek asylum." However, neither interpretation is compelling.

of those who seek refuge in him (מָעוֹן, "refuge," in Pss. 90:1 and 91:9), a theological affirmation illustrated by a plethora of powerful metaphors. The psalm can be divided into three parts, with each section clearly marked off by a change in the poetic voice. The first two verses speak of a person who seeks shelter with God, verses 3-13 are addressed directly to this person (with a possible interruption in v. 9), and verses 14-16 form a distinct didactic poem cast in the first person, with God as the subject.

The opening section of the psalm, verses 1-2, is plagued with difficulties. A central problem concerns the change in the MT from the participle in verse 1 to the first-person singular in verse 2, "He who dwells in the shelter . . . I will say of the Lord." Many interpreters take the first verse to be a subordinate clause placed, for stylistic reasons, in front of the main clause, which follows in verse 2 and also furnishes the belated subject to verse 1, "Dwelling in the shelter . . . I will say."[37] This is a possible, albeit somewhat convoluted, reading of the psalm opening. Others follow the LXX and simply change the subject of verse 2 to the third person, "Dwelling in the shelter . . . he will say to the Lord." NRSV chooses yet a third option. It reads verses 1 and 2 as if they were part of verses 3-13 and changes the subject in both verses to the second person, "You who live in the shelter . . . will say to the LORD." The problem with the latter two renderings is that the first is based on the LXX, thus sidestepping the textual problem in the MT, while the latter option has no textual support for it at all.

The problem of verses 1-2 may best be solved by changing the vocalization of the first-person verb in verse 2 to a participle. This does not require a change of the consonants, and it retains the use of the participle in verse 1. The text would then read as follows:

> 1He who dwells in the shelter of the Most High:
> in the shadow of Shaddai he will spend the night,
> 2saying of the Lord, "My refuge and my stronghold,
> my God in whom I trust!"

Support for this reading comes from one of the Qumran fragments, which we will examine in greater detail below, and which reads the problematic verses in precisely this way. 11QPsAp[a] adds a definite article to what is vocalized in the MT as a first-person verb and hence reads the form as a participle, "He who dwells . . . saying. . . ." The Peshitta, too, has a participle. The implication

---

37. K. Seybold, *Die Psalmen,* Handbuch zum Alten Testament I/15 (Tübingen: J. C. B. Mohr, 1996), 362.

here is that the same anonymous individual who "dwells in the shelter" (v. 1) is "he who says of the Lord, 'My refuge'" (v. 2).[38]

Psalm 91, like several other psalms of Book IV, has probably preserved at least parts of a liturgical formula and most likely originated in the cult. Reading through verses 1-2, it is not immediately clear whether the person in question is a worshiper who has found sanctuary in the Jerusalem temple and intends to remain there, or whether we should understand the imagery of the psalm to be metaphorical, so that the psalmist here merely refers to all people who have found security in God. While during the long reception history of the psalm countless believers undoubtedly have read these words in the second manner, believing themselves to be living "in the shadow of Shaddai," most interpreters nowadays agree that the psalm originally derived from a concrete setting at the temple. Even the fact that as early as the Targum Psalm 91 was assigned to different voices points to its liturgical use already in the institutionalized worship in ancient Israel.[39] In sum, the first two verses serve to introduce the liturgical setup of the psalm and to articulate its main themes.

A man enters the temple, seeking the shelter of the Most High (v. 1). The choice of words is noteworthy here: the metaphors "shelter" (סתר) and "shadow" (צל), as well as the ancient epithets "Most High" (עליון) and "the Almighty" (שדי), both divine names possibly of the pre-Israelite period and only secondarily conferred upon the God of Israel,[40] are closely associated with the temple in Jerusalem and describe the sacred realm in which the worshiper seeks to find shelter. The precise meaning of "dwelling" (ישב) is not clear,[41] though the parallelism with יתלונן, "he will pass the night," at the end

---

38. The change in the consonantal text of 11QPsAp[a] hardly implies, as Eißfeldt claims, that the first two verses were spoken by a temple official. The use of the participles is deliberately impersonal and serves as a liturgical directive, which is not part of the spoken exchange. See O. Eißfeldt, "Eine Qumran-Textform des 91. Psalms," in *Bibel und Qumran: Beiträge zur Erforschung der Beziehungen zwischen Bibel- und Qumranwissenschaft*, ed. S. Wagner (Berlin: Evangelische Haupt-Bibelgesellschaft zu Berlin, 1968), 83.

39. In the Targum, the different speakers are not the suppliant and the temple official but David and Solomon. V. 1 is seen as a superscription to the psalm, vv. 2-8 are spoken by David, v. 9 is a reply by Solomon, and vv. 10-16 (*not* vv. 14-16, as most modern commentators would have it) are spoken by God. See, e.g., A. Weiser, *The Psalms: A Commentary*, OTL (Philadelphia: Westminster, 1962), 605.

40. Seybold, *Die Psalmen*, 362.

41. Following the lead of H. Birkeland, A. Bentzen, and B. Gemser, Dahood, *Psalms II*, 329, argues that the worshiper in this psalm is the king. The participle ישב would then have to be translated "Let him who sits enthroned . . . ," and the psalm would be classified as a royal psalm. Dahood finds further support for his reading in the use of the third person in v. 1, which he takes to be typical of "the court style."

of verse 1 helps to clarify the intention of the asylum seeker. He will spend one or several nights in the temple, hoping to receive a word of affirmation from God.

Upon entering the temple the worshiper says a brief prayer of confession asked of the one who looks to the Lord for shelter: "My refuge and my stronghold, my God in whom I trust" (v. 2). Again, the images are closely associated with God's protective presence in the Jerusalem temple (מחסה, "refuge," in Pss. 46:2; 61:4; 62:8, 9; and מצודה, "stronghold," in Ps. 18:3; 2 Sam. 5:7). Another first-person prayer introduced with "I will say" (אמר) occurs in Ps. 102:25 [Eng. 102:24]. In both cases the insertion, probably a fixed liturgical formula which the psalmist incorporates into his composition, interrupts the literary flow of thought, and so the LXX and other witnesses change the grammatical forms in order to make them conform with the present context.[42]

The middle part of the psalm, verses 3-13, presents a cluster of metaphors extolling God's protective powers. This section is marked off from its context by a change of speakers in verses 3 and 14. Beginning in verse 3 the suppliant, who upon entering the temple utters a brief prayer, is now addressed in the second person. The change of voice is underscored by the use of the emphatic personal pronoun (v. 3, "Truly, He will deliver *you*," and another nine times in vv. 7-13). The whole segment (vv. 3-13) is a concatenation of four, possibly five individual pronouncements of consolation (vv. 3-4, 5-6, 7-8, and 11-13; vv. 9-10 are more difficult to assess). Given the autonomous nature of these sayings, the possibility should not be excluded that they originally circulated independently, though there is no way of knowing. In their present context they are tightly woven together and well integrated into the fabric of the liturgical procedure.

The movement within the poem immediately points to its didactic purpose. God alone provides adequate protection (vv. 3-4), no matter how threatening the forces of evil may be (vv. 5-6), as the sufferer is sure to witness for himself (vv. 7-8). What is more, God will guard and protect him by means of his angels well beyond the immediate bounds of the temple district (vv. 11-13). Clearly we are dealing with a liturgical sequence. Who the speaker is we are not told, but in light of the language (e.g., the assurance formula in v. 5, "Do not fear . . .")[43] and the nature of the assurances (e.g., a blessing for future protection, vv. 9-10, and 11-13), the officiant speaks with considerable authority. He may well be a temple priest.

---

42. E. S. Gerstenberger, *Psalms, Part 2, and Lamentations,* FOTL 15 (Grand Rapids: Eerdmans, 2001), 164 (with extensive bibliography on Ps. 91 on pp. 167-68).

43. Gerstenberger, *Psalms,* 164.

In addition to the change of speaker, the כִּי of asseveration serves as a second rhetoric device to indicate caesurae in the psalm.[44] It is used for the first time in verse 3, "*Truly,* He will deliver you," and then again in verse 14, "*Truly,* he loves Me," to introduce both the middle and the final sections of the psalm. The exclamatory כִּי also appears in verse 9, "*Truly,* O Lord, you are my refuge," and divides the poem further into two subunits, verses 3-8 and 9-13.[45] This formal division is supported by the content of the pronouncements. Verses 3 and 8 frame the first unit: it begins with "the snare of the fowler" (v. 3a) from which God will deliver the suppliant and ends with the punishment of the culprits, here identified plainly as "the wicked" (v. 8b). All affirmations so far are concerned with the worshiper's past, i.e., with the fear and terror that brought him to the temple.[46] Now turning to the future, verses 9-10 and 11-13 promise him protection for times to come. These blessings reach well beyond the present moment, both as far as place and time are concerned, and anticipate, as it were, the ultimate promise of "long life" in the final verse of the psalm (v. 16).

Verse 9 marks the turning point in the poem. The verse presents us with several problems, not unlike the problems in verse 2. Most puzzling is the use of the first person in 9a, just as in 2a, only this time in the form of a suffix ("Truly, O Lord, you are *my* refuge"). This does not fit the second half of the verse, "You have made the Most High *your* dwelling place." In other words, there is a seemingly unmotivated switch to the first person in 9a, whereas 9b reverts to the previous situation in which the worshiper is being addressed by the temple official. Most interpreters, including the NRSV, simply change the suffix in 9a to the second person in order to eliminate the change of voice, "You have made the LORD *your* refuge." However, the MT makes good sense and does not need to be emended. The statement, "The Lord is my refuge," clearly is a deliberate allusion back to the prayer of confession in verse 2 (מַחְסִי in vv. 2a and in 9a), which is also cast in the first person. It seems most

---

44. P. Joüon, S.J., *A Grammar of Biblical Hebrew. Part Three: Syntax,* ed. T. Muraoka, Subsidia Biblica 14,2 (Rome: Editrice Pontificio Istituto Biblico, 2001), 616-18 (§164, "assertive clause").

45. Most modern commentators do not see a change of voice beginning in v. 9, though it is noteworthy that the Targum puts v. 9 in the mouth of Solomon, finding here Solomon's reply to David.

46. The imagery of the Lord's sheltering wings is frequently used in the Psalter and beyond, as many interpreters point out. See Pss. 36:8 [Eng. 36:7]; 57:2 [Eng. 57:1]; 61:5 [Eng. 61:4]; 63:8 [Eng. 63:7]; Deut. 32:11; Isa. 8:8; Ruth 2:12. In connection with the temple in Jerusalem, one is inclined to think of the wings of the wooden cherubim (1 Kings 6:23-28 and 8:6-7; Ps. 17:8); W. Dommershausen, "כָּנָף," in *TDOT,* 7:229-31.

likely, therefore, that verse 9a is a second confessional statement, spoken by the supplicant in response to the promises made to him thus far, in which he renews his own commitment from verse 2 to see the Lord as his only refuge.

Psalm 91 ends in verses 14-16 in another sequence of divine assurances. The blessings of verses 3-13 are confirmed and carried even further to culminate in this final benediction. God will rescue and protect the sufferer and satisfy him with a long life. This last segment, introduced in 14a by the asseverative כִּי, is distinct from the rest of the psalm in several respects. Whereas in 3-13 the anonymous voice addresses the worshiper directly, all of 14-16 is spoken in the first person. The subject is undoubtedly God, whose promises are here communicated by a temple official, either the same person we detect behind 3-13 or, more likely, a different liturgist. The blessings are arranged in strict parallelism. They are concise, rhythmic, and lend themselves to be recited orally.[47] A total of seven first-person singular verbs underscore the wholeness of both the benediction and the promise. The recipient of the blessings is referred to only in the form of suffixes in the third-person singular. This could be the worshiping community as it participates in the liturgical ceremony and now receives the closing benediction. It seems more likely, however, that the beneficiary of the divine benevolence is the supplicant himself, in which case verses 14-16 may well be the salvation oracle that brought him into the temple in the first place. The use of such oracles as an expression of divine protection in combination with the assurance formula (v. 5, "Do not fear") is reminiscent of Second Isaiah (Isa. 41:10-14; 43:1, 5; 44:2; 51:7; 54:4) and further strengthens the case for liturgical use of our psalm.[48] The absence of any proper lament, petition, or individual confession of sin hardly makes the assurances unconditional. To the contrary, the blessings make it clear that they are offered in reply to the believer's unqualified confession of faith in the God of Israel (v. 14b, ". . . *because* he has known My name"). Other psalms, such as the "liturgies of entrance" to the Jerusalem temple (Pss. 15 and 24), spell out in no uncertain terms the conditions of admittance to the temple.[49] In Psalm 91, the presumed duress of the supplicant as well as his two prayers of confession in verses 2a and 9a will have been a sufficient demonstration of his immediate need.

The psalm ends in verse 16 with the promise of a long and fulfilled life

47. See Deut. 28:3-6 for a similar sequence of six blessings on fertility and prosperity (J. H. Tigay, *The JPS Torah Commentary: Deuteronomy* [Philadelphia and Jerusalem: Jewish Publication Society, 1996], 258); also Lev. 26:3-13.

48. Gerstenberger, *Psalms*, 167.

49. N. M. Sarna, *On the Book of Psalms: Exploring the Prayers of Ancient Israel* (New York: Schocken Books, 1993), 102-3.

("With a long life I will satisfy him"). The pronouncement succinctly captures both the longevity ("With a long life," אֹרֶךְ יָמִים) as well as the quality of the suppliant's earthly life ("I will satisfy him," אַשְׂבִּיעֵהוּ; see also Gen. 25:8; Job 42:17). The ultimate blessing, finally, promises the worshiper no less than to see God's salvation (v. 16b).

The focal point of Psalm 91 is verses 5-6. Even a casual perusal through the reception history of Psalm 91 quickly reveals that the interpretation of these two verses determined how later interpreters understood the psalm as a whole. Verses 5 and 6 threw the switch, as it were, to determine the direction much of the interpretive history of Psalm 91 was to take.

> ₅Do not fear the terror in the night
> or the arrow that flies by day,
> ₆the plague that stalks in the darkness,
> or the pestilence that ravages at noon.

In this brief pronouncement, the worshiper is assured that he need not fear the various perils that trouble him. The dictum is self-contained and formally marked off from its context. Verses 4 and 7 form a frame of two tricola, while 5 and 6 each consist of two lines of bicola, arranged in strict symmetry and introduced by the assurance formula. The formal parallelism is underscored by the parallelism of the times of day during which the perils strike (v. 5 night-day; v. 6 darkness-noon).

The expression "terror in the night" occurs only here in the Hebrew Bible.[50] The cause of dread (פַּחַד)[51] is here appended as a genitive, "the terror in the night" (פַּחַד לָיְלָה), even though its exact nature remains unclear (similarly in Ps. 64:2 [Eng. 64:1], and 4QpNah 2:5, מִפַּחַד אוֹיֵב, "terror evoked by an enemy"; 1QHª 10:36, מִפַּחַד הַוּוֹת רְשָׁעִים, "the terror of destruction evoked by the wicked"; and Deir 'Alla I, 10 [12], "terror evoked by the abyss").[52] The "arrow that flies by day" forms the second half of the parallelism in verse 5 and is equally enigmatic. As an instrument of hunting and war, the arrow often serves as a metaphor of various calamities and afflictions, which God resolves to bring against Israel (Ezek. 5:16; Pss. 7:14 [Eng. 7:13];

---

50. However, see Song of Sol. 3:7-8, "Look, it is the litter of Solomon! Around it are sixty men . . . each with his sword at his thigh because of terrors by night (מִפַּחַד בַּלֵּילוֹת)."

51. Dahood, *Psalms II*, 331, wants to translate "*the pack of the night*. Namely, the pack of wild dogs that marauds at night," though the semantic basis for this in the MT is slim at best. Dahood is followed approvingly by O. Keel, *The Symbolism of the Biblical World: Ancient Near Eastern Iconography and the Book of Psalms* (New York: Seabury Press, 1978), 84.

52. See also H.-P. Müller, "פחד," in *TDOT*, 11:517-26.

18:15 [Eng. 18:14]; 38:3 [Eng. 38:2]). As a divine punishment it is also mentioned in Deuteronomy 32:23-24: "I will sweep misfortunes on them, use up my arrows on them: wasting famine, ravaging plague, deadly pestilence, and fanged beasts. . . ." Two of the four perils mentioned in Psalm 91:5-6, the arrow (חץ) and the pestilence (קטב; see Isa. 28:2; Hos. 13:14), also occur in Deuteronomy 32:23-24. The two perils listed in verse 6, "the plague" (דבר) and "the pestilence" (קטב), are both deadly epidemics found elsewhere in the Bible.[53]

The precise nature of these perils remains elusive and is difficult to determine. It is feasible that all four terms should be taken literally, as some interpreters hold. According to Artur Weiser, for example, the reference is here to the danger of being "in broad daylight when the burning sunbeams hatch out diseases";[54] others have proposed that the worshiper has come to the temple to seek protection from an epidemic.[55] It is much more likely, however, that the four terms are to be understood metaphorically. The "terror" and the "arrow" could stand for the enemies of the psalmist who pursue him and from whom he seeks asylum in the temple. Understood that way, Psalm 91 belongs to the so-called imprecatory psalms, i.e., to those psalms in which the psalmist flees from and, once within the secure realm of the sanctuary, curses his enemies. This would explain neatly why the dictum in verses 5-6 is followed in verse 7 by what, understood in this way, would seem to be a call to arms, promising that the persecuted will ultimately prevail over his pursuers: "A thousand will fall at your side, ten thousand at your right."

However, the majority of interpreters, both ancient and modern, have understood the metaphors in verses 5 and 6 to stand not for the psalmist's enemies but for malevolent spirits, or demons. This reading is suggested as early as in the versions. Already the translators of the Septuagint understood verse 6 to talk about evil spirits: "[You will not fear] the concern that travels along in the darkness, the misfortune and evil spirit of midday." "Misfortune" (Gk. σύμπτωμα), here rendering Hebrew קטב, has negative connotations already in classical Greek. The Greek translators added yet a second source of fear in 6b, "the misfortune and evil spirit" (δαιμόνιον). This reading is probably based on Hebrew ושד instead of MT ישוד. Greek δαιμόνιον does not necessarily designate an evil spirit, though this meaning is well established in the

53. Whereas the "pestilence" (קטב) is attested only here, in Deut. 32:24, Isa. 28:2, and Hos. 13:14, the "plague" (דבר) is attested frequently.

54. Weiser, *The Psalms*, 608-9.

55. Delekat, *Asylie und Schutzorakel*, 237, "In diesem Psalm wird einem Mann verheissen, er und seine Familie (10b) würden von einer Seuche nicht betroffen werden (5ff 10b)."

LXX. Most relevant for our psalm are Deuteronomy 32:17 and Psalm 106:37, where, in analogy to our case, δαιμόνιον translates Hebrew שדים (see also Matt. 7:22).[56] The Peshitta follows the MT in that it, too, speaks of one peril in verse 6b only, yet similarly to the LXX renders it as *rûḥā dᵉšāydā*, "a devastating spirit." The interpretation that verses 5-6 speak of evil spirits has therefore its origin in the versions.

Half a century ago Caquot proposed that underlying the Hebrew terms קטב ,רשף, and דבר we can detect the proper names of deities known from the ancient Near East.[57] His proposal has found widespread acceptance, and others have subsequently argued that these demons are here associated with fixed times during the day: nighttime, daytime, evening, and noon, though this reading may be based on a misunderstanding of the poetic structure of the dictum. The breakup of the word pairs "day-night" (v. 5) and "darkness-noon" (v. 6) hardly means that the worshiper was tormented by the demons during specific times of the day; it is merely a poetic way of expressing his constant state of anxiety.

Many ancient interpreters, too, saw in verses 5-6 a prayer against demonic forces. This is not to say that the psalm participates in demonology or encourages the belief in demons. To the contrary, the psalm makes clear that demons have no place in the realm of God. "We always confront demons with this psalm," commented Cassiodorus (490-583) in his *Explanation of the Psalms.* "This psalm has marvellous power, and routs impure spirits. . . . So this psalm should be recited by us when night sets in after all the actions of the day; the devil must realise that we belong to Him to whom he remembers that he himself yielded."[58] Early Christian renderings of Psalm 91 are predicated on the understanding that the psalm speaks about "the righteous man" *(vir justus),* who is none other than Christ and every person who lives in Christ.[59] This reading can easily be derived from the way in which Psalm 91 is

56. שד is an Assyrian spirit or demon representing the individual's vital force; see *CAD* Š/II, 256-59.

57. A. Caquot, "Sur quelques démons de l'Ancien Testament: Reshep, Qeteb, Deber," *Semitica* 6 (1956): 53-68; on Ps. 91 see pp. 66-68.

58. *Cassiodorus: Explanation of the Psalms. Volume II: Psalms 51–100,* translated and annotated by P. G. Walsh, ACW 52 (New York: Paulist, 1991); the quotes are from pp. 380 and 387. The allusion is, of course, to Luke 4:10-13 par.

59. This understanding of Ps. 91 is succinctly captured in one of the interpretive glosses added in the Christian Psalter, "Propheta generaliter de omni viro justo, nunc eodem loquente, nunc Deo." The *titulus* of series III according to P. Salmon, *Les "Tituli psalmorum" des manuscripts latins* (Rome: Abbaye Saint-Jérome, 1959), 106, quoted from P. Hugger, *Jahwe meine Zuflucht: Gestalt und Theologie des 91. Psalms* (Münsterschwarzach: Vier-Türme-Verlag, 1971), 316. Hugger's book provides the most extensive treatment of the

used in the New Testament. After Jesus had appointed seventy of his followers and sent them out ahead of him, they return to him with joy and say, "'Lord, in your name even the demons submit to us!' He said to them, 'I watched Satan fall from heaven like a flash of lightning. See, I have given you authority to tread on snakes and scorpions, and over all the power of the enemy; and nothing will hurt you'" (Luke 10:17-19; see also Mark 16:18). In the Gospel of Luke, Jesus confers the assurance of Psalm 91:13 upon the seventy. What is interesting here is the explicit connection between the quote of Psalm 91:13 and the earlier statement of the disciples that they were able to overcome demons. The reference to Psalm 91 is hardly fortuitous. It assumes that the reader is aware not only of the larger literary context of verse 13 but also of the interpretive history of the psalm, according to which those who receive its assurances derive from it the power to ward off demons.

The same connection between the words of comfort found in Psalm 91 and the psalm's antidemonic force is implied in Luke 4:10-11 (par. Matt. 4:6). Having fasted forty days in the wilderness, Jesus is tempted by the devil. In his third and final attempt to put Jesus to the test, the devil takes Jesus to Jerusalem and, standing on the pinnacle of the temple, recites words of comfort from our psalm, "'He will command his angels concerning you, to protect you,' and 'On their hands they will bear you up, so that you will not dash your foot against a stone'" (Luke 4:10-11; the quote is from Ps. 91:11-12). By quoting Psalm 91, the demon par excellence inverts the intention of the dictum, originally spoken to console those haunted by evil spirits, and now turns it into a tool for temptation. The point here is not so much that the devil quotes Scripture out of context, as is often remarked. To the contrary: the audacity of the satanic trial can be appreciated to its fullest only when the larger, antidemonic context of the quote is realized. In his commentary on Psalm 91, Gerstenberger speculates whether the pronouncement in verses 11-12 originally circulated independently. "Again we may ask — especially in light of NT quotations of the passage as in Luke 4:10-11 [. . .] — whether vv. 11-12 once had been an autonomous saying, for example, a toast to a young man or woman beginning their adult-life's journey, or a blessing for a recuperated patient."[60] This is possible, though the quote in Luke makes it much more likely that precisely the opposite is the case. When taken out of context, the devil's quote loses its edge, seems arbitrary and could be replaced by any number of passages from the Hebrew Bible. The force of the temptation lies

---

reception history of Ps. 91 in early Judaism and early Christianity available, excluding the findings from Qumran.

60. Gerstenberger, *Psalms*, 165-66.

precisely in the implied context of the quote, i.e., its antidemonic connotations which undoubtedly would have been known to Luke and his original audience.

Early Jewish readings of Psalm 91 follow much the same route as Christian interpretations. R. Berechiah, an *amora* from the fourth century, comments on verse 5, "There is a demon that flies like a bird, darting forth like an arrow."[61] Similarly, in the Midrash on Psalms the majority opinion of the rabbis holds that verse 6 refers to demons as well.[62] Other talmudic and midrashic sources supply ample evidence that the rabbis regard Hebrew קטב, which we have translated with "pestilence," as a demon (see *Num. Rab.* 12:3; Rashi ad loc.).[63] The Talmud classifies Psalms 3 and 91 as "antidemonic songs" (שירי פגעים). Even though it is forbidden to use words of the Torah for purposes of healing, "to protect is different" (*b. Šebu.* 15b; *y. ʿErub.* 10:11 [26c]). In the Jewish liturgy, Psalm 91 has traditionally had its place in the Sabbath morning service as well as at the end of the Sabbath.[64] Since the Middle Ages Psalm 91 has been part of the evening prayers of both Jews and Christians. Hugger may have put it best when he wrote, "Ps 91 ist das liturgische Abendgebet schlechthin."[65]

Psalm 91 at Qumran

The first texts we need to consider from the Qumran corpus are the *Songs of the Sage*. These are two sets of liturgical songs (*Songs of the Sage*[a], 4Q510, and *Songs of the Sage*[b], 4Q511), both attributed in their respective superscriptions to the Sage, or משכיל (4Q510 1:4; 4Q511 2:1). The opening lines of the first song provide a summary of the Songs' intention. These are "Bless[ings to the

61. *The Midrash on Psalms,* on Ps. 91:5 (trans. W. G. Braude, *The Midrash on Psalms* [New Haven: Yale University Press, 1976], 102). Commenting on v. 6, the midrash describes the demon further, "R. Huna said in the name of R. Jose: The demon 'Bitter Destruction' (Hebr. קטב) is covered with scale upon scale and with shaggy hair, and he glares with his one eye, and that eye is in the middle of his heart. He has no power when it is cool in the shade and hot in the sun, but only when it is hot in both shade and sun. He rolls like a ball, and from the seventeenth day in Tammuz to the ninth day in Ab he has power after the fourth hour in the day and up to the ninth hour."

62. See *The Midrash on Psalms,* on Ps. 91:6.

63. T. H. Gaster, *Myth, Legend, and Custom in the Old Testament* (New York and Evanston: Harper and Row, 1969), §§242, 275, and 298.

64. I. Elbogen, *Jewish Liturgy: A Comprehensive History,* trans. R. P. Scheindlin (Philadelphia and New York: Jewish Publication Society, 1993), 95 and 102.

65. Hugger, *Jahwe meine Zuflucht,* 336.

Ki]ng of glory. Words of thanksgiving in psalms of [splendour] to the King of knowledge" (4Q510 1:1-2).[66] The "words of thanksgiving" (דברי הודות) have extensive parallels with the *Hodayot* (esp. 4Q511 18; 28-29; 52-59). God is praised for being the God of gods and the Lord of all the holy ones, i.e., for his ultimate dominion over all divine beings. So powerful is his might that the entire celestial realm is terrified and flees from before him.

At this point the Sage begins to pronounce his praises in the first-person singular. It immediately becomes clear that the praise of the Songs is not simply laudatory in nature but follows a distinct purpose: to ward off evil spirits. In reciting these hymns the Sage assumes a liturgical role, the pronouncement of an apotropaic prayer.[67] "And I, a Sage, declare the splendor of his radiance in order to frighten and terr[ify] all the spirits of the ravaging angels and the bastard spirits, demons, Lilith, owls and [jackals . . .] and those who strike unexpectedly to lead astray the spirit of knowledge, to make their hearts forlorn" (4Q510 1:4-6; repeated, albeit in fragmented form, in 4Q511 10:1-3). The passage is intriguing for several reasons. First, the detailed formulaic catalogue of demons named by the Sage does not appear to be an ad hoc formulation but implies that the community had a coherent and complex demonology, which included different orders and classes of evil spirits.[68] And secondly, the context of this list is a hymnic declaration that God rules over all gods, angels, and in particular, spirits. This declaration is at once a praise of God, a statement of confidence that those who are counted among the righteous, a common epithet for the members of the community, will not be harmed by evil forces ("Rejoice, righteous ones, in the wonderful God!"

---

66. The translation is taken from F. García Martínez and E. J. C. Tigchelaar, *The Dead Sea Scrolls: Study Edition*, 2 vols. (Leiden: Brill; Grand Rapids: Eerdmans, 1997-98), 1027.

67. "And on the eighth I will open [my mouth . . .]" (4Q511 42:4) is a further indication that we are dealing with a liturgical text. Presumably the reference is to the eighth day of a certain festival (Lev. 23:36, 39; Num. 29:35; Neh. 8:18). See M. Baillet, "Cantiques du Sage (ii)," DJD 7, 241.

68. This point has been made convincingly by P. S. Alexander, "The Demonology of the Dead Sea Scrolls," in *The Dead Sea Scrolls after Fifty Years: A Comprehensive Assessment*, ed. P. W. Flint and J. C. VanderKam, 2 vols. (Leiden: Brill, 1999), 2:331-53. See also A. Lange, "The Essene Position on Magic and Divination," in *Legal Texts and Legal Issues: Proceedings of the Second Meeting of the International Organization for Qumran Studies, Cambridge 1995, Published in Honour of Joseph M. Baumgarten*, ed. M. Bernstein, F. García Martínez, and J. Kampen, STDJ 23 (Leiden: Brill, 1997), 377-435. Two hitherto unpublished texts from Qumran, 4Q230-231, described by E. Tov as a "Catalogue of Spirits," can potentially add important information about the nature of this inventory once they are published.

4Q510 1:8), and a verbal shield to deter and keep away the harmful demons. The very recital of these praises is intended to keep the malevolent spirits at bay.

The *Songs of the Sage* draw on biblical material much the same way as other liturgical and poetic works of the community we have examined do. The language is thoroughly biblical. A few times entire passages from Scripture are incorporated into the Songs. Thus the sequence of rhetorical questions in Isaiah 40:12-13 underlies 4Q511 30:3-4, and the formulaic self-disclosure of divine identity in Exodus 34:6-7 stands behind 4Q511 52-59. Divine epithets such as "King of Glory" (4Q510 1:1; 4Q511 52-59:4) are taken from the Psalter (Ps. 24:7, 8, 9, 10).

There are two possible allusions to Psalm 91 in the Songs, though neither is certain or even amounts to a direct citation. In his initial list of evil spirits to be deterred, the Sage lists "bastard spirits, demons, Lilith" (4Q510 1:5). The Hebrew term for "demons," שדאים (or שדים in Biblical Hebrew), resembles Hebrew ישוד in Psalm 91:6, which, as we have seen above, the translators of the LXX took to be a noun that they rendered δαιμόνιον, analogous to שדים in Deuteronomy 32:17 and Psalm 106:37. It is far from certain, however, that the word "demons" in 4Q510 is an allusion to Psalm 91. A little later in the text the Sage uses the phrase "in the secret of Shaddai" (בסתר שדי; 4Q511 8:6). This could be a conflation of the longer expression found in Psalm 91:1, "in the secret of the Most High, in the shadow of Shaddai," though this, too, seems strained. The words may be found in Psalm 91, but the idiom is not.[69]

While it appears that the demonology of Psalm 91 would have lent itself to be adopted by the Sage for his antidemonic liturgy, we find no textual evidence that this was the case.[70] None of the dangers listed in verses 5-6 or any of the psalm's distinct terminological clusters appear in the *Songs of the Sage*. Instead, the list of malevolent spirits in the Songs points to a different provenance. Heading this list are the spirits of the angels of destruction and the spirits of the bastards. These are known from the Book of the Watchers (*1 Enoch* 10:9; 15:8–16:1) as well as from the book of *Jubilees* (10:1-11; see also 1QM 13:10-12), where they are said to have risen from the bodies of the slain

---

69. The word שדים (demons) also occurs in Pseudo-Daniel (4Q243 13:2 + 244 12:2).

70. I was unable to find any textual evidence that 4Q510-511 directly quote from, or explicitly refer to, Ps. 91. For a different view, see E. Chazon, "Psalms, Hymns and Prayers," in *Encyclopedia of the Dead Sea Scrolls*, 712, who characterizes 4Q510-511 in the following way: "This prophylactic function as well as the hymns' form and content, including the citation of *Psalms* 91 and naming of demons (related to the Fallen Angels of *Gn.* 6.1-4) qualify them as incantations."

Nephilim.[71] According to these early apocalypses, which have enjoyed significant authority at Qumran,[72] these spirits are active during the present age of the dominion of wickedness until the final day of judgment.[73] It is this tradition of the fallen watchers that stands in the background of, and furnishes the material for, the description of the evil spirits in the *Songs of the Sage*. Psalm 91, by contrast, belongs to a different strand of demonology, which has a different origin. Psalm 91 is conspicuously absent from 4Q510-511, as it is from the Book of the Watchers.

Parts of the text of Psalm 91 are preserved in two scrolls from Qumran, 4QPs[b] (4Q84) and 11QApocryphal Psalms (11Q11). 4QPs[b] is a fragmentary psalm manuscript, which in its first two columns has preserved the text of verses 5-8 (col. 1) and verses 12-15 (col. 2).[74] More important for our purposes is 11QApocryphal Psalms, a very small and highly fragmented psalms scroll attested in one manuscript only from Cave 11 and dating to the early decades of the first century c.e. The editor of the *editio princeps*, van der Ploeg, maintained that 11Q11 originally contained four compositions, three hitherto unknown psalms, which are followed by a variant form of Psalm 91.[75] Due to the poor state of the manuscript's preservation, however, neither the number of four compositions nor the exact transitions from one composition to the next can be determined with any degree of certainty.[76] It seems likely that the

71. The literature is considerable. See L. T. Stuckenbruck, "The 'Angels' and 'Giants' of Genesis 6:1-4 in Second and Third Century BCE Jewish Interpretation: Reflections on the Posture of Early Apocalyptic Traditions," *DSD* 7, no. 3 (2000): 354-77.

72. See, e.g., P. W. Flint, "'Apocrypha,' Other Previously-Known Writings, and 'Pseudepigrapha' in the Dead Sea Scrolls," in *The Dead Sea Scrolls after Fifty Years*, 2:24-66. On *Jubilees* specifically, see J. C. VanderKam, *The Book of Jubilees*, Guides to Apocrypha and Pseudepigrapha (Sheffield: Sheffield Academic Press, 2001), 143-46.

73. Note in particular Gabriel's commission to destroy the giants in *1 Enoch* 10:9-10; see G. W. E. Nickelsburg, *1 Enoch 1* (Minneapolis: Fortress, 2001), 222-24, with further discussion about the origins of the giants.

74. P. W. Skehan, "A Psalm Manuscript from Qumran (4QPs[b])," *CBQ* 26 (1964): 313-22.

75. J. van der Ploeg, "Le Psaume XCI dans une recension de Qumran," *RB* 72 (1965): 210-17; pls. 8-9. Van der Ploeg later published the rest of the scroll in "Un petit rouleau de psaumes apocryphes (11QPsAp[a])," in *Tradition und Glaube: Das frühe Christentum in seiner Umwelt. Festgabe für Karl Georg Kuhn zum 65. Geburtstag*, ed. G. Jeremiah, H.-W. Kuhn, and H. Stegemann (Göttingen: Vandenhoeck & Ruprecht, 1971), 128-39; pls. 2-7. A revised edition was later prepared by E. Puech, "11QPsAp[a]: Un rituel d'exorcismes. Essai de reconstruction," *RevQ* 14 (1990): 377-408; see also his "Les derniers Psaumes davidiques du rituel d'exorcisme, 11QPsAp[a] IV 4-V 14," in *The Dead Sea Scrolls: Forty Years of Research*, ed. D. Dimant and U. Rappaport, STDJ 10 (Leiden: Brill, 1992), 64-89.

76. F. García Martínez, E. J. C. Tigchelaar, and A. S. Van der Woude, eds., "11QApocryphal Psalms," DJD 23, p. 183, speak of a total of "at least three songs" in the manuscript.

number four has gained widespread acceptance because of a supposed connection between our scroll and the large Psalms Scroll from Qumran, 11QPsᵃ. 11QApocryphal Psalms is a collection of songs against demons (שדים), who are mentioned repeatedly throughout the scroll (1:10; 2:3, 4; 5:12). The scroll speaks of "the possessed one[s]" (הפגוע[י]ם in 5:2), who, according to the context, may well be those over whom the psalms were intended to be recited as a means of cure. As mentioned above, a few rabbinic texts (*b. Šebu.* 15b; *y. Šabb.* 6:8b) call Psalm 91 a "song for the possessed" (שיר של פגעים). The same term occurs in "David's Prose Composition" in 11QPsᵃ 27:9-10, where we read that David has composed a total of four songs "to be sung over the possessed" (לנגן על הפגועים; note Flint's discussion of this passage in this volume). Van der Ploeg therefore suggested that 11QApocryphal Psalms has preserved the four psalms for the possessed mentioned in 11QPsᵃ.

The precise nature of the compositions preceding Psalm 91, too, is difficult to determine. There are no fixed apotropaic formulas like those found in incantations and folk adjurations. Instead, the songs include general assurances of assistance and healing (5:1-3). Nitzan surmised that this may well be the result of their relationship with Psalm 91 that follows, which contains similar assurances.[77] At the very least it can be said that the noncanonical psalms are in harmony with the reassuring nature of the biblical psalm that follows. The entire scroll is rather "biblicizing," i.e., its language and tone are closely modeled on biblical poetry. God promises to protect "all the proge[ny . . .] who st[a]nd in service before [him . . .]."[78] He will send his angels and will commission a mighty angel to strike down the demon who threatens the worshipers of God (2:3-9), a promise reminiscent of the assurance in Psalm 91:11-12. The opening section of 11QApocryphal Psalms is also connected to Psalm 91 by a verbal parallel in fragment A 4 and Psalm 91:13, both of which refer to the sea monster (תנין).[79]

Even though both the *Songs of the Sage* and 11QApocryphal Psalms are apotropaic poems discovered at Qumran whose purpose is "to frighten and terr[ify]" harmful spirits, the two compositions are rather different in a number of respects. The first difference is the use of the Tetragrammaton in 11Q11

---

77. B. Nitzan, *Qumran Prayer and Religious Poetry,* STDJ 12 (Leiden: Brill, 1994), 235.

78. 11Q11 2:6. The translation is taken from J. A. Sanders, "A Liturgy for Healing the Stricken (11QPsApᵃ = 11Q11)," in *The Dead Sea Scrolls. Hebrew, Aramaic, and Greek Texts with English Translations: Volume 4A. Pseudepigraphic and Non-Masoretic Psalms and Prayers,* ed. J. H. Charlesworth (Tübingen: Mohr Siebeck; Louisville: Westminster, 1997), 223.

79. As pointed out by Nitzan, *Qumran Prayer,* 235 n. 38, and Sanders, "A Liturgy for Healing," 219 n. 5. See also 5:1 and 12 in Sanders's edition.

(2:10 [?]; 3:3, 9, 10, 11; 4:4, 11; 5:4, 8). The use of the divine name deviates from the usual practice in the sectarian writings at Qumran, as well as from the majority of Jewish magical songs. Puech noted that the divine name, which was also not used by the Pharisees (*m. Sanh.* 10:1), is found only in a small number of Jewish amulets. In 11QApocryphal Psalms, however, the invocation of the divine name serves as a shield against evil spirits, "[l]'utilisation et la prononciation du nom divin étaient nécessaires pour l'efficacité de la practique exorcistique"[80] (see also *T. Sol.* 4:12; 11:6; Matt. 12:22ff.).

A second difference lies in the attribution of all the psalms in 11Q11 to David. The attribution "of David" is preserved only in 11Q11 5:4, but it can be inferred with some confidence that originally the other compositions bore the same attribution. David, the biblical exorcist par excellence (1 Sam. 16:14-23), is an obvious choice for a collection of postbiblical apotropaic songs such as 11QApocryphal Psalms (11QPs[a] 27:9-10) — as is Solomon his son, who is mentioned in 11Q11 2:1 (1 Kings 5:12-14 [Eng. 4:32-34]). Psalm 91 fits the context. While it bears no superscription in the MT, Psalm 91 is attributed to David in the LXX, and in the Targum the psalm is cast in the form of a dialogue between David and Solomon. The tradition ascribing antidemonic hymns to Solomon reaches back to the Second Temple period (Josephus, *Ant.* 8.46-49),[81] and is extended into the rabbinic period, where Psalm 91 is variously ascribed to Moses or Solomon.[82] The *Songs of the Sage,* by contrast, as their title suggests, were composed and recited by the Sage, a high official at Qumran. Instead of using a biblical pseudonym, the Songs derive their authority from the hierarchical structure of the community.

To these two differences discussed already by Puech a third may be added, namely, the type of demonology reflected in either text. As we have seen above, the demonology of 4Q510-511 has close parallels in early Jewish apocalypses such as *1 Enoch, Jubilees,* and 4QVisions of Amram, and is compatible with the apocalyptic worldview of the sectarian writings from Qumran. This, in addition to the fact that the Songs are attributed to the

---

80. Puech, "11QPsAp[a]," 402. It has been proposed that the Tetragrammaton appears in 4Q511 as well, albeit abbreviated as *YOD,* in 10:12, in which case the use of the divine name would not distinguish the *Songs of the Sage* and 11QApocryphal Psalms (G. W. Nebe, "Der Buchstabe YOD als Ersatz des Tetragramms in 4Q511, Frag. 10. Zeile 12?" *RevQ* 12, no. 46 [1986]: 283-84). However, it is not clear that the *YOD* indicates the divine name, which is spelled out fully throughout 11QApocryphal Psalms.

81. J. M. Baumgarten, "The Qumran Songs against Demons," *Tarbiz* 55 (1986): 442-45 (Hebrew).

82. Note, for example, *Num. Rab.* 12:3; for more text examples see Nitzan, *Qumran Prayer,* pp. 250-51.

Sage, strongly suggests that 4Q510-511 were composed at Qumran. 11QApocryphal Psalms, by contrast, does not seem to know of these apocalyptic traditions but derives its demonology from the biblical text, primarily from Psalm 91. It is clear that 11QApocryphal Psalms originally included a list of demons as well. 11Q11 2:4 starts out, "These are [the de]mons . . . ," but the section that follows is too fragmented to tell whether this list is identical with the list in 4Q510 1:4-6 discussed above.

These obvious differences between 4Q510-511 and 11QApocryphal Psalms beg for an explanation. Puech proposed that 11QApocryphal Psalms dates from pre-Qumranic times and possibly stems from the "hassidéen" movement.[83] To account for their differences we do not need to postulate, however, that one of these texts predates the other, let alone to link 11Q11 with the Hasidim. 4Q510-511 and 11Q11 simply reflect two different strands of demonology that converge in the Qumran library.[84] One of these strands, represented by 11Q11, is biblical in origin and closely associated with Psalm 91. It is attested in the New Testament and, at a later point, was further developed in rabbinic literature. The other strand, by contrast, is apocalyptic in nature. It is highly differentiated in that demons appear in lists and are assigned orders and names. Its origins are spelled out in detail in the Book of the Watchers and in *Jubilees*. 4Q510 and 4Q511 are sectarian compositions intended to ward off precisely these evil spirits. Both of these demonologies were obviously known to the community at Qumran, and there is every reason to believe that both were used there for the apotropaic purpose for which they were originally composed.

One of the persistent difficulties any modern reader faces who tries to derive from the scrolls a coherent position on any given issue is that the texts do not always speak with one voice. What we have is a composite of fragments and teachings of diverse origins. The antidemonic texts from Qumran are no exception.

Conclusion

Throughout its reception history in Judaism and Christianity, Psalm 91 has been interpreted as an apotropaic song used to safeguard the faithful from malevolent spirits. Verses 5-6, understood already in the versions to refer to

---

83. Puech, "11QPsApᵃ," 401-3. The alleged connection between 11QApocryphal Psalms and 11QPsᵃ, now also thought to be pre-Qumranic by many interpreters, including Flint, provides additional evidence in support of Puech's assumption.

84. For a different view see Alexander, "Demonology," 345 n. 41, who thinks 11Q11 is sectarian in origin and, like 4Q510 and 4Q511, was recited by the Sage.

demons, provided early interpreters with a hermeneutical key to the psalm as a whole. In the Gospel of Luke the context in which Psalm 91 is used makes clear that the Evangelist knew of the psalm's antidemonic interpretive tradition and skillfully employed it for his Gospel.

The Qumran community, like any other ancient community of the time, believed in the existence of hidden, evil spirits ready to cause harm, as well as in the ability of the believers to shield themselves through the recitation of magical poetry. One group of these poetic texts, the *Songs of the Sage* (4Q510-511), which was most likely composed at Qumran, never refers to Psalm 91 in any explicit way, but is part of the apocalyptic demonological tradition. 11QApocryphal Psalms (11Q11), on the other hand, an apotropaic scroll with no signs of sectarian teaching, has preserved a variant form of Psalm 91 almost in its entirety. Both texts were used at Qumran, though the latter may not have been composed there.

Select Bibliography

The literature on biblical interpretation at Qumran has grown exponentially over the last decade. The following is a sample of the studies that have appeared.

Bernstein, M. J. "The Employment and Interpretation of Scripture in 4QMMT: Preliminary Observations." In *Reading 4QMMT: New Perspectives on Qumran Law and History*, edited by J. Kampen and M. J. Bernstein, 38-46. Symposium 2. Atlanta: Scholars Press, 1996.

———. "4Q252: From Re-written Bible to Biblical Commentary." *JJS* 45 (1994): 1-27.

———. "4Q252: Method and Context, Genre and Sources: A Response to George J. Brooke." *JQR* 85 (1994): 61-79.

———. "Interpretation of Scripture." In *Encyclopedia of the Dead Sea Scrolls*, edited by L. H. Schiffman and J. C. VanderKam, 376-83. New York: Oxford University Press, 2000.

———. "Introductory Formulas for Citation and Re-citation of Biblical Verses in the Qumran Pesharim: Observations on a Pesher Technique." *DSD* 1 (1994): 30-70.

———. "Pentateuchal Interpretation at Qumran." In *The Dead Sea Scrolls after Fifty Years: A Comprehensive Assessment*, edited by P. W. Flint and J. C. VanderKam, 1:128-59. 2 vols. Leiden: Brill, 1998-99.

Berrin, S. L. "Pesharim" and "Pesher Nahum." In *Encyclopedia of the Dead Sea Scrolls*, edited by L. H. Schiffman and J. C. VanderKam, 644-47 and 653-55. New York: Oxford University Press, 2000.

Betz, O. *Offenbarung und Schriftforschung in der Qumransekte*. WUNT 6. Tübingen: Mohr Siebeck, 1960.

Brooke, G. J. "Biblical Interpretation in the Qumran Scrolls and the New Testament." In *The Dead Sea Scrolls Fifty Years after Their Discovery: Proceedings of the Jerusalem Congress, July 20-25, 1997*, edited by L. H. Schiffman, E. Tov, and J. C. VanderKam; executive editor, G. Marquis, 60-73. Israel Exploration Society in Cooperation with the Shrine of the Book. Jerusalem: Israel Museum, 2000.

———. "The Biblical Texts in the Qumran Commentaries: Scribal Errors or

Exegetical Variants?" In *Early Jewish and Christian Exegesis: Studies in Memory of William Hugh Brownlee,* edited by C. A. Evans and W. F. Stinespring, 85-100. Atlanta: Scholars Press, 1987.

————. *Exegesis at Qumran: 4QFlorilegium in Its Jewish Context.* JSOTSup 29. Sheffield: JSOT Press, 1985.

————. "The Genre of 4Q252: From Poetry to Pesher." *DSD* 1 (1994): 160-79.

————. "Parabiblical Prophetic Narratives." In *The Dead Sea Scrolls after Fifty Years: A Comprehensive Assessment,* edited by P. W. Flint and J. C. VanderKam, 1:271-301. 2 vols. Leiden: Brill, 1998.

————. "Qumran Pesher: Toward the Re-definition of a Genre." *RevQ* 10 (1981): 483-503.

————. "The Thematic Content of 4Q252." *JQR* 85 (1994): 33-59.

Brownlee, W. H. *The Text of Habakkuk in the Ancient Commentary from Qumran.* JBL Monograph Series 11. Philadelphia: Society of Biblical Literature, 1959.

Campbell, J. *The Use of Scripture in the Damascus Document 1-8, 19-20.* BZAW 228. Berlin and New York: DeGruyter, 1995.

Carmignac, J. "Le document de Qumrân sur Melkisédeq." *RevQ* 7 (1969-71): 343-78.

Charlesworth, J. H., ed. *The Bible and the Dead Sea Scrolls.* Vol. 1, *The Hebrew Bible and Qumran.* North Richland Hills, Tex.: BIBAL Press, 2000.

Chazon, E. G. "The Creation and Fall of Adam in the Dead Sea Scrolls." In *The Book of Genesis in Jewish and Oriental Christian Interpretation,* edited by J. Frishman and L. van Rompay, 13-24. Leuven: Peeters, 1997.

Chyutin, M. "The Redaction of the Qumranic and the Traditional Book of Psalms as a Calendar." *RevQ* 63 (1994): 367-95.

Collins, J. J. *Apocalypticism in the Dead Sea Scrolls.* London: Routledge, 1997.

————. *Seers, Sibyls, and Sages in Hellenistic-Roman Judaism.* Leiden: Brill, 1997.

Cross, F. M. *The Ancient Library at Qumran.* Sheffield: Sheffield Academic Press, 1995 (1st ed. 1958).

————. "The Contribution of the Qumrân Discoveries to the Study of the Biblical Text." *IEJ* 16 (1966): 81-95. Reprinted in *Qumran and the History of the Biblical Text,* edited by F. M. Cross and S. Talmon, 278-92. Cambridge: Harvard University Press, 1975.

————. "The History of the Biblical Text in the Light of Discoveries in the Judean Desert." *HTR* 57 (1964): 281-99. Reprinted in *Qumran and the History of the Biblical Text,* edited by F. M. Cross and S. Talmon, 177-95. Cambridge: Harvard University Press, 1975.

Dimant, D. "Pesharim, Qumran." In *ABD,* 5:244-51.

————. "Qumran Sectarian Literature." In *Jewish Writings of the Second Temple Period: Apocrypha, Pseudepigrapha, Qumran Sectarian Writings, Philo, Josephus,* edited by M. E. Stone, 483-550. CRINT II.2. Philadelphia: Fortress, 1984.

Doudna, G. L. *4QPesher Nahum: A Critical Edition.* London: Sheffield Academic Press, 2001.

Fishbane, M. "The Qumran Pesher and Traits of Ancient Hermeneutics." *WCJS* 6, no. 1 (1977): 97-114.

————. "Use, Authority and Interpretation of Mikra at Qumran." In *Mikra: Text, Translation, Reading, and Interpretation of the Hebrew Bible in Ancient Judaism and Early Christianity,* edited by M. J. Mulder, 339-77. CRINT II.1. Philadelphia: Fortress, 1988.

Fitzmyer, J. A. *The Dead Sea Scrolls and Christian Origins.* SDSRL. Grand Rapids: Eerdmans, 2000.

Fletcher-Louis, C. H. T. *All the Glory of Adam: Liturgical Anthropology in the Dead Sea Scrolls.* Leiden: Brill, 2002.

Flint, P. W., ed. *The Bible at Qumran: Text, Shape, and Interpretation.* SDSRL. Grand Rapids: Eerdmans, 2001.

———. "David." In *Encyclopedia of the Dead Sea Scrolls,* edited by L. H. Schiffman and J. C. VanderKam, 178-80. New York: Oxford University Press, 2000.

———. *The Dead Sea Psalms Scrolls and the Book of Psalms.* STDJ 17. Leiden: Brill, 1997.

Fraade, S. D. "Interpretive Authority in the Studying Community at Qumran." *JJS* 44 (1993): 46-69.

Fröhlich, I. "'Narrative Exegesis' in the Dead Sea Scrolls." In *Biblical Perspectives: Early Use and Interpretation of the Bible in Light of the Dead Sea Scrolls. Proceedings of the First International Symposium of the Orion Center for the Study of the Dead Sea Scrolls and Associated Literature,* edited by M. E. Stone and E. G. Chazon, 81-99. STDJ 28. Leiden: Brill, 1998.

García Martínez, F. *Qumran and Apocalyptic: Studies on the Aramaic Texts from Qumran.* STDJ 9. Leiden: Brill, 1992.

García Martínez, F., and E. Noort. *Perspectives in the Study of the Old Testament and Early Judaism: A Symposium in Honour of Adam S. van der Woude on the Occasion of His Seventieth Birthday.* VTSup 73. Leiden: Brill, 1998.

Harrington, D. J. *Wisdom Texts from Qumran.* London: Routledge, 1996.

Horgan, M. *Pesharim: Qumran Interpretations of Biblical Books.* CBQMS 8. Washington, D.C.: Catholic Biblical Association of America, 1979.

Klinghardt, M. "The Manual of Discipline in the Light of Statutes of Hellenistic Associations." In *Methods of Investigation of the Dead Sea Scrolls and the Khirbet Qumran Site: Present Realities and Future Prospects,* edited by M. Wise, N. Golb, J. Collins, and D. Pardee, 251-67. Annals of the New York Academy of Sciences 722. New York: New York Academy of Sciences, 1994.

Knibb, M. *The Qumran Community.* Cambridge Commentaries on Writings of the Jewish and Christian World 200 BC to AD 200. Cambridge: Cambridge University Press, 1987.

———. "Rule of the Community." In *Encyclopedia of the Dead Sea Scrolls,* edited by L. H. Schiffman and J. C. VanderKam, 793-97. New York: Oxford University Press, 2000.

Kugel, J. L. *The Bible as It Was.* Cambridge: Harvard University Press, Belknap Press, 1997.

———. *Traditions of the Bible: A Guide to the Bible as It Was at the Start of the Common Era.* Cambridge: Harvard University Press, 1998.

Lange, A. *Weisheit und Prädestination: Weisheitliche Urordnung und Prädestination in den Textfunden von Qumran.* Leiden: Brill, 1995.

Licht, J. *The Rule Scroll: A Scroll from the Wilderness of Judea 1QS 1QSa 1QSb.* 1965. Reprint, Jerusalem: Bialik Institute, 1996 (Hebrew).

Maier, J. "Early Jewish Biblical Interpretation in the Qumran Literature." In *Hebrew*

Bible/Old Testament: The History of Its Interpretation. I/1: Antiquity, edited by M. Saebø, 1:108-29. Göttingen: Vandenhoeck & Ruprecht, 1996.

Milik, J. T. "Milkî-ṣedeq et Milkî-rešaʿ dans les anciens écrits juifs et chrétiens." *JJS* 23 (1972): 95-144.

————. *Ten Years of Discovery in the Wilderness of Judaea.* Translated by J. Strugnell. London: SCM Press, 1959 (1st French ed. 1957).

Murphy, C. *Wealth in the Dead Sea Scrolls and in the Qumran Community.* STDJ 40. Leiden: Brill, 2002.

Sanders, James A. *The Dead Sea Psalms Scroll.* Ithaca, N.Y.: Cornell University Press, 1967.

Schiffman, L. H. *The Halakhah at Qumran.* Leiden: Brill, 1975.

————. "The Temple Scroll and the Halakhic Pseudepigrapha of the Second Temple Period." In *Pseudepigraphic Perspectives: The Apocrypha and Pseudepigrapha in Light of the Dead Sea Scrolls. Proceedings of the Second International Symposium of the Orion Center for the Study of the Dead Sea Scrolls and Associated Literature, 12-14 January 1997,* edited by E. Chazon and M. E. Stone, 121-31. Leiden: Brill, 1999.

Segal, M. "The Literary Development of Psalm 151: A New Look at the Septuagint." *Textus* 21 (2002).

Shemesh, A. "'The Holy Angels Are in Their Council': The Exclusion of Deformed Persons from Holy Places in Qumranic and Rabbinic Literature." *DSD* 4 (1997): 179-206.

————. "'Three Days' Journey from the Temple': The Use of This Expression in the Temple Scroll." *DSD* 6 (1999): 126-38.

Steudel, A. *Der Midrasch zur Eschatologie aus der Qumrangemeinde (4QMidr-Eschat.[a.b]): Materielle Rekonstruktion, Textbestand, Gattung und traditionsgeschichtliche Einordnung des durch 4Q174 ("Florilegium") und 4Q177 ("Catena A") repräsentierten Werkes aus den Qumranfunden.* STDJ 13. Leiden: Brill, 1994.

————. "Testimonia." In *Encyclopedia of the Dead Sea Scrolls,* edited by L. H. Schiffman and J. C. VanderKam, 936-38. New York: Oxford University Press, 2000.

Stone, M. E., and E. G. Chazon, ed. *Biblical Perspectives: Early Use and Interpretation of the Bible in Light of the Dead Sea Scrolls. Proceedings of the First International Symposium of the Orion Center for the Study of the Dead Sea Scrolls and Associated Literature.* STDJ 29. Leiden: Brill, 1998.

Strugnell, J., and D. Dimant. "4QSecond Ezekiel." *RevQ* 13 (1988): 45-58.

————. "The Merkabah Vision in Second Ezekiel." *RevQ* 14 (1990): 331-48.

Swanson, D. *The Temple Scroll and the Bible: The Methodology of 11QT.* STDJ 14. Leiden: Brill, 1995.

Talmon, S. "The Sectarian יחד — a Biblical Noun." *VT* 3 (1953): 133-40.

————. "The Textual Study of the Bible: A New Outlook." In *Qumran and the History of the Biblical Text,* edited by F. M. Cross and S. Talmon, 321-400. Cambridge: Harvard University Press, 1975.

Tov, E. "The Biblical Text from the Judean Desert — an Overview and Analysis of All the Published Texts." In *The Bible as Book: The Hebrew Bible and the Judean Desert Discoveries,* edited by E. D. Herbert and E. Tov, 139-65. London: British Library, 2002.

———. "Scriptures: Texts." In *Encyclopedia of the Dead Sea Scrolls*, edited by L. H. Schiffman and J. C. VanderKam, 832-36. New York: Oxford University Press, 2000.

———. *Textual Criticism of the Hebrew Bible*. 2nd ed. Minneapolis: Fortress, 2001 (1st ed. 1992).

Ulrich, E. "Canon." In *Encyclopedia of the Dead Sea Scrolls*, edited by L. H. Schiffman and J. C. VanderKam, 117-20. New York: Oxford University Press, 2000.

———. "The Canonical Process, Textual Criticism, and Latter Stages in the Composition of the Bible." In *Sha'arei Talmon: Studies in the Bible, Qumran, and the Ancient Near East Presented to Shemaryahu Talmon*, edited by M. Fishbane and E. Tov with the assistance of W. W. Fields, 267-91. Winona Lake, Ind.: Eisenbrauns, 1992.

———. *The Dead Sea Scrolls and the Origins of the Bible*. SDSRL. Grand Rapids: Eerdmans, 1999.

———. "Double Literary Editions of Biblical Narratives and Reflections on Determining the Form to Be Translated." In *Perspectives on the Hebrew Bible: Essays in Honor of Walter J. Harrelson*, edited by J. L. Crenshaw, 101-16. Macon, Ga.: Mercer University Press, 1988.

———. "Multiple Literary Editions: Reflections toward a Theory of the History of the Biblical Text." In *Current Research and Technological Developments on the Dead Sea Scrolls: Conference on the Texts from the Judean Desert, Jerusalem, 30 April 1995*, edited by D. W. Parry and S. D. Ricks, 78-105. STDJ 20. Leiden: Brill, 1996.

———. "Pluriformity in the Biblical Text, Text Groups, and Questions of Canon." In *The Madrid Qumran Congress: Proceedings of the International Congress on the Dead Sea Scrolls, Madrid, 18-21 March 1991*, edited by J. Trebolle Barrera and L. Vegas Montaner, 1:23-41. 2 vols. Leiden: Brill, 1992.

VanderKam, J. C. "Authoritative Literature in the Dead Sea Scrolls." *DSD* 5 (1998): 382-402.

———. *The Dead Sea Scrolls Today*. London: SPCK; Grand Rapids: Eerdmans, 1994.

———. "Exile in Jewish Apocalyptic Literature." In *Exile: Old Testament, Jewish, and Christian Conceptions*, edited by J. Scott, 89-109. Leiden: Brill, 1997.

———. "Jubilees, Book of." In *Encyclopedia of the Dead Sea Scrolls*, edited by L. H. Schiffman and J. C. VanderKam, 434-36. New York: Oxford University Press, 2000.

———. "Studies on the Prologue and Jubilees 1." In *For a Later Generation: The Transformation of Tradition in Israel, Early Judaism and Early Christianity*, edited by R. Argall, B. Bow, and R. Werline, 273-79. Harrisburg, Pa.: Trinity, 2000.

VanderKam, J. C., and P. W. Flint. *The Meaning of the Dead Sea Scrolls: Their Significance for Understanding the Bible, Judaism, Jesus, and Christianity*. San Francisco: HarperSanFrancisco, 2002.

Vermes, G. "Bible Interpretation at Qumran." *ErIsr* 20 (1989): 184-91.

———. *Scripture and Tradition in Judaism*. Leiden: Brill, 1961.

Wacholder, B. Z. "Deutero-Ezekiel and Jeremiah (4Q384-4Q391)." In *The Dead Sea Scrolls Fifty Years after Their Discovery: Proceedings of the Jerusalem Congress, July 20-25, 1997*, edited by L. H. Schiffman, E. Tov, and J. C. VanderKam; executive editor, G. Marquis, 445-61. Israel Exploration Society in Cooperation with the Shrine of the Book. Jerusalem: Israel Museum, 2000.

Wernberg-Møller, P. *The Manual of Discipline.* STDJ 1. Leiden: Brill, 1957.

Zias, J. "The Cemeteries of Qumran and Celibacy: Confusion Laid to Rest?" *DSD* 7 (2000): 220-53.

Index of Modern Authors

Index of Ancient Literature